Situational Writing

SITUATIONAL WRITING

Gene H. Krupa
University of Iowa

WADSWORTH PUBLISHING COMPANY
Belmont, California • A Division of Wadsworth, Inc.

To Jix

English Editor: Kevin Howat
Production Editor: Judith McKibben
Managing and Cover Designer: Adriane Bosworth
Designer: Wendy Calmenson
Copy Editor: Carolyn Davidson

Student essays are used with permission.

© 1982 by Wadsworth, Inc. All rights reserved. No part of this book may be reproduced, stored in a retrieval system, or transcribed, in any form or by any means, electronic, mechanical, photocopying, recording, or otherwise, without the prior written permission of the publisher, Wadsworth Publishing Company, Belmont, California 94002, a division of Wadsworth, Inc.

Printed in the United States of America

1 2 3 4 5 6 7 8 9 10 — 86 85 84 83 82

Library of Congress Cataloging in Publication Data

Krupa, Gene H.
    Situational writing.

    Bibliography: p.
    1. English language — Rhetoric — Ability testing.
I. Title.
PE1404.K7   808'.042   81-16398
ISBN 0-534-01082-2   AACR2

Foreword

This book is so old it is new.

Its intellectual roots are in Aristotle, and its basic methods are those of apprenticeship in a craft. One learns a craft by practicing it. Each product is evaluated by the master, or the users, or even fellow apprentices, in terms of whether it serves its function, and then the apprentice tries again. The craft is perfected and understood in the experience of it.

To say that writing should be functional may seem banal. Of course, one writes to explain or persuade or make known one's views. Often the chief justification for writing courses is that students need to learn to be more effective in school or business. The emphasis on such arguments usually falls on "communication," for writing is described in terms of its social functions, but in school sometimes words like "understanding" or "makes sense" remind one that writing is a tool of learning itself. Either way "good" writing "works" — it gets the job done.

The oddity is that textbooks sometimes treat writing as though it were carried on without content and separate from a situation. In textbooks the "form" is what counts, so the instruction takes place mostly in terms of surface "errors" or failures to conform to some prescribed pattern of organization. In a milder guise the same assumption underlies the practice of using only one sample of writing to provide a measure of a person's total writing skill. Correctness of form in a few sentences may be evidence that one knows what is correct, but it doesn't show how well one adapts writing to fit different purposes.

Writing and speaking are connected intimately to the situations that evoke them. If we must write about subjects we don't quite understand or to people we can't quite imagine or under circumstances we can't quite control, we are likely to write badly. We also may write badly because we don't know much about English. More likely, though, we are so unnerved by people who claim to know about English and who bully us that we go to pieces and write badly.

Gene Krupa's book is based on a different set of priorities. First, one discovers a need that can be satisfied by writing. A situation is defined by a circumstance that requires words. Then a potential writer gathers knowledge. For convenience, most of the knowledge is to be derived from first-hand experience, from the human senses, from memory. Where there is time and need, a writer also seeks the collective memory in the library or conducts various kinds of systematic research. The crucial test for the writers, though, is in recognizing what bits of information really bear on the situation, either in terms of the reality to be expressed or of the need to the reader. The information is shaped by a strategy that produces writing. If the writing turns out to say something the writer finds important, then efforts will inevitably follow to "correct" the text so that it will be easier to read and free of distractions.

The classroom procedures implied by Professor Krupa approximate an editorial conference. Although satirists often condemn "committee prose," much good practical writing today is written by one person, but is edited by a group. The group may cut out some quirky excellence, but it also finds possible miscues, excessive complication, and simple errors. More importantly, the group serves as a test audience; the variety of points of view is in itself informative, and the writer, aware of a community of readers, usually takes care with writing as a matter of courtesy to friends.

Because situations are dynamic, this book encourages revision. Sooner or later writers abandon drafts because they must get on to the next task, but they know that they have not made a perfect statement. All writing is but an approximation of what one hopes to say to a particular person at a given time. Tomorrow the situation will have changed, and the need will be different. If one pretends that writing is merely a matter of mastering some forms from the handbook, then nothing will need revising; merely correcting will suffice.

Life goes on through constant discovery and re-vision. A writing course is the natural workroom for assembling old notions in new contexts and thus for thinking. Writing itself cannot be mastered once for all time in grade school, nor can it be mastered in writing courses, however useful they may be. Each situation calls again for us to build on the previous situations we've thought about in order to write effectively in new circumstances. The effort to master writing is never finished, it is only abandoned at the moment of death, but the writing course is an opportunity to concentrate on how language shapes one's sense of what the world is like.

Those very old and important ideas are what this book is about.

Richard Lloyd-Jones
Iowa City, 1981

Preface

When I was a graduate student I was exposed to a new method of evaluating writing—Primary Trait Scoring.* Briefly, Primary Trait Scoring works like this: students respond to a writing task; by studying the responses, testers try to figure out what rhetorical trait or characteristic is necessary for success with that task (the Primary Trait); testers evaluate the writing in terms of the Primary Trait. In other words, testers using Primary Trait Scoring always ask and answer this question: given a particular writing situation, what makes a good response?

I began to think about the implications of this technique. What would happen if students *knew in advance* what they had to do to succeed in a particular writing situation? Wouldn't their chances of success be greatly improved? *Situational Writing* is an attempt to realize this idea.

Obviously, I am deeply in debt to Richard Lloyd-Jones, Carl Klaus, and the task force who developed Primary Trait Scoring for the National Assessment of Educational Progress. Let me give special thanks to the four students whose work we follow through the initial sequence of assignments: Liz Boenker, Ryoko Miyazaki, Kris Slaymaker, and Tom Wade, my generous collaborators.

I also thank the reviewers: Maureen Andrews of Northern Michigan University, Robert Cosgrove of Saddleback College, John K. Hanes of Duquesne University, Ed Luter of Richland College, Frederick J. Masback of California State University at Long Beach, Lois Rosen of Michigan State University, Mark Reynolds of Jefferson Davis State Junior College, Anne Beaumont of Rock Valley College, Dan Buerger of San Jose State University, James E. Cagnacci of City College of San Francisco, and Sharon Locy of Loyola Marymount University.

I have been up and and down so many times with this project; here's to Gail, who rode that rollercoaster and did not let me give up when I was tempted.

Gene Krupa

---

*For further discussion see Richard Lloyd-Jones, "Primary Trait Scoring," in *Evaluating Writing: Describing, Measuring, Judging,* Charles R. Cooper and Lee Odell, eds. (Urbana, Ill.: National Council of Teachers of English, 1977), pp. 33–66.

Contents

Introduction   1

    What's in This Book?   1
    The Ideas in the Background   3
    Using This Book   5
    Writing Your Responses   6
    What about Grammar and Usage?   7

I.   TWENTY-FOUR WRITING SITUATIONS   9

    1. As I Begin the Writing Course   10
    2. A Time of Your Life   17
    3. A Victim of Injustice   24
    4. Job Talk   30
    5. I Knew a Teacher   36
    6. A Special Place   43
    7. On the Other Hand . . .   51
    8. The Expert Instructs the Beginner   58
    9. Job Advice   67
    10. Teacher Portrait   74
    11. A News Story   80
    12. A Student Problem   88
    13. I Hate to Bring This Up, But . . .   94
    14. The Better Way   101
    15. To Join or Not to Join   109
    16. Letter of Recommendation   116
    17. A Student Complaint   123
    18. Righting a Wrong   129
    18A. A Tongue-lashing   135
    19. Concerned Citizen   139
    19A. Madman or Fool   145

20. Peering into the Future   149
21. A Particular Kind of Excellence   154
22. A Definition of Justice   161
23. The Good Teacher (Or, The Good Student)   169
24. Self-portrait of a Writer   175

II. TIME OUT   183

III. TWENTY-FOUR MORE WRITING SITUATIONS   189

25. Meeting an Old Friend   190
26. A Way You Were   192
27. A Major Change   194
28. At a Crossroads   196
29. A Formative Influence   198
30. A Formative Situation   200
31. Social Identity   202
32. A Wise Person   204
33. Self-portrait   205
34. Your Home   206
35. Explaining Your Politics   207
36. A Family Portrait   208
37. Thinking about the Family Portrait   210
38. A Travel Grant   212
39. A Textbook Critique   213
40. A Musical Debate   214
41. An Exercise in Charity   215
42. A Homecoming Speech   216
43. Specific Advice   218
44. Commercial Consultant   219
45. A Resolution   221
46. Guest Critic   223
47. A Letter to a Hero   225
48. Looking Backward   227

Appendix A. Five Studies in Revision   228
Appendix B. Profiles of the Four Student Writers   243
Appendix C. Classifying the Situations   252

Bibliography   260

Situational Writing

INTRODUCTION

WHAT'S IN THIS BOOK?

Situational Writing consists mainly of writing assignments. The first section of the book is a sequence of twenty-four assignments, each of them presented the same way. First the situation is set up. This, for example, is Situation 1:

The first days in a new class are usually exciting and awkward at the same time because no one knows anyone else. Address part of the awkwardness directly. Write a letter introducing yourself to your teacher. Focus on your past experience in writing classes and on your attitude toward writing. How do you feel about writing? How do you see yourself as a writer? How do you feel about being in the writing course? The purpose of your letter is to give your teacher some information about yourself, your attitudes, and your writing.

Then I suggest guidelines that may help you write your response. These are the guidelines for Situation 1:

1. Say something particular and substantial about your writing.
2. Support your points with details and examples.
3. Express and define your attitude toward writing.
4. Create an honest and cooperative tone.

After the condensed statement of the guidelines comes some discussion of the situation and guidelines.

Next comes an assessment form. These forms are really a restatement of the guidelines that can be used to evaluate responses. The forms are intended to provide feedback to you about your writing. They are designed to tell you whether your response worked, and if not, why not. assessment forms can be used by your teacher, by your classmates, or by you yourself to assess your writing, or they can be used in all of these ways. This is the assessment form for Situation 1:

Writer _____
Self Assessment _____ Group Assessment _____
Teacher Assessment _____ Other _____
Reader (teacher) would have learned something about the student as writer, and would feel more ready to work with him or her. _____

or

Writer needs *more substance,* higher information content. _____
Writer needs to clarify his or her points. _____
Writer needs to support and illustrate his or her points. _____
Writer needs a clearer attitude toward writing. _____
Writer needs a more candid tone. _____
Writer needs a more cooperative tone. _____
Other suggestions: _____

After the assessment form come the responses of four freshman students: Liz, Ryoko, Kris, and Tom. Seeing how some other freshmen have responded to the situation may sharpen your sense of the situation itself and of the possibilities for responding to it.

Next I discuss the four student responses: how I reacted to them, how other students reacted to them, how the writers themselves assessed their work after receiving feedback from others.

This is the basic format of the chapters in the first section: situation, guidelines, discussion, assessment form, student responses, discussion.

The second section of the book, Time Out, is a brief reconsideration of what you have done, of where you are if you have written the first twenty-four assignments. It reviews some of the principles that have surfaced in the situations and outlines several perspectives on writing.

The third section of the book offers twenty-four more writing situations in a stripped-down format: situation, guidelines, assessment form. These situations provide more possibilities for writing; here you are more on your own—no discussion, no student responses.

There are three appendixes. Appendix A discusses revision and offers five case studies—situations in which the student writers try to improve their work by revising. Appendix B profiles the four students as writers after following their work through twenty-four situations. Appendix C

Introduction

classifies the forty-eight writing situations in terms of five different principles: (1) purpose, (2) thematic sequences, (3) traditional modes, (4) level of abstraction, and (5) audience.

THE IDEAS IN THE BACKGROUND

Every writing text should grow from a philosophy of writing and its teaching. Let me outline the philosophy of *Situational Writing* in seven propositions:

1. *You develop as a writer by writing.* There are no shortcuts in writing; you learn through doing. Learning to write means facing the blank page and returning to it until you come near to accomplishing your purpose. To grow as a writer you need to do this regularly and often with different kinds of writing tasks. That is why *Situational Writing* takes the form of a sequence of twenty-four writing situations supplemented by twenty-four additional situations. You can learn through the process of writing responses to those situations.

2. *All writing originates in a situation or context.* Every piece of writing is a complex interaction of writer, reader, and subject. Writing is directed *to* someone; writers write with an audience in mind. Writing has a subject; it is *about* something. And obviously there must be a writer, who shapes himself or herself and the subject to achieve an effect on the reader.

When people have trouble writing, it is frequently because they do not have their audience clearly in mind, or they do not fully understand their purpose in writing, or they do not understand how to achieve that purpose. The situations in this book try to make purpose and audience clear. Finding your specific subject will be up to you, but I believe you will understand what kind of subject will fit the situation. A good part of the book is devoted to guidelines that suggest methods and strategies for achieving your purpose in a given situation.

3. *You write best about what you know best.* All the writing situations in this book ask you to draw upon personal experience. Writers must have a personal stake in any meaningful writing; writing that does not matter to you has no chance of succeeding with your reader. Also, writing that is not based on personal and firsthand knowledge is always in danger of becoming false and hollow and degenerating into a mere academic exercise. The situations in this book explore a number of your personal worlds: for example, play, work, school, an experience involving injustice.

4. *Different situations require different strategies and approaches.* While there may be a number of general principles of good writing—such as unity, coherence, organization, and development—they are too gen-

eral to provide much help to a student facing a particular writing task. Every writing situation is unique; subject, audience, purpose, and the way you present yourself are variables that recombine in different ways each time you write. If you were to drop out of school, how would you break the news to the dean of your college, to your parents, to a boyfriend or girlfriend? The same news would produce three very different letters. Because writing situations present different requirements and demands, each situation needs separate analysis; *Situational Writing* provides discussion and guidelines for each situation you face.

5. *You can write more successfully when you understand what you are trying to do and how to do it.* I have mentioned that *Situational Writing* tries to make each writing situation clear and explicit, so that you understand what you are doing—your purpose in writing. I have also mentioned that the book provides guidelines for each task, to give you ideas about how to proceed. The idea is that you can better solve a writing problem when that problem is focussed, defined, and analyzed than when you are left to your own devices and to trial and error. Still, the challenge of actually solving the problem remains, and the situations are designed to be open-ended enough that you must find your own solutions.

6. *To improve as a writer, you need practice in evaluating writing.* Writers must learn how to judge writing, how to know when their writing works and when it does not. Before you can improve any piece of writing, you must be able to recognize what is wrong with it. With this purpose in mind, *Situational Writing* includes an assessment form with every situation; by using the forms to evaluate the responses of others, to have your work evaluated by others, and to evaluate your own work, you can learn how to evaluate.

7. *Writing tasks should interconnect with and build upon each other, giving the writing course overall direction and structure.* Since you may be asked to write your way through the first twenty-four writing situations (which are designed as a sequence), it is only fair to try to explain where the tasks are heading and by what logic. One pattern is that the situations are initially *expressive* in purpose, become *explanatory,* and then become *persuasive.* For example, the first time that you write about a job situation, you try to express how you feel about that job to a friend; the second time, you try to explain to a friend how to deal with a particular job problem; the third time, you try to persuade your former employer to hire the friend. In terms of *audience,* the assignments generally move from an intimate and friendly reader (a close friend) to an audience that is more distant and impersonal, sometimes even potentially or actually hostile. The assignments also move toward increasing abstraction, from treating things, people, and events to dealing with ideas, generalizations, and theories. For example, the first time you write about an experience of

Introduction

injustice, you will simply try to tell what happened and how it made you feel; the last time, you will try to discuss the principle that underlies the experience. Your writing course should take you somewhere; I hope that you find interconnections and direction as you work through these situations.

USING THIS BOOK

I have recently been asking students to write responses to two situations every week, and I have been spending two class hours a week working with those responses. At the start of a class hour, I spend about fifteen minutes going over the next assignment and its guidelines. Then I ask the class to divide into groups of three, and I collect from each student three copies of the responses due on this day. I give each group one response and its copies (making sure that the writer is not in the group), and I ask them to evaluate those responses using an assessment form. When a group finishes with a response, I give them another, until all responses are evaluated. Then I return the responses to their writers, along with the group evaluations. Writers then assess their own responses, using another assessment form. We usually have about ten minutes left in the hour; I ask for nominations for particularly interesting papers read in group, and I (or the writer) read those responses aloud. At the end of the hour I collect one copy of the response and two assessment forms from each student (one group assessment and one self assessment). I staple this material together and keep it in the student's folder. With so much writing coming in, I don't attempt to return papers at the rate I receive them. I do review the work in the students' folders with them in conference twice or three times a semester.

The process obviously entails a great deal of paper shuffling, but the logistics quickly become routine. Under this system, students receive immediate peer reaction to their papers. They also practice assessing their own work; evaluation is no longer exclusively teacher-centered.

Of course, there are possible alternatives to my routine. For example, each writer can bring his or her response into the group of three. In this case I ask the groups to discuss all three responses; then I ask the writers to fill out a self assessment that balances their judgment of the piece with what they have learned from their readers. Sometimes I have the students ask a friend or roommate to assess their responses, using the assessment form. Sometimes we collect all responses and project as many as we can on the classroom wall, evaluating them as a group of the whole. Sometimes we bypass assessment; I simply ask the students to write a comment on how they felt about their response and about writing it.

I can imagine other possibilities for using *Situational Writing:* responses to the situations could be written in class; the assessment forms could facilitate teacher assessment; students might create briefer sequences out of the forty-eight situations and write them on their own. Obviously, I hope that students and teachers use this book however they like and thrive while doing so; I don't mean to prescribe a rigid methodology.

WRITING YOUR RESPONSES

Writing is a *process*, a complex psychological and physical activity that takes place in stages. It is not easy to generalize about writing as a process, however, because writing habits and methods of composing vary greatly among individual writers. Some writers move torturously from sentence to sentence, unwilling to leave each one until they have it exactly as they want it. Others speed through a first draft with the idea that what is important is to put something on paper. They pursue refinement and slow the pace in later drafts. Some writers do a great deal of composing in their heads and can "spill it out" when ready. Others must put words on the page and then look at what they've said to find out what they think.

Now, even though the writing process differs for different people, I'm still going to offer four suggestions about composing:

1. *Allow for incubation.* When an assignment is made, study it, fix the problem in your mind, and let your unconscious work on it. In most cases an immediate response will not be as good as a response written after you have lived with the assignment a bit, after it has lodged in your mind while you are involved with other things. Inspiration—those sudden flashes about what to say and how to say it—is mysterious, and you should give yourself the best possible chance for inspiration to happen.

2. *Remember that rewriting is natural, continual, and necessary.* Rarely do writers say what they want, the way they want to say it, the first time through. When professional writers write about writing, they talk most about rewriting, about the changes that take place on all levels—from individual word choices to the whole discourse. Professional writers joke about changing six words for every five that they write, and a writer's manuscript often looks like a jungle with crossed-out passages, inserts, arrows, and notes in the margin. A constant dialectic goes on in all writers: saying something naturally engenders the impulse to change what you've said. Whether you like worrying over sentences while you write them or charging through whole drafts before starting over, remember that most people most of the time must rewrite to write as well as they can.

3. *The last and indispensable step in writing is copyreading or editing.* The writing process ends in a product; you eventually produce a piece of discourse, which you offer to a reader. You want your reader to be able to concentrate on your message with as little distraction as possible. This is why you should always copyread or edit your final draft to catch errors in usage, punctuation, and spelling. Part of this process involves training your eye to look "through" your meaning to what you have actually written; writers often let mechanical errors pass because they are unable to "see" them. In some cases you may suspect an error but not be sure because you don't know the appropriate rule. For these cases, you should have a handbook to consult, and you should be willing to ask for advice; begin with your teacher. Errors detract from the readability of your discourse, and a paper that is not easily readable has a poor chance of succeeding in terms of its larger purpose.

When you copyread or edit your paper, look also for problems with style and meaning. Are there sentences that don't say what you mean? Are some sentences unnecessarily tangled in their structure, their syntax? Are some sentences padded with unnecessary words and phrases? Every time I read something I have written, I can find words to cut and phrases to condense. Problems like these will also reduce the readability and effectiveness of your paper. You may want to copyread for style and correctness at the same time; you may prefer to read for style first and then read again for correctness.

4. *Try to formulate your purpose and your methods for any given writing task, and let this formulation penetrate and inform the whole writing process.* From incubation to copyreading, focus on what you are trying to do and how you are trying to do it. This is perhaps the main emphasis of this book and the main way that *Situational Writing* can help you with your writing; each chapter presents *purpose* and *methods* for each writing situation, so that you can hold them in mind while you go through the writing process.

WHAT ABOUT GRAMMAR AND USAGE?

It is important that students learn to follow the conventions of Edited American English, for writing has to achieve at least minimal readability to have a chance of achieving its rhetorical purpose. However, I don't believe that formal classroom instruction in grammar and usage is effective writing instruction for most freshman students,[1] and I have not in-

---

[1] See NCTE Commission on Composition, "Teaching Composition: A Position Paper," *College English*, 36 (Oct. 1974), 219–20.

cluded any apparatus for that purpose in *Situational Writing*. Some students may find a handbook or secretary's manual that treats matters of convention a good supplement to *Situational Writing*. I also think that teachers should explain copyreading or editing as a final and necessary step in the composing process and should work individually with students who have serious problems with conventions.

Although *Situational Writing* does not directly treat problems of usage, spelling, and punctuation, I have found that writing regularly for one's peers creates a kind of pressure that leads students to learn the conventions. One wants one's paper to be as readable as possible; it is embarrassing when a group can't decipher one's syntax. When writing comes under biweekly scrutiny, I have found that most students make significant improvement in editing.

I · TWENTY-FOUR WRITING SITUATIONS

1 · As I Begin the Writing Course

I assume that you are beginning a college writing course. You are in a new situation with a strange group of people, as are your teacher and the others in your class. A main use of writing is to help people work together. Try to address your present situation with this purpose in mind.

SITUATION 1

The first days in a new class are usually exciting and awkward at the same time, because no one knows anyone else. Address part of the awkwardness directly. Write a letter introducing yourself to your teacher. Focus on your past experience in writing classes and on your attitude toward writing. How do you feel about writing? How do you see yourself as a writer? How do you feel about being in the writing course? The purpose of your letter is to give your teacher some information about yourself, your attitudes, and your writing.

What will make your letter effective in this situation? Here and in the situations that follow I will offer some *guidelines*, my suggestions on what you need to write a good response. You may discover other important considerations as you write.

GUIDELINES

1. Say something particular and substantial about your writing.
2. Support your points with details and examples.
3. Express and define your attitude toward writing.
4. Create an honest and cooperative tone.

In one sense this is a *complex* writing situation, for you are trying to do

Situation 1

a number of things at once. You want to provide your teacher with information about yourself as a writer; you want to express how you feel about writing; and you want to establish a good working relationship with your teacher. Part of the challenge of this situation is to pursue a number of aims at once.

As you give information, try to avoid being vague. Think about the situation from your teacher's point of view. Confronting twenty or more new faces, he or she needs to know something that will characterize you individually as a writer. Backgrounds in writing probably vary dramatically among your classmates. Different schools, different school systems, different teachers treat writing differently. What kinds of writing have you done? How much? What aspects of writing have been stressed in your education? You will need to generalize about your particular writing background, and you will need to give details and examples that fill in and support the generalizations. Can you think of particular assignments or kinds of assignments you've had, of particular ways in which a former teacher worked with writing? To be valuable to your present teacher, this letter requires both generalizations and support.

Information is not the only requirement; your teacher will also want to know how you feel about writing. He or she does not, however, want a snow job. It may truly be that writing interests you, that you have always liked playing with language, that you have generally enjoyed and done well in your English classes. On the other hand, you may have hated English classes, you may not have found value and purpose in your writing instruction, and you may be taking this class only because it is required. Or perhaps your main experience with writing has been failure and disappointment; you may feel apprehensive about what will happen in this class, even though you think the class is a good idea and you would like to write better. Whatever the case, try to define and express your attitude toward writing and writing classes. Teachers need to know who you are before they can begin to teach, and in this situation what you feel about writing is an important part of who you are.

There is yet another aim for your letter. It is really a special kind of letter of introduction: you want to establish a positive *working relationship* with your teacher. The tone of your letter establishes the initial terms of that relationship. You want to be honest and open; if your teacher senses that you are being direct, he or she will feel more free to be honest and open with you. You will eliminate game-playing, and the teacher can get down to the business of helping you with your writing. When you reveal something honestly about yourself, other people move toward you; you want this to happen with your teacher.

Your tone should also express willingness to cooperate. Regardless of your writing background, you undoubtedly want to make the best of the writing class. Let part of the *subtext* of your letter (the message between the lines) be your willingness to learn. This will be read as an initial vote of confidence that should start you and your teacher toward mutual cooperation.

Seeing other student responses to the situations may help prepare you to write them yourself. The work of four student writers appears throughout this book; I chose Liz, Ryoko, Kris, and Tom because they are different types of writers. Each sometimes succeeds and sometimes fails with these situations; you will see the individuality of their writing emerge as we proceed through the situations. (This is the subject of Appendix B.) Following the student responses, each chapter will include discussion of my reaction, other students' reactions, and the writers' reactions to what they wrote.

LIZ'S RESPONSE

I could start this paper out by describing my physical features, where I'm from, or even my name, but I won't. Those things really aren't me. What is me is what is deep down inside; the rest is just ways of filing me in the universe.

As a writer I am like a babe not yet conceived. I grew up during the educational revolution when grammar was not taught. Consequently I learned to speak the language but not to write it. In junior high, English class was replaced by film making and doing anything that stimulated you—such as knitting, talking, and spitball throwing, which all participated in, although there were a few who found satisfaction in reading. High school brought a shock to my system. For the next three years I worked on writing, and on interpretations of writings. Although I feel that I worked fairly hard during high school, I am still about three years behind.

I hope that through this course I can further improve my writing and grammar skills. I want to be able to communicate with the rest of the world without voice. To learn how to write in any situation with confidence is my goal. With your help I hope to make my way to fulfilling my wish. Let me introduce myself; I'm Liz B.

Situation 1

RYOKO'S RESPONSE

Dear Mr. Krupa,

How do you do?

My name is Ryoko. I am from Japan.

To tell the truth, I am very scared about taking this course. I came to the United States one year ago to study. But my English was very bad so I took many English classes for foreign students. I took two writing classes in that program and these helped me a lot. But I know it was not enough. I like writing in Japanese, but not in English, because I just don't know how to. I get so frustrated not knowing how to express my feelings in English that I don't want to write anything in English. Besides I know that some people laugh at my writing and speaking because it is too ungrammatical and sounds like a baby is writing or talking.

I'm sure I will have a hard time in this class but I will try my best so this class will help me a lot in speaking and writing in English. And I hope that you can put up with my broken English and me myself.

KRIS'S RESPONSE

Ever since I have been in high school I have remembered one thing about all writing classes. No matter how hard I've worked at writing, I always get the same grade, a B.

I enjoy writing, but only about subjects interesting to me. I have a hard time writing papers on specific topics that don't interest me. When I have to write a paper with a lot of details and specifics, I have a hard time saying what I'm trying to say. I know what I want to say, but I have a hard time saying it in terms of detail and specifics. When a paper doesn't include detail and specifics, I write with very little trouble. It's always been easy for me to say things in a very straightforward manner, excluding the details and specifics.

I have the most trouble writing a paper when the subject is left up to me. It's hard for me to be happy with one subject. I start papers over many times before I'm really happy with what I've done. The easiest things for me to write about are research papers. There is always somewhere I can turn for information to put the paper together. I don't have to rely on my own imagination to make the paper interesting.

I think being in a writing course would help me learn to enjoy other kinds of writing. A writing course would teach me how to handle different subjects and different styles of writing. I also feel that a writing course could help me in the area of expressing myself with greater details and specifics. I feel as if I would enjoy a writing course that would help me learn to become a better writer.

TOM'S RESPONSE

Dear Gene,

I've really had very little experience writing. In the few classes that I did have in writing I performed rather poorly. Writing has always been a chore for me. I have always been a better speaker than a writer. I was a debater for four years. Writing is plain hard work for me. Hopefully, I can improve a demonstrable measure in your class.

What follows is an Assessment Form for Situation 1. Assessment Forms are provided for each situation; they are checklists intended to help you evaluate responses (your own or those of other students).

ASSESSMENT

Writer _____
Self Assessment _____ Group Assessment _____
Teacher Assessment _____ Other _____
Reader (teacher) would have learned something about the student as writer, and would feel more ready to work with him or her. _____
or
Writer needs *more substance*, higher information content. _____
Writer needs to clarify his or her points. _____
Writer needs to support and illustrate his or her points. _____
Writer needs a clearer attitude toward writing. _____
Writer needs a more candid tone. _____
Writer needs a more cooperative tone. _____
Other suggestions: _____

Using the Assessment Form will help you come to conclusions such as these about the responses.

Liz's response and Ryoko's response have this in common: both writers are strongly *there*. Both achieve much through tone; both express candor and cooperativeness, and before they finish, I am interested and enthusiastic about working with them both. Liz comes across as intense, forceful, and serious about her education; Ryoko disarms by her description of her sense of inadequacy with English, by her willingness to reveal feelings. Both Liz and Ryoko could give me *more information* about themselves as writers. I want to know more about the kind of writing that Liz did in high school, what she feels she learned, where she thinks she needs to improve (in addition to grammar). Ryoko makes substantial points when she mentions her frustration in expressing feeling in English and her chagrin at sounding comical and childish. But she could also help me by describing in more detail the kind of writing she was doing and particular problems she encountered. In her assessment of her response, Liz wrote that she needed more substance and more support; the group of students who evaluated her paper thought she needed more support. Ryoko felt she needed more support; her group called for more substance.

Kris's paper is a mirror opposite of Liz's and Ryoko's responses. Concentrating on information, Kris is more successful with that aim than Liz or Ryoko, but in terms of tone, her response could be better. It is encouraging to find a student who is so aware of the need for details and specifics, and who seems to understand that detail is intimately connected with self-expression; this is good initial insight. Kris's tone gives the reader pause, however. The subtext of Kris's first paragraph reads like this to me: "You guys are all alike. No matter how hard I work on my writing, I get a B." My reaction is, "Oh no, we're starting grade combat already, and she's trying to psych me out." Kris's attitude toward her imagination when she mentions research (paragraph three) troubles me; it's as if she's saying, "Don't ask me for imagination; I know I haven't any." I believe that Kris thinks that; I think she's being honest; still, her attitude comes across as too negative, almost as if she's saying, "Don't ask me to change and grow; I know I can't."

There are two other problems with Kris's response. I like the intent of paragraph three because I feel that Kris is trying to give me substantial information about herself as a writer—but what she is saying is not clear enough. I don't understand why it's hard for her "to be happy with one subject" or what dissatisfactions make her start over many times. These generalizations are potentially useful, but Kris needs to clarify what she means, and to support and illustrate her points with examples. Kris's group also mentioned unnecessary repetition in her second paragraph;

this is unquestionably true. Kris thought that her response was successful; her group asked for more clarification and support. I agree with the group; additionally, her tone could be more cooperative and open in places, though I think that Kris is convincingly positive in her last paragraph.

Tom's tone is convincingly direct, straightforward, and unaffected; he sounds candid and cooperative. His points are appropriate to this letter—he addresses experience and attitude, for example. He is heading in the right direction but needs to go further; he needs support, illustration, and development of his points. This was also the judgment of Tom's group.

2 · A Time of Your Life

It may be that we call play "recreation" because it offers moments of intense involvement in which we re-create ourselves, in which we become whole and new people, at least for the moment. Perhaps you recall an instance when the chaotic action on the football field transformed itself into perfectly executed trap blocking, and the play unfolded just as the coach had drawn it on the blackboard. Perhaps it was a jump during which you and your horse became one creature. Perhaps it was a moment at the bridge table when you suddenly saw in your mind where the trumps must be and what you had to play to make them drop. We are very alive in such moments. Can you put a moment like this into language? How close can you come to sharing a rich and personal experience with others?

SITUATION 2

You are talking with a friend about a sport or activity you enjoy. Think back to a particular time or moment when you were totally involved in the activity, and try to write exactly what happened during that moment. Try not to talk about the "thrill of victory" or the *results* of the activity; focus on the *process*, on what actually happened while you were in action. Also, write about one specific time; don't write about what sometimes happens or what usually happens. Your description should establish why you enjoy the sport or activity.

GUIDELINES

1. Use specific details that support your overall feeling about the sport or activity.
2. Use language unique to your sport or activity, if possible.

3. Establish a clear point of view: tell the action as you experienced it as participant. (Put the reader inside your head.)
4. If appropriate comparisons or analogies occur to you, use them.

Your purpose in this situation is to put the reader inside your mind, to re-create your mental state during a moment of intense involvement. *Point of view* is important: you are the center of this situation; tell what happened as you heard it, as you saw it, as you did it. What was going on in your head during this moment? That is what we want to know.

There is a paradox in this situation, however. You want to convey your feelings at an intense moment, but perhaps the best way to convey them is by describing the outer world as carefully as possible. The reader needs to know the conditions surrounding you: specific details, sharp physical impressions. Make your world real and vivid and concrete; put the reader there with sharp, close description of the physical facts.

Now you must consider *selection*. How will you know which specifics to select and use? Choose *those details that support your main feeling*, that contribute the most to your particular state of mind. Remember that you are building around the feeling of the moment: what details fit with that feeling, express it, embody it? A good response will probably bring together many small and telling facts that add up to your particular feeling.

A point about language: many sports or activities have a unique vocabulary of words and phrases. For example, a blitz happens in football; a crop is used in riding; a finesse takes place in bridge. Using the language of your sport or activity should help you keep your description specific and detailed. It should also help you capture the flavor and the atmosphere of the sport.

You will likely find yourself comparing your feeling during the special moment to something else. When asked for our feelings, we often respond, "It's like. . . ." Asked about his writing, novelist William Styron said, "Writing is hell." Coach Woody Hayes often compared football to war. People in the Nixon administration frequently compared politics to football, with game plans and team players.

Feeling is often intangible and elusive; comparison is a way to capture it. Brief comparisons are called *metaphors* and *similes;* extended comparisons are called *analogies;* all these forms are called *figurative language*. You may find that the right figurative language can help you express your feeling in Situation 2. Remember: don't force comparisons; don't use a figure of speech unless it feels natural and right for the situation. And don't use old, stale, worn out comparisons (also called clichés). Those dangers recognized, be aware that fresh and inventive figures of speech can often capture the shape of your feeling and bring it to life.

LIZ'S RESPONSE

Bicycling is a sport in which the mind can wander while the body remains firm but not tense. When I look back on my cycling life, I feel most excited when I recall the climb of a big hill. My body prepares itself by storing the needed energy. The heart begins to beat slower but with an invigorating force. A short glance tells me that I have an incline of about fifty feet. In my mind I calculate for a short time the difficulty of the challenge ahead of me. After all the calculations have been thought over and the bike is in the appropriate gear, it is time to free my mind of any thought. Music fills my ears and my legs respond to the never-ending beat. Although I never look up, my legs feel the rising roadway. I see in front of me only the cracks of the ever-swelling pavement. Sugary juices of energy pour through my veins to relieve the tormented tissues. But my mind continues to sing like a bird on a windowsill. Slowly the chains begin to quicken as the body bursts forth in a gallant finish. There is a oneness between my body and mind, one cleansing the other. With every breath the muscles revive themselves to go one step further. Then as the air grows lighter the legs grind much slower until finally an easy pace resumes. I lift my head to observe my new surroundings. Now I once again hear the sounds of the awakening life of nature. The heat from within is cooled by the beads of sweat. Now I am free of any physical or mental anguish. I am reborn.

RYOKO'S RESPONSE

I have been missing going to the sea very much. I remember one day on which I went to the beach alone.

The waves were just rolling in as I arrived at the beach. I put down a lemon yellow blanket, set up a bright orange parasol to make a shadow, and threw my clothes and shoes on top of it.

The waves were calling me so strongly that I did not even sit down on the blanket. I grabbed my inner tube and ran toward the sea. The cold water covered me gently and the pebbles tickled my feet.

I swam far from the beach pulling the inner tube behind me. When I had gotten so far from the beach that I could not see the orange parasol, I mounted the inner tube and relaxed. In the cobalt-blue sky hanging over my head floated a few cumulus clouds that resembled marshmallows. The sharp, straight sunshine beat down on my body little by little as I lay with my eyes closed. The sea breeze whispered across the water, disturbing no one. The inner tube cradle let me indulge in daydreams. The seagulls floated through the sky, breaking the overwhelming silence of my peaceful world.

Although the sun was pleasant, it was too hot to tolerate. So I gradually let my body sink into the chilly water that surrounded my heated body very severely. I swam back toward the seaside. Before I reached the beach, I found a little pink seashell that made a wish come true.

When I walked on the sand, my chilled feet gradually turned to red. I ran to the blanket and fell on top of it. My eyes were so heavy that I could not keep them open. The lukewarm wind stroked my body and I dozed off.

KRIS'S RESPONSE

I remember three years ago when I was playing softball for Regina High School. It was my first year to play softball, and I was scared to death. Softball had been my favorite game from the time I was able to catch and throw a softball.

I had waited years for this moment, and it had finally arrived. All the practice and hard work I had done were now going to come to the surface. It was finally time for that first game in that new blue uniform.

It was a breathtakingly hot Thursday afternoon when the rest of the team and I strode out on the field at City Park, clad in uniforms and spikes. We warmed up for about fifteen minutes, and then we were ready.

I was positioned at shortstop, one of the fastest places on the field. The first girl was up to bat. I watched her warm up with the bat, and it looked like she was going to hit it out of the ballpark. Well, now I could find out; she was ready.

She stepped up to the plate and crouched into her batting stance. The pitcher was ready; she wound up and delivered the pitch. I watched it cross the plate knee high, and I saw the batter's bat come around. Crack! I heard the wood hit the white, and saw the ball coming straight toward me.

Situation 2

It was a hard grounder coming toward me like a bolt of lightning. I put my glove to the ground, praying that I would scoop it up. I felt the ball hit my glove and I lifed it up, reached into my glove, pulled the ball out and threw it to first base. She's out! With the first batter out, it was time to move on.

TOM'S RESPONSE

While at my first debate tournament I encountered a unique situation. As the first affirmative began his speech about the problem in the status quo, I suddenly realized I had no evidence on this subject.

After the first affirmative gives his speech about the problem in the status quo, I must refute his accusations with evidence. I had no evidence on this subject to refute his allegations, so I looked up at my partner and he just laughed at me. Quickly I found some evidence cards that vaguely fit the subject. After the debate the judge was wondering how I refuted this subject with such vague evidence for such a long time. I shook my head and said with a little luck and a lot of b.s.

Although it was a valiant effort, I did lose the debate. But, since the whole purpose of the thing was to have fun and learn something, I believe it was a good experience. I like debate because it poses a challenge that is exciting. I also believe it is a fun activity.

ASSESSMENT

Writer _____
Self Assessment _____ Group Assessment _____
Teacher Assessment _____ Other _____
Reader would understand the writer's feeling for the sport or activity. _____

or

Writer needs more specific details that express his or her feeling. _____

Writer might use more of the unique language of the sport. _____

Writer needs to clarify point of view. _____
Writer needs more or better figurative language. _____
Other suggestions: _____

The major problem in Tom's response is very clear: Tom needs to be more specific to make his predicament vivid and real to the reader. Both Tom and the group evaluating his response checked "more specifics" as the problem. An old story tells of a prison in which the inmates have told all their jokes so many times that everyone knows them by heart. So they number them all, and they tell jokes simply by standing up and shouting out a number. Tom is shouting out "Number 102," but our problem is that we haven't been in jail with him (or rather, at the debate), so we don't know what he is talking about. For example, what was the topic of the debate? What was the irrelevant evidence on the evidence cards? I did like Tom's use of actual debate terminology; it lends authenticity to his response. Notice that Tom has a good strategy: he wants to give us an incident that will show that he enjoys debate because of the challenge of thinking on his feet, regardless of the outcome. Executing that strategy is his problem.

Ryoko's response is definitely successful for me. I feel that I understand her feeling about going to the beach—that through this activity she relaxes to the point that she can settle deep within herself. Ryoko handles both specific details and figurative language well. The little pink seashell—wish come true—is a detail that suggests a small kind of perfection in the experience. She repeatedly *personifies* the elements: waves call, the sea breeze whispers, the wind strokes. The inner tube is a cradle, suggesting the peace of infancy. All these metaphors help her express her feeling. Ryoko felt that she needed more specific details; her group felt that the response lacked focus—they didn't understand what her main feeling was. I disagreed with these critiques, but later in the course Ryoko did write a revision that improved on this piece.

Kris felt that her response was successful; her group felt that she needed more specifics. I agree with the group, although Kris starts to come up with the right kind of detail in the last part of her second-to-last paragraph. Kris might try doing more with figurative language. Consider her last paragraph. She uses one simile—"like a bolt of lightning"—but that simile is too familiar. The rest of the description is too flat: her language tells what happens, but it doesn't really suggest the feeling of the action.

Both Liz and her group thought that her response was successful. I agree that it is powerful writing—Liz uses evocative and expressive details and figurative language—but it creates some problems for me as a reader. In undertaking the difficult job of conveying her inward state, Liz raises some confusing contradictions and inconsistencies. She is hearing music with a never-ending beat, but then her mind is singing like a bird. Is birdsong characterized by a powerful beat? At one point, her mind is peaceful while her body is tormented; a little later, she says that "there is a oneness between my mind and body." When she has her body "burst forth" and the air "grow lighter," we are not really sure what she means. Liz needs to bring her language under more control, though the power of her language is undeniable.

3 · A Victim of Injustice

One basic human characteristic is a sense of fairness—of how reasonable people should deal with one another, how people should be treated. It gives us a standard, a code of conduct, and we learn to get along in the world by treating others as we would like to be treated. The world, however, is not always a reasonable place, and other people don't always act according to our codes, standards, and expectations. Inevitably, events happen that shock and upset us because they violate our sense of fairness; when they do, they usually leave us angry. This assignment asks you to tell about such an event that happened to you.

SITUATION 3

Think of a situation in which you were treated unfairly, in which you were a victim of injustice—a situation that made you angry. Tell what happened, as if you were writing to a sympathetic friend or acquaintance. Make your feelings clear.

GUIDELINES

1. Select the facts you need to keep your story clear and the facts that support your side of the story.
2. Sound angry and indignant.
3. Make sure that the reader understands what you expected as well as what happened, so that he or she knows why you are angry.

Your purpose is to express the anger that the incident made you feel. You want your reader to hear your anger and to understand what made you angry and why.

The reader needs certain information to grasp the situation as a whole: what happened? Another set of questions involves what happened from your point of view: what facts are basic to your side of the story? What does the reader need to know to understand how the event struck you? Use these two categories in deciding what material to include.

How to sound angry is a difficult question. Consider that every time you write, you create a personality out of words. Your word choice, the way you build your sentences, your attitude toward your subject, your reader, and yourself — all these factors combine to make a speaker, a personality, a *persona*.[2] A number of intangibles together create a convincingly angry speaker, one who would make the reader conclude, "Yes, this writer is really angry."

Although an exact technique for sounding angry is elusive, let me list some ways you *don't* want to sound: factual (like a police officer making a report), mock-angry (like someone playing at being angry), wistful and apologetic and sorry (as if somehow you were to blame). When someone's sense of fairness has really been violated, you can hear the outrage and indignation trembling in his or her voice. To capture that note, relive the situation in your imagination. Often your anger will arise again, unlocking the right words.

Your reader may understand the situation and find your anger convincing, but one other element is necessary. From your description of the incident, the reader must understand why your sense of fairness was violated. The reader must understand, in other words, why you feel that this is a question of injustice. Otherwise the reader knows what happened, hears the anger in the writer's words, but still reacts with a puzzled "Huh?" because he or she doesn't understand what the writer thinks is unfair. You must give the reader a sense of your psychology, of your expectation within the situation.

LIZ'S RESPONSE

Ever since I can remember, my parents have been telling me that honesty and kindness to others are always best. I always thought that if there was anyone in this world you could trust, it would be our beloved Iowa City police. Anyone who believes in the stereotype of the strong man ready to protect us from danger, but still gentle enough to get Aunt Polly's cat out of the tree, has been horribly deceived. The only thing the blue uniform and bright shiny badge do is cover up the yellowness underneath. Last summer I found out what the true police person was like. For some reason we had been pulled over to the side of the road. When we asked what was the matter, all she would reply was that we were stupid high school kids

[2]For more discussion see Walker Gibson, *Persona* (New York: Random House, 1969).

out for what she determined was a joy ride and she would get us for that. Although we still weren't sure what we had been charged with, we gathered it was drag racing because they pulled another car in with us, and they didn't have any radar or anything else to get us for. After we were badgered for an hour with harsh, one-sided questions, we were allowed to leave. This sure wasn't the kind officer I remember seeing in the movies.

For the next three weeks while we waited for the court appearance, the two cops continually followed us. They would even go so far as to follow us to my home. Weeks went past as court appearances were continually canceled by the officers. Then one night we were pulled aside by our shadow officers. Within three minutes we were arrested. We didn't know what for, nor were we read our rights. When we got to jail, he told us, finally, that we had skipped our trial like hardened criminals. After a long speech on how we were ruining our lives, he told us we had to remain in jail till we could find someone to bail us out. So at twelve o'clock at night we had to call our parents and explain the problems to them. Until one o'clock we were filed under hardened criminals. It just isn't that easy to find 150 dollars in cash. The strange part about this whole episode is that we never received the letter because the officer had made an error in the address on the charges. So there was absolutely no way the letter ever could have reached us. But we still had to be subjected to interrogation by the police and stay in jail. Not even the lawyer had received a notice, because of another foul-up by the police station, and it was through him that we had received all the other notices.

When the trial finally arrived I was shocked to find out that not only were the officers harsh, but they also lied to save their own face. Under oath the officers made statements that were unprovable. This whole situation taught me one thing: the Iowa City police don't work on the safety of the city. In turn they will do anything and I mean everything to better their own records. Officers such as this have no place in the human race.

RYOKO'S RESPONSE

I do not remember what I was doing when my mother scolded me. But I do remember that I said to my mother to shut up and that I did not want to have a mother like her. Right after I said so, my mother's face turned blue and she was almost crying. I knew how much I had hurt her, but since I was very perverse and too shy to show my apology to her, I could not stop acting as if I were still very mad at her. The more I said something bad to her, the more I was mad at myself. And the more I was mad at myself, the more I said something bad to her. I hit the floor and went to my room. I cried and felt so frustrated that I wanted to die. Everything was my fault and I made my situation worse.

After a while, I tried to say "Sorry" to her. But I could never say so. So I washed the dishes and cleaned the room, acting as if I were still mad at her.

KRIS'S RESPONSE

Throughout my entire high school years I held a 3.0 gradepoint or higher. I was active in cheerleading, yearbook, and student council. All of the above are the requirements for the National Honor Society, a group of honor students.

No matter how hard I tried, I never made it into the National Honor Society. The students who made it were picked by the teachers, whom I personally feel don't know a thing about their students.

Half of the people I know who are in the National Honor Society don't meet all the requirements. Many are only bookworms and don't participate in any outside activities. If they don't meet all the requirements they don't belong! But then if you're a teacher's pet I guess it doesn't make any difference whether you meet the requirements or not; you're in!

Then there're those of us who do meet all the specified requirements, but just don't meet the teachers' standards! Just how do they explain their justice in picking the members? They don't because they can't! There is no way for them to justify whom they pick and whom they don't. I've asked several times why I wasn't a member and nobody can explain it to me—because there really isn't any reason.

After learning what the National Honor Society really is like, I can honestly say I'm glad I don't belong to such a Mickey Mouse club that really is unrespected!

TOM'S RESPONSE

During a debate tournament last winter, I felt a grave injustice was imposed upon my partner and myself. Before the third round of debating, my partner and I were conversing with two girl debaters from Davenport West Junior High School. They congratulated us on our big victory from last week. They left us to go talk to a debate judge they knew.

A few minutes later our coach told us where we were to debate and who our judge was. To our surprise it was the same judge who knew the girls from Davenport West. He told us that he expected a lot out of us if we wanted to win. As the debate began, it soon became obvious to any normal human being that we were beating our Junior High opponents. The coach who was sitting in on the debate agreed with me.

But contrary to our beliefs, we did not win that round and consequently lost the tournament because of that round. The girls from Davenport West won the tournament. (Gee, what a coincidence! Something was rotten in Denmark.) We appealed to the tournament director, and he investigated the matter and said all he could do was suspend the judge. So we went home, empty-handed, broken-hearted, and really pissed off.

ASSESSMENT

Writer _____
Self Assessment _____ Group Assessment _____
Teacher Assessment _____ Other _____
Reader believes your anger and understands why you are angry.
_____
or
Writer needs better selection of essential facts. _____
Writer doesn't sound genuinely angry. _____
Writer needs to make clearer the expectations that were violated.
_____
Other suggestions: _____

Ryoko's response is moving and insightful writing, but there is a problem in evaluating it: it doesn't really answer the assignment. Ryoko is not the *victim* of injustice here; she feels like the perpetrator of injustice.

Situation 3

Perhaps she is an actor in a complex situation in which no one is purely innocent or guilty.

Kris's response seems successful to me. Kris explains the situation very clearly; we know what happened and why she feels anger. Kris and her group both checked "writer doesn't sound genuinely angry," but it seems to me that her deep bitterness over unfair exclusion runs through the whole piece.

In assessing Tom's response, both Tom and his group check "not genuinely angry"; I am not sure whether this is a true evaluation of the situation. I think that Tom could improve this piece in the same way that he could improve his response to Situation 2. If Tom showed us in detail some of the things that happened during the debate, and showed us why he was sure that his side had won, I think his anger and indignation would come across more forcefully.

Liz's group felt that her response was successful; Liz checked "selection of facts" and "not genuinely angry." Liz does need a clearer presentation of the overall situation. While she gives us detail in some places, she is very vague in others. For the reader, the incident begins on the side of the road; we aren't sure what happened before. The villainous police officer changes from "she" to "he"; the victims are just "we"; we aren't sure of the identity of the participants. We *do* need a clearer situation. On the other hand, when Liz describes being jailed in the night or being called "stupid high school kids out for a joy ride," her use of detail makes us experience her anger. It is interesting that when Liz tries to express her feeling directly, it slips out of focus: the problem with these police is not that they are "yellow" or subhuman. Liz expresses the unfairness, but has trouble when she tries to label it.

4 · Job Talk

Writing is important in the world of work. In fact, one could define white collar jobs as paperwork jobs, jobs in which people work with written language in one form or another. Later in this book, you will do some kinds of writing required in the world of work. Now, however, our interest is in writing as a means of sharing experience, of expressing your personal view of the world. Therefore the next situation asks you to write about a job (whether paid or unpaid) from a personal perspective, in a way that throws light on your feelings and values. In Situation 4, work will be the topic, but your *relationship* to a particular job will be the real subject.

SITUATION 4

Think about the jobs you have held, paid or unpaid (such as working on the yearbook staff or serving as a team manager). Single out a job that you liked or hated. Imagine yourself in a conversation with a friend who is going to take over that job. Try to express in writing how you felt about the job and why. Don't limit yourself to "externals"—such as pay and hours. Try to take your friend "inside" the job, into your subjective and personal feeling about it.

GUIDELINES

1. Define your attitude toward the job.
2. Use specific details that support and explain your attitude.

In a good response to this assignment, your attitude toward the job must be both clear and developed rather than general and undefined. It is clear enough to tell someone that you liked or didn't like a job, but this is too general an attitude to be very informative; you are not telling the reader enough. A situation can be pleasant or unpleasant in a million different ways; you must focus on the particular feeling or combination of feelings that a job creates in you. Do not settle for generalizations like "boring" or "satisfying." What kind of boredom or satisfaction? Sharpen your feeling.

As part of defining your attitude, show your reader your work in specific detail, so that he or she can see what you mean. Select details that support your attitude; once again, the reader should feel that everything "fits." Without the right specifics, your job will not become real and vivid to your reader.

One qualification: making your attitude sharp and clear does not necessarily mean that you must make it simple, unqualified, black or white, love or hate. It may be that you were enthralled by the job or that you totally despised it; if that is so, write your description to reflect your feeling. It is more likely that your attitude was mixed, qualified, ambiguous — that you liked the job in some ways and disliked it in others. It is even possible that you were deeply committed and involved with the job, yet at the same time you found the work difficult and frustrating. (Many professional writers feel this way about writing.) Don't make your attitude clear by simplifying or falsifying; take the harder and more honest route of making a complex attitude clear.

LIZ'S RESPONSE

After working at Randall's for a year and a half, I can honestly say there can't be a better part-time job. Marv Hain makes the store so carefree with his easy-going attitude that it is a pleasure to work for him. During my senior year I participated in basketball, golf, and other outside activities that required a lot of time. Because of his kind nature, Marv worked me only on Saturdays and Sundays during the five months of basketball. Even when I asked off for a two-week trip to France, Marv just smiled and told me, "You're only young once so live it up now." The rest of the store is also run in the same easy manner. Everyone is willing to help everyone else. Randall's is run in a family effort.

I have learned a lot from working. Everyone always told me that working teaches you responsibility, which is true, but at Randall's I have also learned to deal with all types of people. No longer do I become tense when customers blame me for the inflation problem. With time I have been able to communicate with the various different personalities.

The shifts vary in time span. Even on those long, boring days when you think your legs are permanently embedded in tile, the pain quickly dissipates when you think about that sweet paycheck. Because the store isn't in the union, we are given continual raises just to keep the union out. For a part-time job, Randall's pays extremely well.

Although I do admit there are days when I dread going to work, and sometimes things don't go quite so smoothly, looking at my situation as it is, I wouldn't trade my job for anything.

RYOKO'S RESPONSE

A couple of years ago, I worked for deaf or hard of hearing people in my hometown. Because of the old educational system in which deaf or hard of hearing people were taught only sign language, many have difficulty communicating to normal hearing people.

For three months, I was in an intensive training group where I studied sign language. After that, I started working as a minor translator in our city volunteer group. I went to a hospital, a police station, a city office, or a civil court, wherever some hard of hearing or deaf people needed help. Sometimes I got upset going to those places with them, because usually nobody got good news from those places. On the other hand, I learned something about the complex organization of society that I would never have learned if I hadn't been forced to.

What I liked most was working with children who wore hearing aids. They were three to five years old and could neither read the alphabet nor use sign language; besides, they should not use sign language, which might hinder the development of their ability to speak verbally.

What I had to do was to play with them and to let them use their voices to make a good impression on them. Smiling a lot, making funny faces, jumping, running, and drawing cartoons, gradually I could get into their minds. My volunteer mates and I would blow hard or gently on small pieces of paper. We often enjoyed making soap bubbles, too. These were good exercises to control their breath. Pouting our mouths, we practiced the "V" sound. Opening our mouths as much as we could, we practiced the "A" sound.

One boy who called me "Grandma" was interested in anything moving, a train, an airplane, a fly, or even some dust curling. Whenever he started watching things, he did not pay attention to anything else.

A girl who could hardly hear her voice, even though she wears two hearing aids, often cried very hard and hit anybody when she could not do what she wanted to do. There was no way to know exactly what she wanted, and her sharp yellow voice drove me crazy.

Another boy, who could hear much better than these two children, always wanted me to pay attention especially to him. He clung to me like a duckling.

After working with these children for two months, I had to work with a junior high school student who was going to a normal school, even though she could hardly hear anything. When I played with these children on the last day, I could hardly smile. Although they gave me a lot of trouble and sometimes I almost shouted at them, they taught me many important things and gave me a wonderful time.

Now, I am looking forward to working with children after I become a teacher.

KRIS'S RESPONSE

The job I currently hold is that of a cashier in a grocery store. I find my job very interesting and educational—interesting because I meet all kinds of new people and educational because I work with money and numbers all day.

One of my friends works in another store where they have to work their way up to cashier. They start as a courtesy clerk, a person who helps bag groceries. Then they move up to a stocker, a person who puts the stock on the shelves. Finally they get the chance to move up to cashier.

When it was finally her turn to move up to cashier, she came to me for advice. I advised her that it would improve her position to a much higher level and also increase her salary. I informed her of the different things involved in running a cash register: such things as how you handle checks, food stamps, bottle refunds, coupons, and all the different departments.

The strongest point I could stress was that when you begin to run the register it may seem complicated. But as you learn more about the register, you will catch on quickly and begin to enjoy the job.

I've held my job for two years and can only begin to express how much I enjoy my job. I learn new things every day and meet a vast variety of new people every time I work.

It's fun and exciting and is a way for me to escape many of my problems.

TOM'S RESPONSE

For the first job, working at the Dairy Queen is a good experience. If you don't have a lot of work encounters, this job could be a big asset.

One of the advantages of the job is that all of the tasks are very simple. Being a friendly person helps, because you get to meet a lot of different people. Most of your fellow workers are your age, which helps in getting to know the place. The hours you work aren't very long. Usually the place isn't that busy.

But since the place is not that busy, they cannot pay you good wages. This is a good job to start out on, but I wouldn't stay at the job more than a year. It gets old quickly.

ASSESSMENT

Writer _____
Self Assessment _____ Group Assessment _____
Teacher Assessment _____ Other _____
Reader understands how the writer feels about the job and why he or she feels that way. _____
   or
Writer needs to define his or her attitude toward the job more clearly and precisely. _____
Writer needs to support his or her attitude with more specific details.
_____

Other suggestions: _____

Again, the problem with Tom's response is very clear. He has defined an attitude: the Dairy Queen provides a good first job because its demands are limited, although its rewards are correspondingly limited. However, Tom's response is very generalized; he gives no supporting detail, and consequently the job doesn't become real to the reader. Tom's group checked "supporting detail"; Tom felt the response was successful.

Kris's response involves a different problem. It has detail, but that detail doesn't really support and illustrate her attitude. Kris defines her attitude in the first paragraph: she likes the job because of opportunity to meet people and to learn through working with money and numbers. This attitude needs further definition through supporting details and examples, but Kris's response lacks these because she turns her attention to describing the basics of being a cashier for her friend. She does not support and develop her original statement of attitude. Kris felt her response was successful; her group checked "definition of attitude."

Liz's group felt her response was successful; Liz checked "supporting detail." I would agree with both; that is, I think that Liz supports her initial point about accommodating and friendly management very well, but her other points need more detailed illustration.

Ryoko has dug much more deeply into her feelings about her job than the other writers. This may be partly because of the nature of the job, which demanded a strong emotional commitment. But look what Ryoko does with specific details: paragraphs four through seven make the job and her attitude toward it real. And consider how well Ryoko defines her attitude: she is not sentimental about these children, who are less than angels, but she sees them as they are, and she sees their needs, and the clarity of her seeing makes us believe and understand her compassion. Both Ryoko and her group felt that this response accomplished its purpose.

5 · I Knew a Teacher

All students are experts when it comes to teachers; they have known many teachers, good and bad. This assignment asks you to draw upon that knowledge.

SITUATION 5

You are talking with a friend who wants to become a teacher. In the course of the conversation, you think of a teacher who made a strong impression on you, a teacher who was effective and inspiring or ineffective and perhaps even destructive. Write a portrait of this teacher, with the purpose of giving your friend a positive or a negative example.

GUIDELINES

1. Pinpoint the quality or qualities that make or break this teacher. Use "high content" generalizations that say a lot.
2. Use particular situations and typical behavior to illustrate the person's best or worst teaching qualities.

Human character is difficult to write about because it is abstract and intangible. Personality is a complex network of drives, ideas, feelings, and ways of relating to the world and to other people. Further, personalities can be contradictory and changeable: the same person may have a large capacity for love *and* hatred *and* indifference; the friend you knew last year in high school may be very different today in college.

Though this assignment asks you to draw a portrait of a personality, it simplifies that task by asking you to write about a person playing a specific role in a specific social situation — a teacher in a classroom. The question is not "Who is Mr. or Ms. X.?" but rather "How does Mr. or Ms. X. act as a teacher?" (Obviously, X.'s larger identity affects how he or she acts as a

Situation 5 37

teacher.) You can write about *behavior* for this assignment. The question then becomes, what behavior do you select?

First you need to identify what makes this teacher successful or unsuccessful, what key quality or set of related qualities makes or breaks this teacher. Work toward *high content generalization*—generalizations that say a lot about the teacher. For example, if you simply say that a teacher relates well with students, you haven't made a high content generalization. There are a number of ways of relating well: a teacher could relate to a class like an authority figure, like a friend, like a comedian, like a gadfly—good teaching is possible within all those roles. Your generalizations about your teacher's essential qualities may be *explicit* (stated) or *implicit* (hinted) in your examples, but the sharper and more informative they are, the more helpful your discussion is for your friend.

In supporting your generalizations, you can use two basic strategies for describing your teacher's behavior. You can show the teacher in action in one or more concrete and actual situations—what he or she did or said; or you can write on a more general level about the way he or she would act, typical remarks, actions, ways of relating to students. Either strategy can create good portraits. The advantage of writing about concrete situations is that you need to be specific and detailed in a way that will show what you mean about the teacher. The advantage of writing more generally may be that you can express ideas and feelings about a teacher that are more subtle than you can capture in an example of actual behavior. The danger of this strategy is being too vague, not giving enough information about the teacher, not making your sense of the teacher sufficiently sharp and individual. Of course, the two strategies are not mutually exclusive; you can use both in the same paper.

Remember that your generalizations and illustrations must connect to a judgment; it must be clear whether you find this kind of teaching good or bad. There should be a clear lesson for your friend the prospective teacher.

LIZ'S RESPONSE

To be a truly good teacher is a very difficult task. It takes not only time, patience, and a good knowledge of the subject, but also the natural ability to portray an idea to all levels of students. Out of all my past teachers I can think of only one person who can even come close to the ideal teacher.

Each morning Mrs. Petersen entered our English class with the vim and vigor of a night bug ready to light up our minds with knowledge.

Through her many years of teaching she has acquired a certain knack for knowing just how much information a student could handle at one time. She never threw out more homework than a person could do, but she did make each assignment a challenge. I believe a teacher can be judged only by the amount of knowledge each student retained in his or her mind. Mrs. Petersen had such an incredible desire for knowledge herself that every student couldn't help but want to experience that same excitement from thoroughly understanding a poem or novel. Unlike some teachers who throw out facts, Mrs. Petersen ran her classes much like a discussion group. She allowed us to first interpret the novel, poem, or essay as we saw it; then she would give us her opinion and find facts to support each statement.

I think what impressed me the most about her was her organization. Each day she had an activity ready and she herself was prepared for just about any question. If at some time there was something she couldn't answer, her notes were so great that somewhere in her files she would surely find the answer.

One quality a good teacher possesses is understanding. Because Mrs. Petersen is also a student at the University, she is able to relate to the tension of exams or papers. Consequently she did as much as she could to help us through some of the rough times of learning, like helping us to comprehend a novel or helping with the idea for a paper. She was also the type of person who believed that there was more to life than studying. Frequently she attended concerts, plays, and sports activities. Although she was kind, she never let the class take advantage of her. You weren't overpowered by her, but we all knew who had charge of the class.

Mrs. Petersen possessed all the qualities of an excellent teacher. She was understanding, stern but kind, knowledgeable in her field, and well organized. Her desire for knowledge was passed on to each of us, which is probably the best fact supporting her outstanding teaching ability.

RYOKO'S RESPONSE

What? Are you going to be a history teacher? It reminds me of my teacher when I was a junior in high school. The teacher always embarrassed some particular students, including me, during his class, as if he were enjoying doing it.

The class president said to us, "Stand up" when the teacher came into our classroom. We made a bow to him and tried to sit down on the chairs. "Do it again," suddenly the teacher said. "Wait, wait. These guys. How many times have I told you to take off your caps in the classroom?" At that time, I had a hunch that the day was going to be bad for us. After some boys took off their caps, we made a bow to him again.

"Well, it was better than before. However, why can't you do it well the first time? You are not babies, so behave yourselves. Anyway. Last time, we studied about the Middle Ages. And I gave you some work sheets, didn't I? Who forgot the homework?" He started checking our assignments, walking around the classroom, saying, "Come to the front if you cheated or forgot to do it."

It was a day right before the big carnival in school, so we were very busy getting ready for the carnival. However, he gave us four pages of work sheet. There were about eighteen students who forgot to do or did not complete the assignments, including me. "For Heaven's sake! How come there are so many lazy students in the class?" Complaining, he found me, standing in front of the blackboard. "I see. Ryoko. You are the class vice president, aren't you? Look at your classmates. They are imitating your bad example. Why didn't you finish your homework?" Even though I wanted to laugh at his nonsense words, I answered him seriously. "I was drawing pictures for tomorrow's carnival all day yesterday, so . . ." "You should say that you are sorry. I don't want to listen to your explanation." It sounded so ridiculous to me that I grinned, looking at the floor, as if I were showing my apology.

"Everybody, turn your back and make a bow." Strange to say, he always had a very thick book. He began hitting our hips very hard with the book. When it was my turn to be hit, he said, "You are the worst in class. Do you think that I don't know that you are laughing?" Saying this, he hit me very hard three times. He was enjoying it very much as if it were a kind of recreation.

Since I had not slept the night before, when he started the lecture, his low, monotonous voice sounded just like a monk reading a sutra. My eyes were getting so heavy that I could hardly keep them open. Suddenly something hit my head. It was a piece of chalk that the teacher threw at me. "Good morning," he said, grinning.

We students could hardly know what he was thinking or what he would do next. But, little by little, we figured out how to protect ourselves from his sudden emotional changes. But one thing we could do nothing about was that when he gave back our exams, he always read our scores loudly.

KRIS'S RESPONSE

When I was in high school I had a teacher named Nancy M. She taught math courses, namely Algebra I and Geometry. I think she was the worst, most unfair teacher I've ever had!

I stuck it out through Algebra I and her runaround way of teaching, but had many run-ins with her during that course. It was during the first semester that the first run-in occurred. I had been sick for a couple of days and when I came back to class she had decided to punish me for being ill. There were about eight assignments sitting on her desk with my name on them. She handed them to me and told me to have them completed and turned in within three days. Then she informed me that I had to figure out how to do them by myself.

After that first run-in with her she did nothing but give me flak. She must be some kind of teacher to punish students for something that wasn't even under their control.

When I finally decided that I wanted to go into accounting as my profession, I knew I would have to take all sorts of math courses. The last thing I wanted to do was to take Mrs. M. as a teacher, but at least I had to try.

I enrolled in Geometry, the biggest mistake of my life! She was no different toward me than when I had her for Algebra I. She'd throw the assignment on the board without any explanation of the procedure. After she had done what she considered to be teaching, she'd hand you enough assignments for three days and expect you to have them done the next day.

The next day she'd tell you to correct your own papers, find your own mistakes, and hand them in. If you had questions, you were supposed to know how to answer them. When you walked up to her desk for help, she'd give you the answer but never explain how you got it. It's no wonder that nobody ever learned anything from her, and nobody could really stand her.

I hacked her through the first semester of Geometry, but after that I couldn't hack it any longer. I dropped out of Geometry after the first semester and vowed never again to take a class from Crazy Nancy. To put it bluntly, she was the worst teacher I've ever had, and I hope never to have one like her again! If I did I think I would rather drop out of school than try to learn something from nothing.

TOM'S RESPONSE

A dream of every teacher is to have his or her students feel they have learned something from that class. I believe Mr. H. accomplishes that dream.

Mr. H. accomplishes that goal by putting the straight facts into a recent situation that relates to the main idea of the class. For example, in American History class we read about how the presidents during the early 'twenties began to pay off the national debt. Mr. H. interpreted this fact to mean that if our families can't constantly borrow, the government shouldn't, either. He also emphasized that eventually we all have to pay this money back.

This example basically shows how he takes the facts and tells the students how the facts relate to their everyday lives. He also knows the feelings of the student body and can relate to the students on their terms. This is why Mr. H. is a good teacher.

ASSESSMENT

Writer _____
Self Assessment _____ Group Assessment _____

Teacher Assessment _____ Other _____
Reader understands why the writer found this person a good or bad
   teacher. _____
      or
Writer needs sharp generalizations that tell us more. _____
Writer needs more and better illustrative examples of behavior: typical or
   particular. _____
Writer needs a clearer connection between generalizations and examples.
_____

Other suggestions: _____
_____

   Kris's response has a high degree of focus. The problem is Mrs. M.'s inability to teach the process of mathematics; she is interested only in the product, the answers to the problems. Note that Kris basically describes *typical behavior,* though she also uses one particular example concerning her illness. Both Kris and her group felt that her response was successful.
   Tom's response also has focus and is built around a high content generalization: the idea that Mr. H.'s particular excellence is the ability to connect ideas to personal experience. I don't think that Tom's example conveys this idea very well; he needs more and better examples. Both Tom and his group felt that the response needed sharper generalizations; I disagree.
   Liz's group felt that her response was successful; Liz felt that she needed more specific examples, actual situations. I think that Liz might have done more with particular examples—for instance, instead of talking about help with novels, Liz could show us how Mrs. Petersen helped her to understand that the main character in *The Great Gatsby* is really Nick Carraway. On the other hand, Liz's generalizations are thoughtful, and in a number of places Liz describes Mrs. Petersen's *typical behavior* well.
   Ryoko re-creates a particular classroom scene very vividly through detail and dialogue; her group liked her response and felt that it was successful. Ryoko was concerned that her piece might be confusing. I like the piece also, but I think that there might be a problem with the connection between the main example and her generalizations. I am not sure whether Ryoko has quite found her focus. Is the teacher's problem his emotional changeability, as Ryoko indicates at the end? Or is it a general attitude of sadism?

6 · A Special Place

Everyone understands when you say that a place has a certain atmosphere; you are talking about a particular feeling or feeling-tone that permeates the whole scene, influencing everyone and everything in its domain. It is something in the air, a spell that colors perceptions. Each of us has known places with atmosphere. This assignment asks you to re-create the atmosphere of a place in words.

SITUATION 6

Sometimes place has a strong effect and influence on people. Describe a place that affects you strongly (a room, a building, an outdoor setting). Show the place so that the reader has its image in his or her mind's eye. The image should create a particular atmosphere and express a particular feeling.

GUIDELINES

1. Build your description around a particular feeling.
2. Use specific details that suggest and support that central feeling.
3. Find metaphors and similes—comparisons—that capture your feeling.
4. Order your description by *controlling the point of view.*

How does one capture an abstract and intangible atmosphere? Atmosphere is created by the way the parts of a scene fit together. While atmosphere may be intangible, the parts are not. Name the parts. Describe the physical features of the room, the building, the setting, as closely as you can. There is a good chance that if you can reconstruct a detailed picture of the place, you will capture its atmosphere in the process.

Of course, in writing the description, you will find yourself making choices. Which parts of the scene will you describe? What details will you include, what details will you skip over? Of the million and one physical features of the scene, which belong in your sketch? Include those features and details that connect with your feeling for the place, contributing to its mood. You might try making a list, then checking those details that evoke the atmosphere.

At some point you will need to define the basic quality of the atmosphere, so that you can *select* details that support that quality. Is a place peaceful? How so? Is it peaceful like a graveyard, where all activity is done and ended? Is it peaceful like a busy classroom or beehive, with a humming sense of harmonious, cooperative activity? Or is it peaceful like the ocean during a calm, when one senses a mighty force temporarily at rest? Pinpointing the nature of the atmosphere can help you select detail.

Another way to characterize the atmosphere is through the use of metaphors and similes (figurative language). In the paragraph above I used figurative language in comparing a peaceful atmosphere to a graveyard, to a busy classroom, to a beehive, to the calm ocean — these comparisons suggest different kinds of peace. You may find that you can help characterize your atmosphere by using metaphors and similes. However, don't force figurative expressions; don't use them unless they seem particularly fitting and helpful. Remember that you can't rely on them completely; the reader must see your place on its own terms, in its own detail, before comparisons will be meaningful.

There is one new problem in this assignment. When you were describing an activity in Situation 2 and an incident in Situation 3, organization was largely predetermined. You could rely on *time*, on chronological order, on "this happened, that happened, and then that happened." In this assignment, dealing with *space*, you will probably have to be more actively involved in making an organization, an order. You need to find a principle of organization to keep your description from being a random collection of details.

Remember that you are controlling the reader's *point of view*. Point of view can have at least two meanings: (1) physical location (where the writer places the reader with regard to the scene), and (2) the writer's subjective attitude toward his subject. (Thinking about the movies is one way to get a feeling for point of view as physical location. In every shot, the director determines the viewer's point of view by deciding where to place the camera.) In Situation 6 you must control point of view in the first sense very carefully.

Once the perspective is fixed, you are the one who moves your reader's attention. What will he or she see first, then next? Suppose you have positioned your reader in front of a tall building. Perhaps you will have the reader study the entrance and then move his or her glance upward. Perhaps you will start at the top and have his or her attention move downward. Perhaps you will start your reader with some unusual second floor window detail, then show him or her that the shape of the windows is echoed in the entrance. There are many effective ways of organizing space, and you may discover an effective pattern for your description naturally. If your description seems confusing, however, you may need to impose a pattern. You may find the natural movement of your attention when *you* are in the place — what you notice first, next, and so on — a good place to start.

LIZ'S RESPONSE

After dragging my overstuffed suitcases up five flights of the narrowest circular staircase possible, I turned to my left and viewed at the end of a long hall room 24. This I believed to be my little home away from home for the night. Slowly I pushed my body toward the pale yellow door. Upon reaching my destination, I pulled out the enormous key and took notice of the rather small keyhole. After fiddling with the key for a while, I finally heard the latch break through the rust, dirt, and grime that had formed over the last thirty years. Now it was time to peek into my little dwelling. I took a firm grip on the scratched-up knob (it was evident that rust had finally eaten its way through half of the bolts) and thrust the warped door open. To my surprise I was met with yet another small entryway. I thought to myself that it was such a tranquil little area. There was wallpaper with little pink and green flowers on two of the walls. It was fascinating to me to see how these little flowers even seemed to age on the wall: as I scanned toward the peeling ceiling, the flowers seemed to change colors, wither, and finally die at the top. On the third wall was again another semi-yellow door. When I had retrieved my luggage from the hallway I turned around and shut the door. After hearing the old knob fall on the other side, I was astonished to find that the wallpaper on the door in no way matched the other two walls, and neither did the paper underneath it, which could be seen under the unruly paper in the corners. Looking down to the floor I noticed underfoot a red piece of carpet, which matched neither of the two, or should I say three, types of wallpaper. Upon opening the door I saw my *très petite chambre*. On the walls was a stunning wallpaper of orange, blue, and green, which seemed to grab you, strangle you, and kill you with one look. I did have a small plywood closet, equipped with one bent hanger, set out from the wall. To its side was the bed. It reminded me of a bale of straw covered by one of Granny's old quilts that had since lost its print and form. I somehow found room to bring in my suitcases and place them on the bed of nails. Finally noticing the window, I ran over to check out the view. It was difficult to open because the paint that covered part of the windows also covered some of the latch. Breaking through to the outside of our soot-covered hotel, I saw a few pieces of drying underwear, a dead geranium, and a great view of the bathroom. I then turned around to see that yes, my room did come with its own bathroom. Jumping over the bed (there was no room to walk because of the luggage), I took one step into a black-tiled room, no bigger than the closet. The plumbing was the first ever invented, with the original rust stains, and the shower came without a curtain or nozzle. Even though the floor was wet and cold, the plumbing old, and the walls blank, I did notice the cutest little window above the toilet. Happily I jumped on the toilet and opened the sticky window, only to find a man sitting on the ledge looking in. It was nice to know that someone was looking out for me. I immediately sat on the bed (no other furniture would fit) and looked over my situation. Once I had opened my big window it became impossible to shut again, so not only could I see out but everyone else could see in. Although the curtain did help some, the moths had seen to it to provide an adequate view. The door knob had fallen off so there was no protection from outsiders, the lights didn't work, and if the wallpaper didn't kill me the bathroom surely would.

I wouldn't have minded the room so much if it had been clean. The bathroom was color-coated with rust stains and dirt on the floor. I guess what bothered me most was the ant and roach convention in one corner and the dust bunnies under the bed who had no conception of birth control. For the first night I stood prepared with my flashlight to battle whatever came my way, be it roach, bunny, or the man in the bathroom window. I think I know why they say there is no place like home.

RYOKO'S RESPONSE

Whenever I was so sad or frustrated that I could hardly stand anything, I wanted to be alone and to let myself be more and more miserable. So when I was very blue, I visited many times a temple that was on a mountain. As a matter of fact, I could have gone anywhere, to the sea, to a shrine, or to the lake. However, as if I were fascinated with the devil's sweet words, I went there to think about myself.

I left my home, saying "See you later" to my mother, as if I were going to school as usual. I wore a dark brown raincoat closed tightly to hide my school uniform, unless the sky was infinitely cobalt blue. I got on a train that went in the opposite direction of the school. For about forty-five minutes, my eyes were following the outside view, which looked like senseless, inanimate things.

When the train arrived at the station, a few old ladies and I got off the train; it was early in the morning, and also it was on a weekday. I walked through a farm for about fifteen minutes and slowly went up a long hill toward the mountain. Then I stepped onto a dark path to the temple. The path was surrounded by a bamboo grove, so sometimes the chilly, moist breeze passed over my shoulder, whispering a tale of birds.

The temple, which was a tiny old nunnery, was settled down in the bamboo grove like a shadow. The eighty-two-year-old nun was gathering pale brown leaves tenderly, with rustling sounds. She looked up at me as I walked into the garden and asked me, "How are you?" with a warm smile. So I closed my eyes for a moment instead of answering her. Then I went round to the back of the temple.

Sitting on a veranda under the eaves, I stared at a Chinese bellflower in front of a big stone. The cricket sang me a song quietly. Teardrops were running down my cheeks. The delicate illumination among the trees reflected on the small pond in the garden. A carp made a splash, and gradually the water rings expanded. My melancholy feelings dissolved into the rocking waves.

After a while, the nun treated me to a cup of dark green tea as usual. She never asked me any questions until I began talking to her, as if she had understood my mind. While a leaf was trembling in the air, I found myself again.

KRIS'S RESPONSE

My favorite place to go whenever something is bothering me is my grandmother's house. It's an old farmhouse that sits along the back side of Lake McBride in Solon.

I don't think there's any place like it in the entire world. At least not a place that is as special to me as this one.

I enjoy walking down the hill behind the house to the edge of the water. It gives me a feeling of freedom and aloneness, yet I'm still aware of the life that surrounds me. It really is a breathtaking experience!

You walk down a hill covered with green grass and clover leaves, as if you were walking across the blanket of heaven. Never in my life have I seen a place that glows with such beauty and freshness. This glow of beauty and freshness is the same exact feeling I have after walking through the grass and clover leaves.

The atmosphere around you is so full of life, yet there is still a hushed relaxation, as if it were really two worlds in one. You can hear the rush of the water as it hits the banks of the land, yet you're not really aware of the life going on in the water. You can hear the birds sing, but they're more like a chime that lulls you into your own little world of peacefulness.

Above you there's a blue sky that's a cover from all harmfulness. There's a feeling of life unending, as if you can just go on forever. This feeling stems from the ability to see forever, as if the beautiful land doesn't end.

Walking back up the hill I carry a feeling of refreshment. It's as if you've been to the world beyond and now you're coming back as a new person. It's like no other feeling you've ever felt before. In fact, I'd say it's almost like a feeling of eternity.

TOM'S RESPONSE

When I want to be alone to think, I go to my bedroom. As I open my bedroom door I feel as if I am opening the gates to a world filled with peace and solitude.

The first thing I notice when I enter my room is my large stack of records. I pick out of the stack my favorite record, "Old Dan's Record" by Gordon Lightfoot. I place it on my small stereo and turn it on. The music from the speakers begins to wake up my sleepy paradise. I sit down on my couch and stare at my poster of the Grand Tetons. When I stare at those mountains I feel a hundred times stronger, a thousand times wiser.

Situation 6

For now these mountains are only a dream, a glimmer of hope that keeps me going. But sooner or later we must accept the grim face of reality that strikes us all, that dreams can't come true. So now I must leave my dream world and enter the real world once again and face harsh reality.

ASSESSMENT

Writer _____
Self Assessment _____ Group Assessment _____
Teacher Assessment _____ Other _____
Reader understands how you feel about the place and why. _____
  or
Writer needs a clearer focus upon a particular feeling. _____
Writer needs more specific details. _____
Writer needs controlled use of figurative language. _____
Writer needs better control of point of view. _____
Other suggestions: _____

Kris's response calls our attention to an important mistake. Kris repeatedly uses a powerful metaphor to express her feeling for the place: she compares the atmosphere to heaven, the world beyond, eternity. This metaphor conveys the *power* of the experience for her, but she gives us almost no detail; we have only the vaguest, most general idea of her place. Both Kris and her group found this description successful; I suspect they were under the influence of the powerful religious metaphor. I feel frustrated and dissatisfied with the piece because I want to know what it is about the place that makes it like heaven; I want more of the earthly reality.

Tom's response suffers from similar problems. Two specifics—the record and the poster of the Tetons—are good, but they are far too few. What does the poster look like, what does the music sound like? What about the rest of the room—what makes it a "sleepy paradise"? The last paragraph is a particular problem because Tom's figurative language is heading toward cliché—"grim face of reality," "harsh reality"; his language is also slipping out of control—can a face strike us? Tom recognized that the last paragraph was a problem, and his group asked for more specific details.

Liz's paper, which turns description into story, is packed with specifics, and she has certainly found a focus: the repulsion and disgust evoked by the tacky room. The energy and humor of the piece make it hard to be critical of it, and Liz's group judged it successful. Though I, too, like its spirit, I find it difficult to read; the extremely long first paragraph needs to be broken up so as to divide the experience into natural sections for the reader. Also, Liz has to take better care of the reader in terms of perspective in some places; for example, what is happening in the small entryway is quite confusing. And the piece seems to move too slowly and awkwardly through its first part — a problem Liz was aware of. Liz checked focus and specifics on the Assessment Form, but I would turn her attention to paragraphing and sentence work.

I don't understand everything in Ryoko's response, but I think that I do understand her central feeling and the atmosphere of the temple, and that feeling and atmosphere are beautifully expressed in and supported by specific details. Ryoko checked focus, but her group felt the response was successful.

7 · On the Other Hand . . .

Point of view in the second sense—as the subjective attitude of writer toward topic—is obviously important in writing. Every time you write, you express a view of the world—through what you say, through what you leave out, through the purpose for which you are writing, through your attitude toward the subject, through your attitude toward the reader, through the speaker you create as your mouthpiece. The more coherent and well defined your point of view, the better your writing holds together around a way of seeing the world, and the greater your chances of holding your reader's attention.

Situation 7 poses a challenge in working with point of view. Not only does it ask you to create a viewpoint other than your own (much like a novelist seeing the world through the eyes of one of his or her characters), but it also requires that that point of view run counter to your natural way of seeing things.

SITUATION 7

Return to Situation 3, in which you felt yourself a victim of injustice. Often, one's idea of justice is heavily influenced by one's role in a particular situation. For this assignment, shift roles. Put yourself in the role of the person whom you regard as primarily responsible for the injustice. Imagine that he or she is telling a friend about the incident, and tell what happened from his or her point of view.

GUIDELINES

1. Tell the story clearly, giving the reader the facts necessary to understand what happened.
2. Make sure that your speaker's viewpoint differs in important ways from your actual viewpoint.

3. Create a definite and consistent attitude toward the incident. (In other words, create a convincing personality for your opponent.)

One requirement for this assignment is direct and straightforward: give enough information that your reader understands the basic situation. Nothing is more frustrating than listening to a story without having enough background to understand what is happening. The trick is to work this essential information into the narrative so that the reader can pick it up as the event unfolds.

The other two requirements are more difficult: how does one successfully create a point of view? Actually, you are trying to put the reader inside another mind — in this case, a mind that looks at things differently from you. You must re-imagine the whole event. The same things happen, but they take on a different meaning because you are seeing from a different perspective. You are devising a different *interpretation* of reality.

To succeed in creating this point of view, you will need consistency and thoroughness as well as imagination. You must see the whole event through the eyes of the other party; your narrator must play a consistent role. It won't do to jump back and forth between your original view of things and the new view you are creating. And you must *find a voice* for your narrator, a way of talking that convincingly expresses his or her point of view. You may find point of view and voice so closely connected that finding one means finding the other.

LIZ'S RESPONSE

If there is one thing I can't stand, it's big-shot teens trying to show off their cars. Last night I caught these two kids, one in a Z28 and the other in a Trans Am, trying to see who could hit the pedal the hardest. Well, little did they know I was a block away. I didn't even have to see their start to see they were in hot competition. I pulled both of them over and took their licenses. I didn't even bother to tell them what was going on. I just figured—let 'em think about it. Then I put them up against the cars and ran questions by them so fast that they got all nervous and almost confessed right there in the street. I had those kids so scared when they left that they would have kissed my foot for forgiveness.

This one kid in the Z I thought might give us a little flak, and I was right. He and some big-shot lawyer contested the case. I sure wanted to nail this punk so I followed him for two months. I looked for everything

Situation 7

but found nothing to charge him for, until he missed his court date. Then I looked all over until I found him. Then I treated him as if he were a murderer. I just hate it when these kids think they can get something past me. It looks bad on the record.

When it came around to court, I knew this kid was going to lie so I beat him to it. I said I saw the start of the race, with their hands signaling the match. I even said that they were going over 95, by my speedometer of course, and that he had confessed his guilt. I knew I had the judge eating out of my hand. I tell you, with lawyers you just have to do anything to save your record.

RYOKO'S RESPONSE

Since my parents were very conservative, as most other parents were in those days, I was raised very strictly by them. When we seven brothers and sisters talked to our parents, we had to use polite sentences. We were afraid of our father, because a father was the greatest and the most powerful person in a family. We children and our mother had to obey whatever he wanted us to do.

My husband did not like the way in which he and I were raised. He let our children be much more free than we were. Of course, the basic manners and rules we taught them were the same, though. Since my husband was a very busy person, he was rarely at home when the children were young. He scolded the children when they did something extremely bad or when they were completely wrong. So, as a mother, I had to advise them what to do or not to do. I knew that nobody wanted to be told some little things again and again, but I had to tell them, especially our oldest daughter.

Because she was our first daughter, sometimes I was not sure what to do. Besides, she did many things she should not do as a girl. I was worried about whether she would grow up as a feminine lady. She thought that I worried too much about trifling things. But I kept telling her.

When she was fifteen years old, because she was a member of a school swimming club, she had very hard training every day. And the date of an entrance exam for a high school was coming closer. But she could not handle both swimming and studying; she was often angry at herself and frustrated about her uncomfortable situation.

One day, when she came home, she was very tired and stressed. She lay on a sofa and watched TV without changing her school uniform. I told her to change her clothes and help me fix supper. However, she was still watching TV carelessly. Then she tried to change a channel by using her toes. I was so amazed that I said to her, "Are you a girl? How can you do such a shameful thing? Shame on you! Change your clothes and do your work!"

After a while, she started saying nonsensical, ridiculous things. "Do you mean that just because I am a girl, I have to have shame on myself? Who decided that girls had to cook or do the housework even if they are very tired, but that boys don't have to even if they don't have anything to do? What are men? What are women? I don't care about whether I am a boy or a girl—because I am a human being." So, I had to convince her that she was saying ridiculous things and nothing was wrong about my thoughts. She listened to me just for a few minutes and said, "Shut up. I told you I do not care about my sex. I would never have wished on myself an old-fashioned, traditional, conservative mother like you."

While she was criticizing me as a mother, I felt so empty that I almost fainted. Until that moment, she had never said anything bad about me myself, even though we argued a lot. I thought that I was wrong, because I knew that she was very tired and frustrated at that time. Besides, she hated being lectured about traditional good manners by me. She kicked the floor and went to her room.

After the other two children and I finished supper, I went to my room and thought about the way in which we had raised her. Then I noticed that she was cleaning the kitchen, acting as if she were still mad at me. But I knew that was her way to apologize to me, because she was very perverse; she could never have made an apology verbally. I was still shocked about what she had said to me, though I was sure that we had not raised her in a wrong way.

KRIS'S RESPONSE

I can see Kristy's point in saying that she has been treated unfairly when she is talking about the National Honor Society. It is a fact that she does meet all the requirements specified for membership, but for some reason she has been considered to be an undesirable candidate for membership in the National Honor Society.

I, as a counselor, have no control over who is elected to be a member or who is not. It is the teachers' role to elect the members, but they have their own little ways of picking their favorite students, whether they meet the requirements or not. I have no control over the way of choosing members; I just give them the list of students who fit the requirements. After that it is out of my hands.

Kristy has come to me many times not understanding why she hasn't been chosen as a member. I have asked the members of the selection committee several times why they feel she isn't satisfactory as a member, but they can give me no reason. It seems to me that they can think of nothing right off hand. It is my feeling that a terrible injustice has been done, not only to Kristy but to several other students who have been treated the same way.

The last time eligibility came up for the National Honor Society, Kristy was once again not selected. She came to me furious with anger. The only thing I could tell her was the same thing as before: there was no reason she should not be a member! I also told her that the National Honor Society was not as highly regarded as it used to be. In the past few years it has lost some of its respect; therefore, I wouldn't call it any honor to belong to such a group. Kristy accepted this but still felt hurt and betrayed.

I believe Kristy has every right to feel treated unjustly, as well as do many other students who were treated the same. The National Honor Society should have some set of formal rules that teachers have to follow no matter who the student is. With these rules it would allow students who are eligible for membership to get in, and also push out those students who don't meet the requirements, but are teachers' pets.

TOM'S RESPONSE

The task of judging debates is a thankless, never-ending endeavor. About a year ago, I judged a debate between Iowa City High School and Central Junior High of Davenport. The guys from City High were effective speakers, but I don't think they were arguing on the same subject that the team from Davenport was arguing on. But the issue was the matter of my conspiring with the two Davenport Central girls to unfairly judge debates of others, and to make sure they would win the tournament. I admit that I did know these girls quite well, but this fact is not conclusive evidence that I did anything wrong. The accusation is definitely untrue. My job was to judge debates by the rules.

The duty of the negative team is to refute the propositions of the affirmative; since they did not refute the affirmative's contentions, they did not win the debate.

Although I did talk to these girls during the tournament, I didn't discuss with them any wild scheme to make sure they won the competition. I think before these guys start accusing me of being unfair, they better have the evidence to prove that I am unfair, and not just have their own opinions.

ASSESSMENT

Writer _____
Self Assessment _____ Group Assessment _____
Teacher Assessment _____ Other _____
Reader finds this to be a clear, plausible, and different version of the original incident. _____
or
Writer needs to make clearer what happened. _____
Writer needs a viewpoint that differs more sharply from his or her viewpoint. _____
Writer must make the speaker more vivid, convincing, and authentic sounding. _____
Other suggestions: _____

Liz's response and Ryoko's response make an interesting contrast. Liz skillfully brings to life a policeman who thinks of teenagers as his natural enemies and who rationalizes his unethical conduct as necessary to win his war. The personality that emerges is unattractive but believable. Liz convinces us by creating language that expresses an insensitive and prejudiced outlook. Ryoko, on the other hand, makes her mother very sympathetic—a woman with values and background much different from Ryoko's, concerned with her daughter's happiness, able to see the pressures on her daughter, and willing to admit herself at least partially in the wrong. The result is a strong and moving portrait of generational conflict, conflict too complex for simple judgments of right and wrong. Both writers create convincing viewpoints, though those viewpoints have different effects on us. Liz and her group thought her response was successful. Ryoko's group felt the same way, but Ryoko was worried about the clarity of her situation. It does take the reader a little time to find his or her bearings in Ryoko's piece, but the situation becomes clear in the fifth paragraph. Ryoko might consider *beginning* with the incident, then having her mother develop the background.

Tom also does a good job of seeing his incident through someone else's eyes. His debate judge raises the cogent point that the evidence against him is merely circumstantial, and he sounds convincingly professional and indignant. Tom and his group found his response successful.

Kris gives us a weak, ineffectual person who sees an injustice but doesn't seem able or willing to act. Kris's speaker sounds authentic, but the problem is that his or her attitude toward the situation is too close to Kris's. The real challenge for Kris would have been to write from the viewpoint of one of the blackballing teachers. What *could* their thinking be? In imagining that, Kris could learn something about herself, other people, and the way she is perceived by other people.

8 · The Expert Instructs the Beginner

While we sometimes write to share our private worlds, there are other writing situations and other purposes. Sometimes we write to convey information, to explain something about the common world, and on these occasions we want the reader's attention on the *subject,* away from *us.* In terms of the communications triangle of writer, subject, and audience, our emphasis is on the subject. Writing a textbook is a good example of writing for this purpose. You won't be asked to write a textbook, but this assignment asks you to fill the role of explainer.

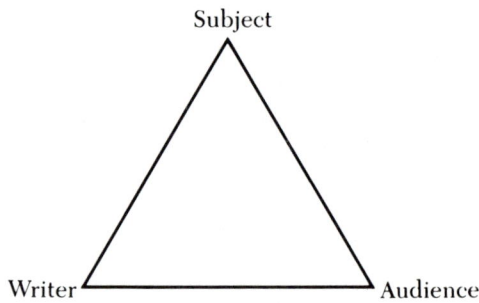

SITUATION 8

In Situation 2 you described one especially satisfying moment of participation in a sport or activity. Think again of that sport or activity (or of another you like). Assume that you are introducing a beginner to that activity. Single out one process within the activity (like getting up out of the water in waterskiing or hitting a serve in tennis). Write instructions that would help a beginner to learn that process.

GUIDELINES

1. Select one limited and relatively self-contained part of your activity.
2. Make sure that the reader understands your focus, knows what you are teaching—both the activity and the process within the activity.
3. Determine the most essential parts of your process and present them as a series of steps.
4. Write the instructions as clearly and simply as possible. Putting your steps into a list and using parallel structure may help you do this.
5. Make sure that your instructions are geared to a beginner's level of understanding.

Seeing clearly often involves looking closer. In writing these instructions, you want to focus your reader's attention on one part of your sport or activity; it would be unrealistic to try in one lesson to teach a beginner how to play football or how to do any other complex activity. Before breaking your process into steps, you need to identify that process and to separate it from the larger activity.

Analyzing the physical world—describing objects that exist in space and processes that occur in time—requires us to perceive natural divisions, natural "breaks." For example, we often tend to see human figures as composed of three parts—head, torso, legs. We divide the motion of a baseball pitcher into two parts—windup and delivery. Much of your success with this assignment depends on your ability to see the natural breaks, first in selecting a part of your activity, and then in subdividing that part. Try to select a part of your activity that seems relatively self-contained, in some way complete in itself, so that your instructions seem to your reader like a complete unit, a satisfying block.

Once you have identified your process, make an initial division into steps. Then consider the quality of your analysis. Are you identifying the essential steps? Are you leaving out anything important? Are you repeating yourself unnecessarily or including steps that might be too obvious to need mentioning? Are the individual steps treated in enough detail? Is each step sufficiently specific?

Stating the steps clearly is as important as identifying the steps. Be clear and direct; make your instruction as easy to read as possible. Check for deadwood; do away with unnecessary words and sentences. Check for tangled sentences that might confuse. Search for any places where your meaning might be ambiguous; instructions that can't be easily understood defeat their purpose.

One stylistic device may be particularly useful to you here: *parallel structure*. Sentences in parallel structure have the same syntax; they follow the same grammatical pattern. Do you see why the following sentences are in parallel structure?

When writing to explain, think first of organization and clarity.

When writing to express yourself, think first of voice and figurative language.

Parallel structure simplifies reading because the reader does not have to contend with a variety of sentence structures. By staying with one pattern, you free the reader to concentrate on your message.

When you are satisfied with your analysis, back up to make sure that your reader is not so lost in trees that he or she can't see the forest. Have you clearly labeled your instructions? Does the reader know what part of what activity you are describing? In other words, is there a clear context for these instructions?

Also, are your instructions at the right level for a beginner? There may be complexities and refinements in your activity that matter only after one has had considerable experience. For example, a beginning golfer doesn't need to know how to "fade" a shot; hitting the ball straight is problem enough. In the same vein, be careful about using technical or slang terms when a beginner might have trouble determining your meaning.

LIZ'S RESPONSE

The most important function of a forward is her ability to shoot the ball and make it score. Of all the different types of shots, the jump shot is the most widely used and the most difficult to master.

The first step in learning how to perform the shot successfully is to relax and think only about putting the ball through the hole. Now when your mind is cleared, take the ball in both your hands. Put the forefinger of your right hand on the air hole, spreading your fingers out for a good grip but still maintaining the ball on the fingertips. The left hand in turn should be placed at the side of the ball, also using the fingertips, but instead of gripping the ball, the left hand is used only as a balance. The left arm should be pointed at a slight angle while the right elbow is pointing straight down to ensure a straight thrust of the ball.

Legs prove to be a very important function of the jump shot. As you are ready to start the jump, remember once again the importance of relaxa-

Situation 8

tion. With the right foot take one step forward while at the same time bending both knees downward. With a push off your right foot, extend your legs, back, and head straight upward. If one were to extend either forward or backward, one would run the risk of charging into the defender or becoming so off-balance that the shot would be more of a throw. At the very peak of the jump, the ball is released, but the shot is not complete until there has been a successful landing. The knees must bend slightly on the way down, so the landing is soft, like the bouncing of a ball. To ensure a sense of balance it is also important to land on the balls of your feet since they are the widest and most centralized position of the foot.

After knowing the position of the ball and the functions of the body, it is time to learn how to release the ball. Bring the ball up to about your chin, an inch or two from the body, keeping it in the correct hand position. At the same time the body thrusts upward, the ball moves to the forehead and the right wrist becomes cocked backward. When the jump is at its peak, the wrist uncocks, putting a reverse spin on the ball, enabling it to die on the rim. This uncocking of the wrist is a soft, rhythmic movement, not a harsh jerk. The right forefinger should be the last piece of flesh to be in contact with the ball.

With the knowledge of each of these basic functions of the jump shot, anyone can become an all-star with practice. Just remember continually to keep your eyes solely on the front rim and your body square to the basket. If you can put all of the above together smoothly, no defender will stop you from putting the ball through the hole. Remember, the rim is two basketballs wide.

RYOKO'S RESPONSE

Swimming has been my favorite sport since I was six years old, when I was taught to swim by my father. In swimming, if you know how to dive, it will be more and more exciting. I don't know how to dive from a very high place, but I can tell you about the beginning dive.

1. Stand up on the pool side close to the surface of the water and simply jump into the water as you jump from steps to the ground.

2. Straighten your arms, keeping them close to your head. Then do the same jump you did in step one. When you do this, you should probably go to a little deeper place so your head will be in the water too.

3. Go back to the shallow place and sit down on the edge of the pool as if sitting on the edge of a chair. Straighten your arms, keeping them close to your head; slowly bend your upper body, sinking your hands, head, and body into the water. When you practice, try not to close your eyes, keep your arms straight up, and don't put your chin up. Your eyes should look at a place about five feet from the edge where you are sitting.

4. In this step, squat by the swimming pool and bend your upper body as you did in the previous step. Slightly kick the floor to sink into the water. The distance between your feet should be about the same length as your shoulders. In this step too, keep your head parallel with your arms; otherwise you will hit your breast or stomach. After you get into the water, put your fingers slightly up, so you won't keep going down in the water.

5. Little by little, stretch your bent legs. Relax your body and kick the floor just a little.

The final step should be easy for you to practice if you master these first five steps.

6. Stand up on the edge of the swimming pool; make the distance between your feet about your shoulders' width; hold the edge of the pool with your toes; bend your knees a little; relax; bend your upper body slightly; and then kick the floor. As soon as you kick the floor, straighten your arms as you practiced in the previous steps.

I hope you enjoy practicing these steps and have more fun going swimming.

KRIS'S RESPONSE

The sport I enjoy most is softball. The thing I enjoy most about softball is batting. There's just no way to describe the feeling that flows through your body when you hear the metal of the bat hit the ball. There's no other sport that gives me such a feeling of success.

Situation 8

The first time you step up to that plate and have all those people looking at you, it's very nerve-wracking, but after a few times it becomes easier. What it really boils down to is that if you know the procedure you should be able to hit any ball that falls in the strike zone.

Before even stepping up to the plate, you are called a batter on deck. This means that you are the next in line to bat, and are practicing your swing while waiting. While on deck, you should practice your stance, swing, eye contact, and follow-through. You must have all these things timed to the precise second to be a successful batter.

First, the stance of your feet should be shoulder-width apart, and each foot should be facing a different direction. Your knees should be slightly bent so as to make your body crouch a tiny bit. Your back should be bent slightly forward at the waist, and your rear end should protrude just a little bit. These are the only things that fit together to make a good stance.

Second, for your swing your arms should be lightly lifted, about even with your chin, and should be bent at the elbows. If you're right-handed, you should grip the bat with your right hand on top, with your thumb facing the knuckles of your left hand, and your left hand should be below with your thumb facing the knuckles of your right hand. When you begin your swing, your arms should start a gentle arc down and the elbows should begin to straighten out. You should bring your arms through at a straight level, even with your waist.

During the entire time you should always keep your eye on the pitcher and the ball. In order to make anything else work right, you're going to have to watch the ball as if you had the eyes of an eagle.

Finally you come to the follow-through, the part after you've hit the ball, or not hit the ball. No matter which happens, you have to have a follow-through. At this point your back should be coming out of the swing at an even level. Your bat should come around to your back at an even level until it reaches the bottom of your shoulder blades, where it should begin to swing upward. When it reaches the top of your shoulder, you should begin to pull it toward the ground, where you'll set it when you're ready to run.

After practicing these steps a few times, you should be able to walk to the plate and really lay into that ball. Who knows, maybe you'll even become a slugger!

TOM'S RESPONSE

The role of the first negative in a debate is the most important role of the debate for the negative team. To be a good first negative you must deal with the three main factors of the affirmative case: inherency, significance, and solvency.

When you begin your speech you must first deal with inherency. Inherency is the contention that the problem is part of the system. To refute the contention of inherency you must explain to the judge that the affirmative's definition of the problem is not part of the system. Significance is the contention that the problem is very important in the system. To refute the contention of significance you must explain to the judge that the affirmative's conception of an important problem is not very important, because the affirmative does not tell you all the facts about the problem. Solvency is already refuted because you have told the judge that there is no important problem in the system; therefore there is no need for solvency.

In your rebuttal speech you should review the points we have discussed and convince the judge you have won the debate.

ASSESSMENT

Writer _____
Self Assessment _____ Group Assessment _____
Teacher Assessment _____ Other _____
Reader would be likely to learn this part of the activity by following these instructions. _____
or
Writer needs to provide a context for his or her instructions. _____

Writer needs a better analysis. (Steps seem incomplete, redundant, or insufficiently explained.) _____
Writer needs a clearer presentation. (Reader has difficulty following the writer's language.) _____

Situation 8

Writer needs to adjust to a beginner's needs. _____
Other suggestions: _____

Liz's response is difficult to read for a number of reasons. First, she needs to do better at introducing her instructions and giving them a context. We have to figure out for ourselves that the sport is basketball, and we move so quickly into technique of the jump shot that we haven't much sense of how the jump shot fits into the game (except that it's the "most widely used"). Liz has divided her process into parts—grip, body mechanics, and release—but I'm not sure that she *signposts* her organization clearly enough; as readers, we may need to have this organization laid out more clearly (not just at the start of the fourth paragraph). The strength of Liz's response is her obvious knowledge and feeling for basketball technique and the density and thoroughness of her explanation. The danger here is that of losing a beginner in detail; I think this becomes a problem with Liz's instructions. Liz and her group found these instructions successful; I think they need to become more readable.

Kris does better with her set-up; she firmly places the reader in the on-deck circle, learning how to swing a bat in four steps. (The reader might find an explanation of "strike zone" helpful, however.) One question for Kris about her analysis: is it best to include grip under swing, or might it fit better with stance or as a separate category? While Kris has a good breakdown into steps, she sometimes has trouble stating her meaning clearly. For example, Kris says that "each foot should be facing a different direction." Does she mean that? Her description of the grip includes "your right hand on top with your thumb facing the knuckles of your left hand." I have some trouble with *facing;* does Kris mean "aligned with" or "next to"? In dealing with follow-through, Kris says, "your back should be coming out of the swing at an even level." Level with what? Kris needs more precision in stating the instructions; Kris and her group felt the instructions were successful.

Tom has done a good job in choosing and identifying his process: the first negative speech. He does need to provide more *context* to show us how this speech fits into the debate as a whole. But his division into parts seems excellent; the speech naturally divides into parts with different functions. The explanation of the parts needs work, however. I'm not sure that I understand "inherency" because I don't know what Tom means by "the system." I think I understand "significance," but some confused wording of the idea intrudes. Tom avoids explaining "solvency." Tom checked "better analysis"; he recognized that his steps require more explanation. Tom's group checked both "better analysis" and "clearer presentation."

Ryoko has done a very good job of dividing her sport, both in her initial division and in setting up her steps. The entrance dive is a good subject for this assignment, because it does separate neatly from the rest of the sport and because it can be handled in limited space. Ryoko's steps are well set up; each one places the reader on the edge of the pool and has him or her follow a somewhat different procedure. Repetition with variation; each step requires something a degree more difficult, building on the previous steps. Ryoko sometimes has a problem with *clear presentation*. For example, I never felt really clear about arm position, or where the upper body was supposed to bend (forward from the waist?), or what she meant by kicking the floor (pushing off?). Sometimes she needs to find a more direct and economical way of stating her meaning (when she wants the diver's feet about a shoulders' width apart, for example). Ryoko's group felt presentation was a problem, and Ryoko felt frustrated by the reluctance of her language to do what she wanted.

9 · Job Advice

Whenever there are tasks to be done, wherever people must work with other people, explanations are necessary. This assignment again puts you into the role of explainer, this time in the context of a job.

SITUATION 9

In Situation 4 you expressed your feelings about a particular job. Imagine that a friend is about to start working at that job and has asked you for advice. Think of some part of the job that may give your friend trouble, and write your friend a set of instructions for handling the problem. Identify a problem and suggest ways of dealing with it. Assume that your friend has general knowledge of the job, but not detailed awareness.

GUIDELINES
1. Identify and define a problem.
2. Put the problem in the perspective of the job as a whole.
3. Present an ordered set of specific suggestions for dealing with the problem.

In writing Situation 8—instructing a beginner in a sport or activity—you probably became aware of the need for defining and limiting, for staking out the ground you intend to cover, for carefully dividing and analyzing. In that situation you defined your activity by the way you broke it up. For example, if you analyzed the essential parts of bowling as the approach and the release, you gave your reader a particular way of seeing bowling. The better your analysis, and the more satisfactory your division into parts, the better your chances for writing successful explanation.

You face a similar task in Situation 9. In Situation 8 you were analyzing a process taking place in time and space; your job was to arrest and describe part of the process. In Situation 9 you need to analyze your job duties and to select a part of the job that may cause trouble for a new worker. You not only need to divide your job into parts; you need to *think like a new worker* to identify the problem. Of the many job responsibilities, what part of the job might give a new worker trouble? Your acuteness in selecting and defining the problem will determine the value of your advice.

Another similarity to Situation 8: you need to give your reader some *context* for the problem. In other words, the reader needs to know how the problem fits into the job as a whole. Putting the problem into perspective may not require many words, but it is important.

Once your problem is identified and defined and its context established, you should make suggestions that will help your reader deal with it. Are your suggestions relevant to your problem—would they lead to a solution? Are your suggestions sufficiently specific? Do you need examples to show what you mean? Are your suggestions in an effective order so that the reader can follow them as a unit or block? Are your suggestions easy to read? Are your sentences clear and concise? Thoughtful suggestions will be wasted if the reader has trouble understanding them.

LIZ'S RESPONSE

Because Randall's is the only grocery store in Iowa City or Coralville to allow the charging of groceries, our Master Charge system is widely used. It isn't really very difficult to do, but it may take a little time to get used to it.

First, after the customer has given you the card, look to the lower right-hand corner where the expiration date is given. The months are numbered and each card is good through the month stated. If the card has not expired, then pull the bad card book from the drawer under the belt. The book is in numerical order, so it is easy to look up the number on the card. If you don't find the number in the book, then pull out the Master Charge form. Ring out your register as if the person had given you cash. With the receipt tape you have all the necessary information to fill out the charge sheet. In the specific boxes mark down the total, the amount of tax, and your number. Pull out the charging machine, checking to make sure the date is correct. Each number designating the date is on a wheel so it can be easily changed by rotating the wheel with a pen. Put the

Master Charge in its form-fitting spot and then lay the charge slip on top, in its form-fitting place. Move the knobs at the bottom of the machine up or down to punch in the correct total amount. Then pull the side lever across the card and form. Give the customer the card and have him or her sign name, address, and phone number to the charge form. After the customer has done this, tear out the middle copy and with a smile and a thank you, give it to him or her. The two other copies are then put underneath your change drawer.

RYOKO'S RESPONSE

Although there are many things you must know when you take care of hard of hearing children, I will explain some of the most frequently occurring things. In this case, the children are about three to four years old.

When you are in a class, you might be surprised at the way they talk. Most of them who can hear a little tend to speak loudly (it may seem to you that they are shouting) because they can hear a little by themselves. But do not tell them often not to speak loudly. It is very difficult and too early to teach them how to control the volume of their voices. So, only when they scream extremely loudly should you tell them or let them know that their volume is too loud. Otherwise if you tell them very often not to shout, they will be afraid of using their voices and gradually tend not to speak in front of people.

Make a good first impression. It works well to get along with them. Try not to look down at them. When you wait for them in a class, sit down on the floor. When they are waiting for you, assume a low position. Talk to them at the same eye level or lower. It works very well to make them relax and to get along with them in a short time.

Keep trying to catch their eyes. Losing your eye contact with them might let them have anxiety and doubt about you. At first, they may not even look at your face, but keep trying. Not only will you learn many things from them, but also your observation will be more careful and sensitive. When you get a general idea about their characteristics from your observation, it helps you to teach and to play easier.

Give them clear responses to their actions. When you teach them how to make sounds, you must show your response to their learning clearly. This does not mean that you keep saying "Good" to them. But when they do a good job, you reward them with your words, with your face, or by showing how you are surprised at their response.

They take classes during weekdays and have studied hard since they were about two years old. And also we are not professional experts and teachers; we should be like children and enjoy studying with them. Studying must be playful. At this point, keep in mind that they almost read your mind from your attitude and activities. Do not forget that they are watching you all the time. If you are tired or blue, strange to say they can sense what you are thinking or how you are feeling, and they may not obey you. On the contrary, they may oppose you or do something intentionally to make you confused.

I am sure that you will learn many things from them unconsciously and it will surely help you someday.

Be kind and friendly. Good luck.

P.S. Enjoy yourself.

KRIS'S RESPONSE

My main job at Eagle's Discount Supermarket is to be a cashier, but I also do many other jobs. For the past two years I have been what is known as the Strawberry Queen in produce. During the summertime my hours are shared between grocery and produce.

My job is to put strawberries in quart containers. First I set up a table with twenty quart containers, waiting to be filled with strawberries on the cart. I bring the strawberries back out to the table, where I begin to fill the containers.

The easiest way to do it is to pick up single flats at a time and dump the strawberries into the containers. You fill the back containers first and then work your way to the front containers.

After you finish one flat, you pick up all the pint containers and stack them, then you sort through the strawberries looking for bad ones. Then you get a second flat and do the same things as with the first. You keep doing this until you have all the containers full.

When the containers are full, you pull out one at a time and put what is known as a top on them. The top is a piece of cellophane paper with four breathing holes in it. To get the tops to stay on, you take a rubber band and put a corner of it on the thumb and forefinger of each hand, stretching it to make the shape of a square. You lay the piece of cellophane across the top of the container and put the rubber band down over the four corners of the container.

When you have all the containers covered, you put them in what is known as a bread tray. It's just a square tray that holds twenty quarts of strawberries. When you have about three trays of berries done, you go out and fill the table on the floor. Your entire job for the day is to keep the table on the floor full, and to have enough strawberries to last for the entire night.

I enjoy the job very much because it is a break from running my register all the time. Once you get used to it, you get really speedy and have a lot of fun. It really isn't hard to learn if you just follow the steps I have given you!

TOM'S RESPONSE

One problem you will encounter while working at a gas station is that you occasionally get robbed. Since you can't prevent these robberies, you must know how to deal with them. Here are some guidelines to follow.

1. Keep calm. If you're not, the robber won't be, and he'll blow your head off.

2. Be as observant as you can. Try to get the best description of the robber that you can, so that the police can catch him more quickly.

3. Don't try to stop the robber yourself. Odds are you'll lose your life.

4. Give him the money quickly. The quicker you give him the money, the less chance he will blow your head off.

If you follow these tips, odds are that you will live to see tomorrow.

ASSESSMENT

Writer _____

Self Assessment _____ Group Assessment _____

Teacher Assessment _____ Other _____

Reader would recognize the importance of the problem and would understand how to deal with it. _____

or

Writer needs a better analysis, a more significant problem. _____
Writer needs to define the problem more clearly. _____
Writer needs to provide a context for the problem. _____
Writer needs more specific and relevant suggestions. _____
Writer needs to order the suggestions more effectively. _____
Writer needs to state the suggestions more clearly. _____
Other suggestions: _____

Liz's response and Kris's response make an instructive comparison. Both writers sound as if they know what they are talking about; both pay attention to detail and specifics. Both writers are generally clear, though there are places in both responses where I would be lost (for example, when Liz refers to "the drawer under the belt" and when Kris talks about "flats"). A common problem: neither writer really explains why the process she describes would trouble a new worker. While we might infer that these processes are a problem because they are complex, the writers might do more in terms of approaching the tasks from the new worker's viewpoint. Kris probably does a little better than Liz at placing the task into the context of the job as a whole. Kris also does better than Liz with organizing her suggestions. Kris shows you the major divisions in her process by the way she paragraphs; a new major step takes a new paragraph. Because Liz puts all her information into one long paragraph, reading is difficult. I think she could help the reader by putting her information into a list of steps or at least by indicating natural sections through paragraphing. Kris and her group felt her response was successful. Liz's group felt Liz needed to state her suggestions more clearly; Liz felt that she needed to define her process as a problem. I agree with Liz, and I would also suggest work on ordering and organizing her suggestions.

What I like about Ryoko's response is her relationship to her material. Obviously she knows this job and cares about it, and a humanity pervades her instructions. The response is particularly strong in terms of the *specificity* of her instructions. (Interestingly, Ryoko felt that lack of specificity was her main problem.) I think that Ryoko needs a better

Situation 9

definition of the problem; all Ryoko's suggestions center around communicating with the children; she should identify this as her focus. Ryoko's group felt that her response was successful.

Tom has clearly defined the problem, and his suggestions are clear and to the point. Tom could tell us more — should one move quickly or slowly (step 4 implies quickly, but wouldn't that alarm a robber?). Should one talk to the robber or keep quiet? Look the robber in the eye or look down? Keep one's hands in the air? There is a real opportunity for elaboration here; Tom's group called for more specifics, and Tom also recognized the need.

10 · Teacher Portrait

Not often are we called upon to write *pure physical description;* usually, we find ourselves using description as a means for achieving a larger purpose: expressing feelings, or explaining something, or persuading someone. To help you try your hand at extended description, this assignment asks you to embellish your response to an earlier situation.

SITUATION 10

Think back to Situation 5, in which you told a friend who is interested in teaching about a good or bad teacher of yours. Imagine that the friend interrupted you to ask, "What did he or she look like?" Write a description that would let the friend see the teacher in his or her mind. (If the teacher is too hazy a figure in your memory, use someone you know well for your subject instead. Again, describe that person so that the reader can see him or her.)

GUIDELINES

1. Cite striking features, specific physical details.
2. Establish an overall impression.
3. Fit the individual features into the context of the overall impression. Coordinate the two.
4. Organize the movement of your description.

We perceive people physically in two different ways: we form a total impression, a sense of the person as a whole, an overall *gestalt;* and we are struck by individual features that call attention to themselves. When the political cartoonist Oliphant portrays Ayatollah Khomeini of Iran, for example, he gives Khomeini prominent, downward-slanting eyebrows. The caricature as a whole creates a cruel, brooding, obsessed figure. The viewer takes in both the eyebrows and the cruelty at the same time. Parts and whole, details and overview fit together. You want to achieve this same coordination in your portrait of your teacher.

In addition to making sure that details and overall impression match thematically, you must decide when to present what. Are you going to start with an overall impression, then present individual features? Are you going to work the other way around? Perhaps you wish to build to your general impression, then fill in some further details. Perhaps you will never state a general impression explicitly, but will let your details build to an unstated (implicit) conclusion.

You must also decide on an order for the movement of your description; by what logic will you move your reader's attention from one thing to another? Are you moving from head to toe? Or from build to clothes to characteristic postures? The discussion of organization, space, and physical point of view in Situation 6 is relevant to this assignment.

LIZ'S RESPONSE

My parents always told me in order to learn one must look, see, and listen, but then again Mom and Dad never had to learn from Mrs. B. Of all my instructors, Mrs. B. was by far the most competent and interesting. In knowledge she did not lack, but in appearance she needed help. She was one of those people who couldn't get lost in a crowd.

As a usual state of affairs I don't spend my time looking at the figures of my instructors. With Mrs. B., though, observation was an uncontrollable reaction due to just plain fascination. Her head was of normal proportion and contained all the necessities, such as brown eyes, about which a black eyebrow pencil cobraed in the shape of an eyebrow. Her nose was sleek and slim, from which your eyes slid down to the thin, bright red lips. From each of her ears dangled the most hideous earrings. They were so heavy that they seemed to drag her lobes down to her shoulders.

From her narrow shoulders her body scans down in a V shape to her trim waist. At the waist the V flips over and dramatically widens over her hips. Attached to this slightly odd-shaped frame are two spindles with knobs at the knee joints. One might suspect that they had once belonged to a chicken, perhaps Big Bird of *Sesame Street*.

Her clothes fit to her body like Saran Wrap fits to a bowl. The double-knits stretch around her bulging hips and then sharply curve in around the legs. Down to the ankles the pants fall, to show off her varied array of shoes. Above her belt buttons up a plain-colored shirt. To this day no class has ever seen Mrs. B.'s Adam's apple, for she buttons her shirts so high and tight that we wondered for a long time whether she even had a neck. Over that shirt she always wears a jacket that of course is the same printed double-knit as the pants. One can't say that her outfits aren't color-coordinated; they just consist of colors that no one else has ever seen. At times they are so bright and shocking that they seem to devour you as soon as you step into the room.

Probably the most talked about and remembered portion of Mrs. B. was her hair. Atop her head sat a thick black mess of plastic threads. As sophomores it took us about two and a half minutes to figure out that she wore a wig, and then the rest of the year was spent trying to figure out what color her hair really was. It amazed me how through wind, rain, sleet, snow, and hail, not one hair was ever moved on that wig. It was almost as if that half curly, half straight, and three-quarters deteriorated head of hair had been sprayed with glue.

Even with all of her oddities in dress and appearance, there was still one basic fact: she was the best teacher at West High. I went to school to learn, not to judge, and it was with Mrs. B. that I did more than just learn English. I learned the art of concentration on important issues and how to block out the unimportant. In this case one should listen but not look.

RYOKO'S RESPONSE

You want to know what he looks like? If you see him, you can tell how mean looking he is. He looks at his students, maybe not only his students but everybody, from the side of his glasses, smiling a little bit with his lips, showing some of his golden teeth that made me think of a cheap, nasty usurer.

He thinks of himself as a very tidy person. He always has three handkerchiefs, which are clean and neatly ironed, one for drying his hands after washing in the bathroom, one for wiping his hands before he eats something (he never washes his hands in the bathroom before he eats something), and one for emergency use. Even during summer (we have very sultry summers), he wears a summer sack coat and a necktie as other white-collar people do. And in his coat's pocket, there is one more handkerchief for wiping his sweat.

Unlike Americans, we are very small in junior high. So since he is taller than average, he is very tall for us. He looks very muscular, which makes it more difficult for us to disobey him. He can easily beat you up. Besides, he has a black belt in judo.

He walks like an authority figure in school, his jaw pointing up at the sky. If you pass by him without making a bow, he will grab your neck and tell you that you have awful manners.

Did you get a picture of him? Don't worry. Not many people can be like him anyway.

KRIS'S RESPONSE

When I was a sophomore in high school, I had the worst teacher I've had to date. And I think she looked as bad as she taught. Her appearance is something I could never forget; yet somehow I wish I could.

The most memorable characteristic about her was the size of her hips. The size of her back end was wider than two of me put together. All the students used to say that she had the butt of a B-52.

Another thing I remember about her was that she always wore the most outdated clothes. Her clothes were the wildest color combinations, and her pants were always about three inches too short. When she wore a dress, she didn't wear hose, not even in the winter.

I guess you could say that all her students were so amused by her appearance that they thought the idea of her being a teacher was ridiculous. All of us had a hard time sitting down to watch and listen to the B-52 teach class.

TOM'S RESPONSE

When you meet D. H. his large appearance will seem to dominate you. Don't be frightened because his friendly face will show you that there is nothing to worry about. When you talk with him, those brown eyes will show concern and a sincere reaction to what you're talking about. His receding hairline shows his many years in the teaching field. His large shoulders and huge chest show a man who has lifted weights for many years. His proud walk shows his inner pride in himself. The blue pinstripe suit and oxford shoes are evidence of the powerful character he possesses. This unique person is D. H.

ASSESSMENT

Writer _____
Self Assessment _____ Group Assessment _____
Teacher Assessment _____ Other _____
Reader can see the teacher in his or her mind. _____
   or
Writer needs more striking features and specific details. _____
Writer needs a sharper overall impression. _____
Writer needs better coordination of features and impression. _____
Writer needs better organization. _____
Other suggestions: _____

I certainly can see Liz's Mrs. B. in my mind's eye; she cuts a vivid comic figure, strangely built, madly dressed, apparently unaware of the effect of her appearance on her students. Liz wades in with customary thoroughness, and in this case the portrait seems to gather a wild comic energy of its own. Double-knits stretch, shirts button, pants fall, and eyebrow pencils "cobra"; Mrs. B.'s appearance takes on a life of its own, ready to riot. Mrs. B. materializes as an ungainly, bizarrely costumed Big Bird of a person topped off with a "half curly, half straight, three-quarters deteriorated" nest. Liz has a wealth of detail, an overall impression, and an organized movement—her description moves from head down to feet (with a little jumping around in the fourth paragraph), then returns to the wig for the crowning touch. Liz's group felt the response was successful, and so did Liz. (In a way she felt it was too successful; she felt remorseful about her outrageous caricature of her favorite teacher.)

Ryoko's portrait doesn't have the full detail of Liz's, but her detail is well selected to support her overall impression. Her teacher comes off as sly, vicious, compulsive, and petty, and the gold teeth, thin smile, multiple handkerchiefs, and upthrust jaw all fit this character. It is an effective portrait; my one reservation concerns the movement of her description—the fourth paragraph seems out of place, an interruption of the flow. Ryoko's group felt the response was successful; Ryoko thought she needed more specific detail.

"The butt of a B-52" sounds authentic to me, but Kris needs to paint a more complete portrait. Kris gives some good clothing detail in paragraph three, and there are those hips, but I can't really visualize this teacher. Kris thought she needed more details; Kris's group wanted more details and a sharper overall impression.

I'm pleased with Tom's focus on an overall impression. Tom centers his portrait around D. H.'s combination of power and warmth, and shows how those potentially contradictory qualities are united and integrated in D. H. Tom's group felt he needed more specific details, and Tom agreed. I think Tom has created an interesting and effective organization: after some initial awe, Tom brings the reader in for a close-up on D. H.'s face. Then Tom progressively pulls the reader back, so that one finally sees D. H. full-figure from a distance.

11 · A News Story

A reporter tells the public what happened. A reporter digs out and presents the truth. But the truth according to whom? Whose version of what happened? At least in theory, a reporter tells The Truth and What Really Happened. He or she is concerned with facts rather than with interpretations, conjectures, and opinions.

The reporter's stance in relation to the event is one of distance and detachment. Ideally the reporter writes without personal involvement, without taking sides or taking a position. A reporter *describes;* a reporter does not *judge.* A reporter is a *spectator,* not a *participant.* A reporter stands apart from what he or she is reporting and plays no favorites.

Some people argue that such absolute objectivity is not possible, that any account of an event is to some degree an interpretation of that event because of the choices all writers must make: what to include and what to exclude, what to emphasize and what to subordinate. But wave that objection aside for the moment. This assignment asks you to play the role of reporter, to take as objective a stance as possible while describing an event you have already treated from two different and subjective points of view.

SITUATION 11

For Situation 3 you told about an incident in which you felt unfairly treated; for Situation 7 you told the incident again from an opposing point of view. Now take up the matter from another angle. Put yourself in the position of a reporter; you are going to write up what happened as if it were a news story. You have talked with the writers from Situation 3 and Situation 7; you have gathered all the information you can on the incident. In your role as reporter, write an objective account of the incident.

Situation 11 81

GUIDELINES

1. Try to record facts rather than opinions. (The "facts" may be the common ground, the circumstances on which the two parties agree.)
2. Make sure that the reader understands what happened.
3. Maintain your neutral viewpoint; don't slant your language.
4. Follow news story form: headline, subhead, lead.

What does it mean to write a news story? First, it means assuming a point of view that we might call *third-person impersonal.* You the writer never appear in the story; you tell about other people and events while remaining anonymous. For example, if I were to treat the writing of this chapter as a news story, I might use for a headline,

TEXT WRITER COMPOSES OBJECTIVE ASSIGNMENT

and for my subhead,

Students Asked to Play Reporter.

In my story I would try to establish the facts according to an old journalistic formula: *who? what? where? when? how?* Who was involved? What happened? Where and when did it happen? By what means did the action take place? Be careful if you deal with *why?* because it is easy to introduce your speculations when you are dealing with people's motives.

Iowa City—June 24, 1979

A teacher named Gene Krupa today composed an eleventh writing assignment for his proposed textbook *Situational Writing.* The assignment will require students to write up an experience of their own as a news story. Professor Krupa stated that that assignment fits into a larger sequence of assignments, and that he composed it because he wants students to consider one event from a number of perspectives. Professor Krupa revealed that the idea came to him over his morning newspaper.

Granted that the subject is a ridiculous one for a news story. Yours may be also, but what matters is what you may learn from trying to assume an objective, reportorial viewpoint. It may alter and complicate your understanding of the original "injustice."

The idea of headline and subhead is obvious enough (though these are not necessarily easy to write). The "lead" is your first sentence: it should contain as much of the essential information as possible (within the limits of a readable and efficient sentence). Your lead should also be clear in terms of the relationships that structure your information: who are the main actors? What did they do? The rest of your story should be essentially an expansion, an elaboration of the facts in your lead.

Let me illustrate an earlier point about the impossibility of total objectivity. Consider again the headline

TEXT WRITER COMPOSES OBJECTIVE ASSIGNMENT.

Notice that the main elements in my story are the writer and the assignment. I could have written the headline this way:

TEXT INCLUDES OBJECTIVE ASSIGNMENT,

a presentation that changes the meaning of the event because the emphasis is on the textbook rather than on the author. Or I could have written,

STUDENTS TO BE GIVEN OBJECTIVE ASSIGNMENT,

again changing the meaning of the event.

A main consideration in writing a news story is to refrain from explicit judgment. For example, had I said,

BREAKTHROUGH IN ASSIGNMENT DESIGN

or,

STRANGE WRITING ASSIGNMENT,

I would have been evaluating the event, passing judgment. This points out another important consideration in writing this assignment: using *denotative* language — language that simply describes — as opposed to *connotative* language — language that judges and carries emotional associations. In the previous examples, *breakthrough* implies a positive judgment; *strange* expresses some skepticism. A neutral word in this context might be *unorthodox* or *unusual*.

To recapitulate, you want to stay within a third-person impersonal viewpoint, and you want to use neutral, nonevaluative language. These two strategies are closely related. Also, like any other good reporter, you want to be clear, complete, and easily understood. News story form is designed to achieve those ends; see whether you can follow it.

Situation 11

LIZ'S RESPONSE

HOT CARS HIT THE ROAD
Drag Racing Still a Problem

According to police report, Jim Jones and John Stevenson were charged with drag racing following an incident on Saturday, July 23, 1981. Charging officer Kinkle reported that the two cars, one a 1981 Camaro Z-28 and the other a 1980 Pontiac Trans Am, were in a cat and dog race on Riverside Drive, going speeds up to 115 miles an hour, as recorded on his own speedometer. Kinkle said he first noticed the two cars at the intersection of Riverside Drive and Highway 1 where the Z-28 was in the left lane and the Trans Am in the right. After a short exchange of engine revving, each man jumped on the fresh green light. After the smoke cleared, Officer Kinkle proceeded to follow the two vehicles without turning on his siren or lights. The Trans Am was in the lead by a car length as they passed the Wardway Plaza, but as they reached the airport the cars seemed almost even as they reached maximum speeds of approximately 115. It was at this point that Officer Kinkle turned on the siren and pulled both cars to the side of the road. There they were formally charged with drag racing, and they are now awaiting court appearance on September 2, 1981.

RYOKO'S RESPONSE

CHITCHATTING WITH OUR NEIGHBORS

Hi! How are you doing?

Today, I want to chitchat with you about my friend and her argument with her mother, which happened a couple of days ago.

There are lots of problems between a mother and children in everyday life. You might be having one now, too. So, let's see what's happening to them a little bit.

My friend Ryoko is an active fifteen-year-old girl who often has arguments with her mom. Her mom is a forty-seven-year-old lady, a little traditional but understandable. The other day, Ryoko came home after her swimming training at school. She usually helps her mom with cooking and housework. But on that day, she was exhausted and felt very frustrated about everything. So she did not help her mom but lay on a sofa and watched TV instead. She said that she didn't even try to change her school uniform. Once, her mom asked her to do whatever she was supposed to do—helping with the cooking, changing her clothes, and setting a table. But she didn't even answer her and kept doing nothing.

Then her mom said that if she were a girl she would act more female and help her mother with the housework. This was what made Ryoko mad.

Ryoko started acting badly and tried not to listen to her mom. But after a while, she started criticizing her mom, saying, "Do you mean that just because I am a girl, I have to do this and that? You just shut up. I don't care who you are. I will do whatever I want to do and it doesn't matter whether I'm a girl or not. I wish I didn't have a mother like you!"

Her mother's face turned pale and she said nothing. Ryoko kicked the floor hard, went to her room, and didn't show up for supper.

Ryoko came down to the kitchen late at night and started washing dishes. She still looked angry and acted angry too. When she saw her mom, she didn't say anything to her. Moreover she kept acting as if she were still mad at her.

What do you think?

Do you see yourself in here?

KRIS'S RESPONSE

YOUNGER DAUGHTER UPSET WITH POSITION
Wants to Prove Herself to Her Parents

Kris S. is the younger child in a family of two daughters. Her older sister, Kim, is a year ahead of her.

Kim was a sophomore in high school when she was allowed to ride to a boys' basketball game with her friends instead of with parents. It was the first time that she was allowed to go to a game with her friends. Before she left she was warned by her parents to behave herself and not get into any trouble.

Situation 11

Well, as it turned out, Kim did get into trouble. She never showed up at the game, and her parents were to find out the reason when they came home.

One of Kim's friends had decided to buy a twelve-pack of beer for the trip to the game. After a few of those beers, it seems that this friend got a little brave and began to toss the cans out the window. As it turned out, the friend got a little too brave. The group was caught by the authorities and taken to the local police station. At the police station they tried to contact the parents, but none of them were home. All of the youngsters were given a harsh lecture by the police. They were told they must tell their parents because the police would later contact them, and a letter would also be sent home.

One year later Kris became a sophomore, and she thought that it was finally her chance to go to the games with her friends. But, Kris found out she was wrong. She was not allowed to ride to the games with her friends.

Kris felt that she was the victim of injustice. She believed that she had been judged upon her sister's actions. She didn't feel she was allowed to prove herself to her parents.

In this situation Kris felt that she was the victim of injustice because she wasn't allowed to prove herself; she was guilty until proven innocent. She felt her parents were punishing her for her sister's actions, and she was deeply hurt.

TOM'S RESPONSE

BIAS CHARGED AT DEBATE TOURNAMENT
Iowa City Team Up in Arms

Iowa City, Iowa

During last week's debate tournament, the negative team from Iowa City charged their debate was fixed by a judge from Davenport. The team asked for a ruling from the tournament director, but he refused to overturn the ruling. When the judge was asked about the charge, he replied, "No comment." The men from the negative team were still very upset about this grave act of injustice. The tournament director said he could not overturn the ruling because the evidence was much too sketchy.

ASSESSMENT

Writer _____
Self Assessment _____ Group Assessment _____
Teacher Assessment _____ Other _____
Reader feels that this is a fair and objective account of the incident. _____

or

Writer needs to make clearer what happened. _____
Writer needs to stick within an objective viewpoint. _____
Writer needs to eliminate slanted language. _____
Writer should follow news story form more closely. _____
Other suggestions: _____

    Liz reports well: her emphasis is on the facts; she turns the reader into a spectator watching an event unfold; she gives clear and detailed action rather than interpretation. Liz and her group felt her response was successful, but I am bothered by the issue of objectivity. What Liz gives us is an objective treatment of the police officer's version of what happened. As I understand Liz's incident, Liz would deny the validity of this story. What, then, would an objective, reportorial account be? Assuming the reporter had talked to both the police officer and the accused parties, I can imagine this sort of headline:

ALLEGED DRAG RACING INCIDENT
Reckless Driving or Police Harassment?

If the writer has heard several possible versions of the truth, objectivity would dictate presenting the conflicting accounts.
    Ryoko doesn't play newspaper reporter; she takes on the role of a neighbor, and it's hard to say exactly whom the neighbor is addressing — is she retailing gossip, or is she the host of a sort of Ann Landers – Joyce Brothers TV segment? Nonetheless, Ryoko's variation on the assignment achieves the original purpose: Ryoko reports the incident from a third point of view, from the outside vantage point of a spectator rather than that of a participant.
    Ryoko achieves objectivity in much of the piece, but in other places the narrator presents Ryoko's thoughts rather than simply reporting her ac-

tions. In the fourth paragraph, for example, she writes of Ryoko's exhaustion and frustration. This makes Ryoko more central to the story than her mother. In paragraph seven, the narrator reports Ryoko's words directly, while in paragraph six she paraphrases what the mother says; this also tends to highlight Ryoko's role in the incident.

In addition to featuring Ryoko, the narrator occasionally passes judgment on her rather than simply reporting what happened. In the seventh paragraph, for example, "Ryoko started acting badly. . . ." Such judgments aren't passed on the mother. In the last sentence of the ninth paragraph, "moreover" sounds slanted, judgmental, a nail in the coffin of Ryoko's guilt.

Ryoko's group didn't feel that the story was in news story form, and Ryoko was aware of this problem. I also felt that the piece needed more objectivity.

Though Kris tells her story clearly and readably, she misses the object of the assignment because she doesn't step outside her own point of view. Her headlines make this clear:

YOUNGER DAUGHTER UPSET WITH POSITION
Wants to Prove Herself to Her Parents

Kris's story features Kris's state of mind rather than what happened. A more objective treatment might be headed:

SECOND DAUGHTER RESTRICTED IN BASKETBALL ATTENDANCE
Protests Parental Decision

Kris changes the formal point of view—that is, she writes about herself in the third person. But she doesn't change the real point of view: she tells everything from her perspective, and ends with an explicit judgment on the situation. This is not reporting; this is *taking a position*.

Tom begins well; his headlines promise an objective treatment. Toward the end of his story, however, he lapses from objectivity when he talks of "this grave act of injustice." Tom also needs more specific information to make clear what happened. Most important, he should elaborate the basis of the charge. How did the judge throw the debate, according to his accusers? What was the evidence that the tournament director found sketchy? Second, Tom could make his lead more detailed: what tournament? Held where? On what days or dates? Tom's group wanted more objectivity; Tom felt the response was successful.

12 · A Student Problem

Explanation sometimes involves *imagining how others see the world*. This was true in Situations 8 and 9, where you needed to approach an activity or job from a beginner's viewpoint. Sometimes, however, explanation primarily involves discovering what *you* think. Explaining your viewpoint can be very important because others can respond to us as we want only when they understand us. In the following assignment you must draw upon your viewpoint *and* your understanding of the viewpoints of others to identify a common problem.

SITUATION 12

A counselor from Student Services at your college or university has made an appointment to talk to you. She is interested in interviewing students to find out the main problems students face in the school environment. In preparation for the interview, write a discussion of a problem that affects you and other students.

GUIDELINES

1. Identify a school-related problem that you share with other students.
2. State the problem clearly.
3. Show in detail how it affects your life.

What will make the interview productive for both the interviewer and you? First, your problem must relate to the institution, so that official attention is appropriate. Second, the problem should be typical of the experience of many students, rather than unusual and of limited application. A problem that meets these conditions will seem real and convincing.

Once you have identified the problem, you need to state it clearly. Find language that allows a clear, sharp generalization; you need to condense your problem into a phrase, a sentence, or several sentences. The sharper your statement of the problem, the less interpreting for your interviewer.

A good general statement is not all you need, however. A problem becomes real for us when we see its concrete manifestations in particular cases. For example, the concept of poverty tends to remain distant and unreal for one who is not poor until that person walks through a slum. In the same way, your problem requires specific examples, cases, illustrations. If you can show specific instances of the problem and its effect on your life, you make the problem more urgent and immediate for your audience.

LIZ'S RESPONSE[3]

Although West High is considered one of the top schools by scholastic testing, I believe the credit should go to the students, not the administration. The teachers at West have no real interest in their subjects, or they just aren't able to teach in an interesting and informative fashion. Thus each student is faced with the problem of boring classes and teachers who just don't care. Take, for instance, the French teacher. The final trimester was run in a very unorganized fashion. The daily reading assignments were given in one lump sum and never discussed. She was always late to class and never had anything for us to do. She assigned, along with the readings, several large papers. The only problem with this was that she told us she never had time to grade them all, so all we got were check marks for our work. We had one day of review, without the teacher's assistance, for our final. A couple of my friends missed the review because of sickness. Consequently, they hadn't received some vital information needed for the test. The day they returned, they were forced to take the test without this vital information. The teacher said her reasoning was that it wasn't her fault they were sick; they should have known everything anyhow.

The foreign language department wasn't the only division that

---

[3] As a freshman beginning college during the atypical summer session, Liz felt that she did not yet have enough exposure to the institution to write the assignment. She therefore wrote about her high school.

claimed incompetent teachers; every other department did as well. The music department has a band director who comes to school either drunk or with a hangover. The math department carries two teachers who don't even care enough to halt cheating during tests. This became very disturbing to a few people I know. They were forced to take lower grades because the cheaters had raised the class curve. Consequently, they were punished for being honest.

In the physics class, the teacher was a baby sitter. He didn't give lectures or discussions. Correcting papers was his job. The physics tests were a joke because the tests were always out beforehand. The history department is terrible. Teachers are forced to have classes they don't want in order to remain the football coach or just to have a job. The assignments are not well thought out and boring. Because the teacher himself has no interest in the course, the students have no interest.

After talking with quite a few students, I have decided that these are the biggest complaints: the teachers take weeks to grade tests and papers; they aren't willing to stay after to give extra help; there are areas where students have been graded unfairly because of their extracurricular activities; assignments have no learning value—just busy work; and there is a lack of organization. It is amazing to me how I ever attained any knowledge when the teaching system possessed so many problems.

RYOKO'S RESPONSE

Living in a dormitory during a summer session, we students have more problems than we do in a regular school year. I live in Burge Hall with two roommates. In our hall, there are three studying rooms, one big TV room, and some recreation rooms in the basement. However, except for the smallest studying room, none of these rooms is available during the summer session. Before my roommates and I complained about our poor studying environment to the residence director, we could not even use the smallest studying room. Unless we would pay a fee, the residence director would not allow us to use the TV rooms and the recreation rooms in our hall. On the contrary, she told us to go to Daum Hall, which is next to our residence hall. We are very upset about her decision. However, it is getting worse.

Situation 12 91

After we were here for about ten days, many high school students started living in this hall. They are having some experience before they decide whether they want to attend this university or not. Since most of the high school students do not have to study hard, not only are they noisy, but also their manners are quite bad. They float all over the hall and sometimes even do some mischief. So we always have to lock our door whenever we go out. They often gather in the front lobby, so we cannot go there to rest; they always play music loudly and direct bad jokes at us.

And now, we are really mad at the residence director and some other coordinators of the university because we have to put up with some middle-aged men who are having a conference here. Three of the rooms on our hallway are used by the men. So we have to be careful about many trivial things: we cannot walk in our hallway wearing pajamas and we must be sure the door is closed while we are changing our clothes.

Anyway, we hope we can get some consideration from the university for us university students so that we can have both good study conditions and comfortable living in our dormitory.

KRIS'S RESPONSE

The problem I'm thinking of applies mainly to new freshmen and transfer students who are new at the University of Iowa. I know when I first started school here it was a real problem for me.

The problem I'm talking about is how to find your way around campus. When I first started I didn't know where anything was. I didn't know whom to ask or where to find out anything. I guess what I really was was scared and embarrassed.

When I first walked on campus I didn't know where any of the buildings were, and I was afraid to ask. Finally I realized that if I wanted to make it through the University I would have to ask questions.

My advisor helped me answer these questions and work through these problems. Without his help I would still be a scared freshman running around in circles.

I think the most specific problem is the students' fear: their fear of asking questions of either their fellow students or their advisors, fear of feeling stupid, and just fear in general. Sooner or later I think every student will overcome this problem and settle down to the seriousness of a college education.

TOM'S RESPONSE

One problem that faces most college students: how do I make a sufficient amount of money to cover living expenses? Since it does cost plenty of money to go to college today, one must be able to accumulate a sufficient amount of money in a relatively short time span.

There are many major expenses in college. One major expense is the dorm fee. The other outstanding expenses are tuition, activity fees, books, supplies, food, personal items, and entertainment. Since these items affect our daily lives they must all be included in planning. Obviously, they are all important to every student in college, but each expense has a different value or priority for each student on campus. The priority may be influenced by the campus, personal growth at the time, and the conditions of the environment when setting the work priority.

I deal with these problems daily in my life. It affects me from the shirt on my back to the roof over my head. This is why I think this is the biggest problem of most college students today.

ASSESSMENT

Writer _____
Self Assessment _____ Group Assessment _____
Teacher Assessment _____ Other _____
Reader is convinced that the problem merits consideration by the institution. _____
   or
Writer needs a more appropriate and significant problem. _____
Writer needs a *common* problem. _____
Writer needs to state the problem more clearly. _____
Writer needs more illustration and support. _____
Other suggestions: _____

Situation 12

The four student responses give a sample of the various problems this assignment can produce. Tom's response raises the issue of appropriateness. Tom has identified what is surely a major problem for many students: personal finance. Yet, as Tom presents it, the problem seems personal rather than school-related. Tom is not thinking enough of the situation or the audience; his presentation is not really geared to a representative of the institution. What could a counselor do with this information?

Ryoko's response is certainly appropriate; her problem definitely involves the administration of the institution. The issue that her paper raises is significance. While Ryoko details a series of related annoyances, one wonders about their effects on Ryoko and her roommates as students. It is inconvenient to have to share the dorm with middle-aged men and high school students, it is inconvenient to be denied full use of its facilities, but education doesn't seem seriously threatened. Also, the problem seems to be a special case rather than a common institutional problem. Ryoko and her group both felt that the problem needed to be "more convincing." Ryoko does a good job of stating the problem (particularly in her generalization in the last paragraph) and of illustrating it.

Illustration is Kris's weakness. Her problem is stated clearly enough: how to find one's way around campus. The most perceptive and interesting part of the paper is her analysis of the psychological condition beneath the problem—the newcomer's fear. I think this would be helpful to the investigating counselor. But Kris needs specifics. She should show her orientation problems in detail—how the abbreviation JH meant nothing to her; how learning the JH meant Jessup Hall still left her lost; how learning that Jessup Hall was part of the Inner Quad did nothing to resolve her situation; how she finally found Jessup Hall. Kris needs to make the problem real through example. Kris's group felt that she needed a better statement of the problem; Kris felt that her response was successful.

Liz's response, a passionate and sweeping indictment of high school, would stun the investigating counselor. The response has many formal weaknesses: in organization, in word choice and sentence construction, in terms of whether all the charges in the conclusion are supported and illustrated. But the problem is certainly appropriate and important; it is clearly stated; and a number of aspects of the problem are illustrated in detail. The response has force; Liz cares about her subject. She has given the counselor who really desires student perspective on the institution just what she wants. Liz's group felt the response was successful; Liz felt her problem was much too large and needed more support and illustration.

13 · I Hate to Bring This Up, But . . .

Persuasive writing is concerned with your reader's reaction to your words. You are writing to change your reader's thinking or behavior, or both. In this assignment, you have the advantage of knowing your reader personally, but the persuasive task is still a delicate one.

SITUATION 13

We all have bad habits. Think of a bad habit of someone you room with or someone else you know well. Write a letter in which you try to persuade that person to give up the habit.

GUIDELINES

1. Make the habit and your feelings about it real and vivid.
2. Create a tone of empathy; show convincing concern for the reader's best interest.
3. Show benefits of the change, if they are not obvious.
4. Suggest possible ways to change, if appropriate.

This assignment is difficult because it pulls you as a writer in opposite directions at the same time. First, you need to make your reader see, recognize, and acknowledge the problem. To do this, you must make the habit vivid and real. Name the habit clearly; show specific results or specific occasions when your reader was practicing the habit. We all have blind spots, personal characteristics that we don't allow ourselves to see. Your job is to hold up a mirror to make the reader see something that he or she has been ignoring. He or she must be somewhat shocked by the unpleasant truth in order to be motivated to change.

Motivating the person may involve telling the truth about *your* feelings. Be frank about being upset by the habit, and show why you are upset. After all, if your complaint doesn't really matter to you, your reader may shrug it off. If it is a trivial matter, why bother to change?

If, however, you present the habit in strong terms, you face another problem. Since persuasion centers around the reader's reactions, you can see that *tone* — the relationship between writer and reader — becomes very important. How the reader reacts to your letter depends in great measure on the attitude that you project toward him or her. In stating the problem strongly, you can come across as a harsh and hostile critic of his or her behavior. Your criticism may seem to be an attack, and the reader's natural reaction to attack is to defend against it, to fight back. And a person who is being defensive or aggressive is not in the frame of mind to change.

A defensive reaction is not what you want; therefore, try to create a tone of *empathy*. People are most likely to change when they feel understood, when they feel that someone sees their position. Empathy may allow someone to unbend and accept criticism. Empathy means *feeling with* the other party. Show that you are interested in your reader's welfare — that you are writing for his or her sake and for your sake at the same time. Empathy is not incompatible with anger or humor. You may be angry at someone and still convince the person that you care about him or her. Or you can use humor to establish a bond even while you are raising a criticism. The goal is to be close and critical at the same time, a difficult matter.

Obviously, motivation is key to change; we need strong reasons before we change our habits. If you give a strong enough picture of the destructiveness, wastefulness, or ugliness of the habit, you may provide sufficient motivation. At this point, there are two additional strategies to consider. First, it may be that changing the habit will bring additional benefits, bonuses that provide further reason for change. For example, one could base an argument against smoking on the grounds that the smoker may be killing himself or herself. This powerful reason for stopping could be supplemented by pointing out other benefits: money saved, sweeter breath. Second, a person may be more likely to change if he or she believes that change is possible. It may be appropriate in your letter to suggest methods for making the change. Such suggestions may make the change seem more possible, and they also show the sincerity of your concern about the habit and your reader. If you are willing to go beyond complaint to active help with the change, you are obviously trying to take up the problem *from the reader's standpoint*.

LIZ'S RESPONSE

My dearest friend Tammy,

I am writing you this letter because what I have to say needs my full, unbroken concentration. Besides, if I spoke to you, I would probably say all the wrong things.

In the past two months some of your other friends and I have noticed a habit of yours that is becoming an increasing problem. It is your drinking. Do you realize that the last three weekends, when you have come home, you have been totally plastered? What worries me most is the fact that now you don't seem to go through a day without a drink. Tam, you are no longer a social drinker; you are an alcoholic. Please don't hate me for saying this; it is just that I care what happens to you. Each time you leave, I wonder if you will ever come back or if you'll get into trouble and lie dead on the curb. I worry that you will get into your car and injure yourself and someone else.

I know that your past has been less than cheery, and the present sometimes puts up what seem to be less than passable barriers. I probably understand that better than anyone else. I too looked for a way to forget my past, but drinking just wasn't it. I tried getting drunk, and I do admit that while I was smashed I felt like I could conquer anything. But each time I became sober I found that my problems hadn't changed and neither had I. There are the other ways to deal with your problems. Talk to us, your friends. We can maybe help you deal with your difficulties. If you don't want to talk to us, please go to the student center and talk to a professional. It could really help. Or maybe you could find as I did that God has the answer for everything. When I am depressed I turn to Him and He gives me comfort. If you would like, I could tell you what I have learned and from there I can take you to someone else who knows even more. But that choice is up to you. Just remember, drinking can only compound your problems, not help.

In this day and age, drinking is considered very sociable, but intoxication is not. You have told me how many drinking friends you have, but do they really care about you? I think the guys are just one-night stands who take advantage of your position. I have found that life is the only catalyst a person needs to be happy. Remember, we care.

If you won't stop drinking for us, do it for yourself. You are ruining your body. Each time you have beer you are destroying brain cells that can never be replaced, not to mention what damage you are doing to your liver. There are even studies now that support the idea that women who have been heavy drinkers, even if they have since stopped, risk the chance of hurting the health of their unborn children. Alcohol is supposed to disturb the makeup of genes, thus causing defects. Tammy, you could be destroying the lives of your children. For us, for you, for your unborn children, find help to stop now. We'll always be there to help if you'll help yourself. Please.

RYOKO'S RESPONSE

Dear Jerrie,

Although I have no right to talk about your habits or activities, since I am worrying about you as a roommate, I will tell you my opinion about your dancing habits.

You go dancing almost every night. You love dancing, don't you? However, you said that you go dancing so often to forget something and to release your stress. Dancing makes you feel refreshed. However, can you forget something by dancing?

Why don't we go swimming or jogging instead? This would be better exercise. While you are dancing, you breathe such dirty, smoky air, and after dancing, you drink so much beer that has many calories. Doesn't that sound awful? It's nothing good for your body, is it? You always come back in the middle of the night and sleep for about four or five hours. You have to go to classes and to work in the cafeteria three times a day. Aren't you tired? You will be sick if you continue going dancing so often.

Take care of yourself. As adults, or at least as university students, we have to solve our problems; we can't avoid them or hide from them. If I can help you, I will do my best. Take it easy.

KRIS'S RESPONSE

Dear Roger,

Every day of your life I can see you take extra minutes off your life by smoking cigarettes. It greatly disturbs me to see you take away minutes,

minutes that may mean the difference between seeing or not seeing your grandchildren.

I've watched my grandmother waste away day by day from cancer caused by cigarette smoking. It's one of the most terrifying and sad things I've ever witnessed. I've observed her gradual destruction each day, and can honestly say that she would be much better off if she were not living any more.

Cigarette smoking was the cause, and cancer was the ruler. The cancer hid itself for about a year, but finally it caught up with her and was determined to be the ruler. Well, the cancer has become the ruler and now the minutes of her life are gradually decreasing.

I'm asking you as a favor to yourself and your family to give up cigarette smoking. It's a habit that can be broken if you are really determined to quit. I don't want to see what is happening to my grandmother happen to you! I'm sure that I couldn't live through the ordeal; it's much too heartbreaking.

You know that I'm here willing to help you; all you have to do is ask! I would gladly hold your cigarettes for you, allowing you so many each day until the habit is finally broken. All I want to do is help you kick the habit so we'll have more time together, time that may mean so much.

Cigarette smoking is a bad habit and can only harm you and others around you! It's easy to see smoking is bad because the bad aspects outweigh the good by miles.

Please think hard about what I have told you and what I'm trying to get you to do. If you won't do it for me, at least do it for yourself! At least make a start at trying to kick the habit; that's the hardest part.

TOM'S RESPONSE

When people room together, they have to share lots of things. Since we have been roommates, I have shared many things with you, but there are some things I do not want to share with you.

My diary is one of those things I don't want to share with you. You

Situation 13

know if you had a diary I would not read it. Therefore, I see no reason why you need to read my diary.

Since you don't need to get into my personal articles I would appreciate it if you would quit going through my personal belongings. If you stop this bad habit I think we could maintain a better relationship in the future.

ASSESSMENT

Writer _____
Self Assessment _____ Group Assessment _____
Teacher Assessment _____ Other _____
Reader might well be motivated to change the habit. _____
   or
Writer needs more display of the habit (details, examples, consequences).
_____

Writer needs to soften the tone. _____
Writer should show benefits of change. _____
Writer should suggest ways and means for change. _____
Other suggestions: _____
_____

Liz's response and Kris's response are notable because of the writers' extreme concern and involvement. It would be hard to ignore a friend this earnest and this worried. Both letters are achievements in tone because of the persuasive relationship they establish between writer and reader. Kris's main tool is the frankness and force of her feelings, her worry over Roger's health and future. Kris actually sent her letter, and Roger was persuaded to stop smoking, so her piece of writing was a practical success. Liz does much more with empathy than does Kris; she shows that she understands the attractions of drinking, yet she maintains that it doesn't achieve the desired results. She also suggests more means for change. I like Liz's way of suggesting a number of sources for help; Liz is the opposite of pushy and bossy—she leaves Tammy room to make her own choices. Liz and Kris could both do more with specific display of the habit—they could "hold up the mirror" better. Remind Tammy of the morning she couldn't remember where she had been the night before and of the nights when she pulled out of the parking lot into oncoming traffic. Remind Roger how he couldn't catch his breath at the top of the airport steps. The writers and their groups felt that these letters would accomplish their purpose; specifics could strengthen these successful responses.

Like Liz, Ryoko expresses empathy. She tries to show that she understands Jerrie's attraction to dancing, and—like Liz with Tammy—she tries to persuade Jerrie to think analytically about the possibility that the habit is an evasion and escape. Ryoko's group felt that the response needed more work on tone; they felt that Ryoko was being too maternal. I'm not sure on this point; I think that Ryoko's good will comes across, but the question is whether it comes across in an annoying way. Ryoko's group also felt that there was a problem with *focus*: is Ryoko worried mainly about the dancing itself, or the late hours and drinking, or the possible problem behind this behavior? This lack of focus leads to jumpiness and lack of continuity. I would also suggest more display of the results of the habit: circles under the eyes, falling asleep over books, inability to answer the alarm clock. Make the consequences of the habit real. Ryoko agreed that she needed more specific details.

Tom's response is a sharp reprimand, and it's easy to see why he is angry at his roommate's invasion of privacy. However, if in this situation maintaining good relations is important as well as expressing anger, Tom's letter needs work on tone, as his group pointed out. Tom also needs to explain more clearly why he is upset. He states that he would never do something like this, and that his roommate has no need to do so, but he skirts the issue of his feelings about privacy, and they are what he needs to express. For example, Tom could explain how he learned that his diary had been read and how he felt at that moment. Could anyone help being ashamed when the action was replayed? Such additions also would provide specifics, and Tom and his group agreed that his response needs them.

14 · The Better Way

Sometimes argument becomes technical. That is, the parties involved agree about goals, principles, and the rules of the game. They accept the same framework. But they disagree about methods and procedures, about the best *means* for achieving their *ends*. The issue is *how;* given several ways of doing something, which is better? This assignment asks you to make such an argument.

SITUATION 14

In all sports and activities there are disagreements over technique. In tennis there are defenders and opponents of the two-handed backhand; in baseball one can argue the merits of an open or a closed batting stance; in slalom waterskiing some skiers come out of the water with both feet in the ski while others get up on one foot and then put the free foot in the ski. Take a stand on a particular technique in a sport or activity that you know well. (You may use the sport or activity you wrote about in Situations 2 and 8, or you may switch to another.) Make the best case you can for your technique, as if you were trying to convince a friend who is also involved with the sport.

GUIDELINES

1. Find a genuine issue and present it clearly.
2. Sound like an expert. This may involve using the language of the sport.
3. Make arguments for your position *and* recognize the opposing position.

The challenge in responding to this situation may be to find a good issue. Support a technique that is genuinely controversial. That is, there should be at least one alternative to your technique that is accepted and endorsed by other serious, knowledgeable people. For example, some serious basketball players and fans argue that zone defense is superior to man-to-man defense; other basketball devotees argue the opposite. This, then, is a genuine issue. Don't try to make an argument for dribbling with your head up or keeping your hands up on defense, however, because there is no legitimate opposition; everybody agrees with you before you start.

When you have an issue, make sure you present it clearly — both your position and its alternative or alternatives. The reader must understand what you are arguing for (and against) before you begin your argument. Even though you assume that your audience knows the sport or activity, you still need to identify the issue; otherwise the point of your argument won't be clear. For example, I might write eloquently that defensive pressure on the basketball leads to many turnovers, but unless I first make it clear that this argument is intended to support the superiority of man-to-man defense over zone, my reader won't catch my drift.

Your arguments must relate to your issue and be appropriate to your issue. For example, I could include a long section on the general importance of defense in basketball, but this would be beside the point; the issue is *what kind* of defense is best.

Keep in mind the need for a *balanced argument*. Give reasons that support your position, but also recognize the logic of the opposition. I want to convince you that man-to-man puts more pressure on ball-handlers and shooters, leading to more mistakes; that it makes a team more aggressive and alert; and that it makes it easier to block the opposition off the backboards. But in addition to backing up my own case, I should recognize the arguments for the opposition. In this case I should state the main arguments *for* zone defense: that it can protect players from foul trouble; that it can protect the area around the basket and force long-range shooting; that it makes setting picks more difficult and allows for extra help on star players. What do I do after recognizing these arguments? I may take issue with them, try to show that they are wrong. I may try to *qualify* some points — to show that they are only partly true or true only under certain conditions. I may *concede* other points — admit that they are true, but contend that my side has points and arguments that outweigh them. What is important is that I try to anticipate and deal with the opposition; otherwise my reader may likely say to himself or herself, "Yes, that's true. but what about. . . ."

Arguments are important, but so is the way you present yourself. Write with confidence; write from your experience; write in the language of your sport or activity. Readers believe not only arguments; they also

Situation 14

believe writers who sound as if they know what they are talking about. This leads us back to your choice of topic: make sure you know the sport and care about the technical issue you have chosen. This is the best way to ensure your credibility.

LIZ'S RESPONSE

In all sports there are different styles of playing the game. Look at all the ways you can sink a putt or shoot a free throw. But after looking at all the successful styles, what it really boils down to is what feels right and works for each individual. No matter what any "rule book" says about how to shoot a free throw, if a coach has a kid who makes ninety-five out of one hundred attempts doing it the "incorrect" way, there is no way that coach will show him the "right way." What a rule book does tell you is how the game is to be played.

For the last five years politicians, coaches, and players have been arguing over the equality of Iowa Girls' Basketball. The point in question is whether Iowa girls should play the traditional boys' style (with five players) or continue with the traditional Iowa style (six women).

In this day and age of falling into the footsteps of tradition, it seems ridiculous to give up one of Iowa's longer traditions, six-on-six Iowa Girls' Basketball. For three-quarters of a century, Iowa girls have been filling arenas with their excitement and beauty. Each year the State Tournament grows in both profits and spectators, making the girls' tournament more spectacular than the boys'. In today's world where profit and money management are important, it would be hard to justify the switch to five-on-five play. In the surrounding states, like Missouri and Illinois, the girls' programs are costing the athletic departments because of the lack of spectators. Here in Iowa the girls' program more than supports itself; thus no money has to be taken away from the boys' program.

The financial stability and popularity of Iowa girls' basketball are not the only reasons for retaining its existence. It is a known fact that the bone and muscle structure varies greatly between men and women. Because men have small hips and broad shoulders, their strength is centered in the upper body, thus making it easier to lift their bodies high for jump shots and rebounding. On the other hand, women are endowed with large hips and small shoulders. Although women are not necessarily weak in jumping, it is true that this difference in proportion makes their endurance much weaker. So in a game of five-on-five where the players move up and down the court, women have a much more difficult time hustling and shooting. Where there is a break between the forward and the guard court (as in the Iowa girls' game), both the offense and the defense get a chance to rest, so that when it is their turn to play they can do it with the utmost hustle.

Probably the last comment on five-on-five versus six-on-six is a question. Who says the girls must play like the boys? Nowhere has it ever been written that the way men play is the right way. Personally, I find Iowa girls' basketball much more exciting than men's basketball. Why can't women be unique and play with the style of basketball that suits them the best? In this day of women's lib, let's stand up not to play like men but to be unique and continue with Iowa's six-on-six basketball.

RYOKO'S RESPONSE

From my experience, I would say that the best way to read a textbook is to read it once slowly and carefully to understand the content, and then quickly read it again to make sure of what was important.

I do not know that this will work for everybody, but at least for me this is a better way than any of the other possible methods: reading the material quickly to grasp general ideas, and then rereading; or reading quickly three or four times.

Before reading a chapter carefully, I usually look through the headings or the titles to get the main ideas. I check for key words or terms that might be collected at the end of the chapter or written in italics or boldface.

Then I read the chapter slowly and carefully to understand what is going on and to avoid misunderstanding. Sometimes I take notes so hopefully I won't be confused by complex relationships within the materials or difficult terms. I usually don't use markers to make my books colorful because when I do, the next time I see the book I feel that I know everything in it, even if I don't really know it at all.

Of course, there would be a lot of argument about this way to study, but I think I can save my time in the long run and don't have to try hard to memorize the materials later on. Besides, you won't forget things in the book quickly after you have had exams.

KRIS'S RESPONSE

Many people don't consider cheerleading a sport; they just consider it a part of sports. I consider cheerleading a sport because I was a cheerleader for three years, and there is just as much competition and hard work in cheerleading as there is in any other athletic event. As in any other sport, there is a right way and a wrong way to do it. I am just going to give you a brief outline of the right way cheerleading should be done.

To be a good cheerleader, you must do a lot of hard work. You have to work out every day, and you always learn new ways of doing old things. Since it means lots of sore muscles and much discouragement, it really makes being a good cheerleader a hard test. But all of those sore muscles and disappointing practices pay off when you're out there in front of that crowd doing your thing.

Cheerleading takes a certain kind of person. It calls for a person who is happy, peppy, and at ease in front of people. It takes a person who is agile and learns quickly; it also calls for a person who can make some noise.

When a person has these qualities, there are still things that are needed to make that person a good cheerleader—the right cheerleader. To cheerlead the right way, you must go out in front of that crowd and capture their attention. You have to smile even if you don't feel like smiling, but you can't be a put-on. You must at all times be natural.

You must influence the crowd's spirits. Just as a coach is a team's leader, you are the crowd's leader. They depend upon you to lead them, and it is your job to lead them. You must draw out every ounce of their energy, and you must also give every ounce of your energy.

The most important part of cheerleading the right way is showing people how much you enjoy it. You do this every time you go out in front of that crowd and draw out of them every ounce of energy they have. When you have successfully done this, you will know it because that crowd will tell you.

They will be so filled with enthusiasm and energy that it will feel as if the ground you are standing on is shaking. When you get that crowd all riled up and feel the ground begin to shake, all that hard work and those sore muscles seem worthwhile. You have been a cheerleader, and you have done it the right way.

TOM'S RESPONSE

The role of the first negative is the most important role of the debate for the negative team. The technique you use for this role will play a powerful role in determining whether you win or lose.

You must begin your speech by dealing with the three major factors of the affirmative case, which are inherency, significance, and solvency. The correct way is to deal with these factors in this order. You must devote the majority of your time to arguing inherency and significance, leaving the remainder for solvency. You should not concentrate on solvency because that is the duty of the second negative position. As the first speaker, one should really just introduce the factors in the case.

In your rebuttal speech, you should review the points you have made in your earlier speech, summarizing them and convincing the judge you have won the debate.

ASSESSMENT

Writer _____
Self Assessment _____ Group Assessment _____
Teacher Assessment _____ Other _____
Reader would seriously consider this argument. _____
   or
Writer needs to establish the issue. _____
Writer needs to invent appropriate arguments. _____
Writer needs to establish his or her authority better. _____
Writer needs a stronger case for his or her position. _____
Writer needs more recognition of the opposing position. _____
Other suggestions: _____

Situation 14

Liz invents appropriate arguments; she deals with finance, popularity, and women's physiology in ways that are relevant to her issue. Liz develops her position, and in doing so comes to sound like an authority; her reference to the state of women's basketball in Missouri and Illinois and her paragraph about physiology help establish her credentials.

As Liz's group pointed out, Liz could improve this response most by recognizing the opposing position. Her group immediately wanted to know about the disadvantage to Iowa women who want to compete in five-woman basketball in college. For full persuasive effect, Liz must address this strong objection. Also, Liz could explain her issue more fully earlier in her piece. The differentiating feature of Iowa girls' basketball is not simply that there are six women on a side; it is also that all participants are restricted to one half of the court (players are either on offense or defense). Liz mentions this in her third paragraph, but establishing it sooner could clarify the issue.

Let me quibble a bit with Liz's response. Liz's tradition argument seems to lack depth, and I'm not sure that it's compatible with the uniqueness argument in her last paragraph. I would particularly like Liz to delete her "in this day and age" lead-ins. I am intrigued with her physiology argument (paragraph three), but if women are not as well designed as men for jumping, doesn't that imply that their game should be full-court (where there is relatively more emphasis on running and relatively less on jumping) rather than half-court? I am interested in her assertion that six-woman basketball is intrinsically more exciting; I wish she had developed that. But in the end what matters most is Liz's success in inventing arguments that address her issue.

The best feature of Ryoko's response is her detailed description of what she does and why she does it when she reads a text. The problem is that she does not really treat the controversial part of her issue. No one will dispute that at some point textbooks require a detailed, careful, "slow" reading—so the question becomes *when* the detailed reading is most appropriate. Ryoko recommends a detailed reading followed by a fast rereading; her first alternative reverses this order. To establish that her method is better, Ryoko must deal with the question of effective order instead of putting the emphasis on her methods of careful reading. One could see this problem as "more recognition of the opposing position" (as Ryoko's group did) or as "inventing appropriate arguments," or both.

By the end of Kris's response, it is clear that she knows cheerleading from the inside, that she is an authority who cares about her subject. Kris writes with convincing intensity. The problem is that her response is *off the task*; it is not what the situation called for. In many ways this response would fit Situation 21, which will ask you to define excellence in a particular activity. When Kris writes about being natural and yet being perpetually cheerful (paragraph four), I feel convinced that this paradox is close to the heart of cheerleading excellence. When she sees cheerleaders as coaches of the crowd, when she describes the ground shaking, I think she is getting at the inner core of the activity. But Kris is off-target for this situation because she is writing about the right way (and by implication the wrong way) instead of *a better way*. Kris presents no real alternatives; there is really no issue to argue.

Like Kris, Tom doesn't really grasp the idea of the rhetorical situation. What Tom has written is very close to his response to Situation 8 (explaining a process within a sport or an activity). Like Kris, Tom is explaining the right way of doing something; he doesn't present us with an issue and with the best of several feasible alternatives.

15 · To Join or Not to Join

Penetrating the reader's mind, anticipating the reader's needs and reactions—this is one way of describing what the successful writer does. The good writer cares about the reader and makes an effort to see the world through his or her eyes. We have already talked about the application of this idea to explanation. This way of thinking about writing is particularly valuable, however, in writing persuasion, when your goal is to influence the reader's thoughts and actions.

Persuasion implies a difference in views. Even when you are addressing a close friend, your values and his or her values are not necessarily identical. Your viewpoint is at least somewhat different from the reader's viewpoint; otherwise, you would not be writing to persuade. To obtain the reader's attention you must write *with his or her viewpoint in mind*, selecting those arguments and approaches that are most likely to move the audience to your position.

In this assignment you will urge a particular friend to make a certain decision.

SITUATION 15

A friend of yours is considering joining or trying out for a group that you know well (either as a member or as an observer). Write your friend some advice. Try to convince him or her to join or not to join, depending on your attitude.

GUIDELINES

1. Give specific reasons for approving or condemning the group.
2. Connect your reasons with your friend's nature and thinking.
3. Use evidence to support your reasons.
4. Express your feelings about the group.

To be persuasive in this situation, you need reasons for joining or not joining. Two things will determine their effectiveness: (1) your ability to connect your reasons to your friend's nature and thinking, and (2) your ability to support your reasons with evidence. For example, suppose you want to persuade an outgoing, gregarious friend to join a social club. Arguing good times and good company would probably be effective. But assume that your friend is shy and introverted; arguing good times and good company will probably get you nowhere. However, you might argue that the experience might be good for her by helping her to become more socially at ease.

Reasons usually need to be expanded, supported, illustrated. Suppose you are arguing that going to a particular college will give a friend a well-rounded education. What do you mean by well-rounded? Do you mean that he or she will take courses in many different areas? Can you illustrate this claim by naming unusual departments or areas of study, or detailing the liberal arts requirements? Can you show why this college would provide more variety and choice than other colleges? Or do you mean something different? Do you mean that the school will provide both social and educational opportunities? Again, explain and illustrate. Reasons lean on the quality of their support.

Another important factor: your friend will probably be swayed by your feelings, by your personal and subjective reactions to the group. Do you express your feeling for the group—positive or negative? Is your enthusiasm or dislike convincing? Your feeling about the group may be as influential as your arguments. Remember, however, to show that you know the group well by presenting detailed information that proves your familiarity. If you seem to know what you are talking about, your feelings will be much more persuasive.

LIZ'S RESPONSE

I am not the type of person who belongs to many groups or organizations. One group I do belong to is the work force at Randall's. Although some might not think of us as an organization, I think maybe you'll see why we are after you read this paper.

Randall's is like a lot of other organizations in that we have certain requirements that must be met, like being sixteen years of age and having a social security number. The head of our little group, the boss, takes a look at each person and makes a judgment. If the person is kind, polite, full of energy, and responsible, he or she is asked to join us. Consequently we all get along.

As in all organizations, we strive to work together for one purpose and that is to provide a courteous service for the community. Everyone must eat, so we at Randall's try to make the repetitious trip to the store as enjoyable and pleasant as possible. Working together makes our job seem more like a family affair. Each person in every department is ready to assist another member in time of trouble. Because the store wasn't busy last Thursday, I helped the stockers fill the shelves, which allowed them to leave early if they wished. In turn, the stockers and others have assisted me many times in sacking and price checking. The best part about being a part of Randall's is that we help each other and have fun outside of our building. There have been many times when others and I have needed some assistance. During the football season, I had no way to return home, so the stockers each took turns and got me home, even if it was out of their way. To show even more of our unity, our chairperson, the boss, even gives out financial aid to those members who need it if the checks aren't on time.

That brings up one of the biggest advantages to our group, money. Unlike most organizations, we are paid for our services. Each week we receive a check paying us according to the number of hours we have given to the organization. The starting rate is about $3.85 an hour with a thirty-cent raise every three months, not including time-and-a-half for services contributed on Sunday. This organization is profitable not only to the community but also to the members themselves.

I believe I have given you enough information to show the goals and advantages of our organization. We are an enjoyable group who wish to invite all who will fit in well with us.

RYOKO'S RESPONSE

I strongly recommend that you become a member of the International Association. Since you have taken five years of Spanish, it is a very good chance to brush up on your Spanish. From my own experience, the best way to improve a language ability is to talk to many native speakers. There are many students who are from Spanish-speaking countries in the Association, and they are very willing to speak or to teach Spanish to you. Also, you might get interested in learning other languages.

To be a member, when you come to a party or a meeting, you simply sign your name, address, and phone number on the list. There is no admission fee nor a membership fee.

The way of management of the Association is that whenever you can help us or work with us, you may help us and work with us. But if you are too busy or not interested in a project, no one will force you to work for us. And you may go to any parties or events you are interested in. However, if you are interested in the management of the Association, you can put your opinions and knowledge to practical use and be very active in management coordination.

Not only can you enjoy being a member, but also you can extend your point of view and your own world by learning about cultural differences and traditional events and customs of other countries. You might have a chance to find someone who will be very important to you.

I am sure that you will have very useful and enjoyable experiences as a member of the Association.

Our next event is a picnic on July Fourth at City Park after a meeting at the International Center. Please come and join us.

KRIS'S RESPONSE

For two years when I was in high school I was a member of the cheerleading squad. I have to say those two years were among the most exciting times of my life. I found so much enjoyment and pleasure in cheerleading that I wanted to be a member of every squad I could.

Julie, knowing the type of person you are, I think you would find great enjoyment in being a cheerleader! You're the type of person who likes to be with people, and you like to have fun in whatever you're doing. Believe me, in cheerleading you have to enjoy what you're doing in order to be a success. You have a gorgeous smile that catches people's eyes whenever they look at you; you have a figure that would knock any guy flat on the floor; you have gymnastic talent; and your voice carries far and loud. All these are strong characteristics of a good cheerleader.

There are good times to be had when cheerleading. You get to be with a lot of people and you really get to know the student body of your school. There were two really special times during my two years as a cheerleader. The first was when all the cheerleaders got to stay all night in Waterloo after a long game. We were all together and we got to know one another really well. I think this helped us to be a better cheerleading squad. The second time was Boys' State Basketball Tournament in Des Moines. We stayed in a very nice motel and we were always going and doing something fun. I think the best time of the whole tournament was the games. There is just no way to describe the feeling of being in front of all those people, and I know there's no way of describing the feeling of being Number One!

Another thing I gained from being a cheerleader was learning how to cooperate and relate with people. Not only do you have to relate and cooperate with the other cheerleaders, but you have to do the same thing with the crowd. When you have won your crowd's approval, there's really not much left to do except cheer.

Being the type of person you are, I think you would make a fantastic cheerleader and would really enjoy yourself. You're a lot like me, and cheerleading really did a lot for me. I hope with all my heart that you decide to try out for cheerleading and find it as rewarding as I did. If you need any help practicing the cheers, just give me a ring and I'll be there to help. It really would be a lot of fun to run through all those good times one more time!

TOM'S RESPONSE

Joining the Student Council is a waste of time. Nothing is accomplished at the meetings. We were promised a stereo but it was never received. More dances were promised but there were no more dances.

At meetings important subjects are not discussed. The only topic of discussion is when and where the next party is going to be. These are my observations from sitting in on these meetings.

Since you like getting down to business immediately, I believe you'll be very frustrated during these meetings. The factor that would upset you most would be being dependent on the input of the other, ineffective student council members.

ASSESSMENT

Writer _____

Self Assessment _____ Group Assessment _____

Teacher Assessment _____ Other _____

Reader would be likely to be influenced by this argument. _____

or

Writer needs better and clearer grounds for his or her position. _____

Writer needs to adapt the arguments to the friend. _____

Writer needs more support for the case. _____

Writer needs a more direct and forceful expression of feeling. _____

Other suggestions: _____

Liz's response is a good starting place for discussion, because it shows clearly what she does well and what she still needs to do. Liz emphasizes the cooperative spirit and harmony of the work force at Randall's and backs up her sense of belonging to a supportive family with specific examples. Her reasons for liking Randall's, her evidence, her expression of feeling about the organization are all convincing. What she needs to do is to adapt her argument to her particular audience, to show why Randall's and her friend are made for each other. Liz and her group both recognized this need. A sidelight of Liz's paper: Liz's playful comparison of Randall's with typical social clubs carries through her whole piece and *organizes* it. A technical problem: her long third paragraph needs reorganization and subdivision.

Tom also does a number of things right. His points about the stereo and the dances are good evidence to support his contention that the Student Council has no real power. His analysis of his friend's nature seems appropriate and helpful in light of his objections to the organization. The problem is that Tom's reasons for not joining are contradictory. In his first paragraph he indicates that the Student Council does real business but has no real power. In the second paragraph Tom seems to say that the Council does no real business. Tom needs to clarify and explain his position further.

In contrast to Tom, Ryoko has a clear position or set of reasons, but her reasons need support and her argument needs more adaptation to her friend. Developing language ability, learning about other cultures, and making friends who have different backgrounds are all good reasons for joining the Association. What Ryoko needs now is *evidence* — what are the specific activities of the Association that help members achieve the benefits she mentions? Her friend would probably need more specific information about what the Association does. Also, Ryoko could do more with audience adaptation; her reference to her friend's Spanish background is a good start, but she needs to continue. Ryoko thought she needed more support; her group thought she could better adapt her argument to her reader.

Kris's response generally works well. Her enthusiasm for the group is unmistakable, her analysis of Julie is directly to the point, and she presents persuasive reasons for involvement in cheerleading. However, Kris needs better support; she can marshall more convincing specifics behind her argument. Look at paragraphs three and four: Kris needs to give her reader details that will show why those nights in Waterloo and Des Moines were fun. She needs to show what is involved in winning the crowd's approval and what it feels like to do so. Kris and her group both felt that the response was basically successful but could be improved through the addition of detail.

16 · Letter of Recommendation

Mind-reading — using your imagination to put yourself in the position of a reader — is a key element in persuasion. Only from this position will you understand what arguments are likely to move the reader. This assignment presents another situation in which you need to anticipate the reader's thinking.

SITUATION 16

Return to the situation in which a friend is interested in a job you have held (Situations 4 and 9). Assume that your friend wants to apply for that job. Write a letter recommending your friend to your former employer. You may write the assignment with an actual friend in mind, or you may create a fictional friend with an appropriate set of credentials. You want to help your candidate get the job.

GUIDELINES

1. Establish the basic situation immediately. Make sure that your reader knows what job your candidate is applying for.
2. Point out relevant qualities and qualifications.
3. Create an appropriate tone. (This depends to some degree on your relationship with your employer.)

Put yourself in the position of the employer. What would you look for in a candidate for this job? What would constitute appropriate background, training, experience, and education? You would want someone whose history seems to match the job. For example, if you are recommending a friend for an assembly-line job in a factory, you probably should not stress that he or she was an honor student. Academic intelligence is probably not necessary for the job; it may even be a drawback.

Experience with routine work requiring care and endurance, however, would be persuasive.

Second, the more specific the qualifications you list, the more persuasive you will be. It is encouraging to learn that a candidate for a job as an auto mechanic has had some high school shop training and some experience working in garages. But exactly what were the courses? Where and when were they given? Under whose supervision? Who were the previous employers? What kinds of experience did the jobs provide? It would be important to know that the candidate was tuning engines rather than pumping gas. Do you have any *factual evidence* of the quality of the candidate's work performance, such as rapid promotion or repeated or lengthy service? The more specific your information, and the more you sound like an authority, like someone who knows the candidate and the requirements of the particular job, the greater will be the credibility of your letter.

There is another consideration besides qualifications, however: what are the *qualities* of the candidate that make him or her right for the job? Qualities are traits of character or personality. The ability to get along with people, for example, is a personal quality. In writing your recommendation, match your candidate's qualities with the job. To return to an earlier example, the ability to get along with people might not be very important in an assembly-line job. However, manual dexterity and punctuality would interest an employer because they are directly relevant to the work.

It is sometimes difficult to provide evidence of a quality. For example, how can you *show* that your candidate is good at getting along with people? Or that he or she pays close attention to detail? One strategy would be to show your candidate in specific circumstances or situations where he or she demonstrated the quality. If you want to demonstrate the ability to get along with others, mention that your candidate mediated between the team and the basketball coach in a dispute over practice hours. If you are demonstrating your candidate's self-control in public, mention the incident when he refused to fight even when provoked and insulted in a bar. Supporting your claims about your candidate's qualities can be difficult because it may be hard to come up with examples that don't sound forced or manufactured, but it is important that you show *how you know* about your candidate's particular qualities. Good supporting material can serve another purpose at the same time: it can show your real knowledge of the candidate, thus enforcing your credibility.

Your tone should be influenced by how well you know the employer. If you know the employer well, you may be much less formal than if you have never met the employer personally or if you are writing to a firm's personnel office. Most important, however, is that you sound as if you have the best interests of both candidate and employer in mind, as if you want to do a favor for everyone involved.

Remember to state the purpose of your letter clearly at the very beginning. It is an essential courtesy to let the employer know why you are writing, so that the information that follows (qualities and qualifications) will make sense inside a context. Identify the position in question, even if you are certain that the employer will know what you are talking about. Stating your business clearly is important because it avoids misunderstandings and ambiguity, because it puts the situation into immediate focus with a minimum of effort from the reader, and because it shows that you care about structuring your message for the convenience of the reader.

LIZ'S RESPONSE

Dear Marv,

I want to tell you about Jane Smith, who put in an application today to be a cashier. She told me you weren't there when she turned in the application, so I thought maybe I could tell you a little bit about her. I have been close friends with her for years and can tell you just about everything.

She is nineteen years old and has been working since sixteen. Her past work has been as a waitress in a very busy restaurant. This job consisted of bussing tables, taking orders, and running a register that was somewhat similar to ours. After a year of waiting tables she was offered a job at Big V Supermarket. This store was much larger than ours. It included a deli and a drugstore, and the rest of the store is also larger. What made her job difficult was that each item was categorized by section—frozen, deli, drug, etc. Even with all this to consider, she was still extremely quick because she had no need to look at the register. She had the keys memorized and worked it with the speed of a typist.

Working in a big store in St. Louis gives you the chance to meet people of all types. Jane has had to deal with shoplifters and vandals. She has even been held up in her lane, but because of her quick thinking she was able to hit the alarm, which rings only at the police station, without the holdup men realizing it. Consequently, the store was saved a lot of money. One day I was able to observe Jane while working. She was very

Situation 16

polite to each customer even if they became irate about food prices, etc. I think that it is much more difficult to work in a big store like her old store, so she should really fit well into our smaller store. Any problem that could arise I know she could easily handle.

One great advantage to having her work for you is that she will be staying in Iowa City for many years. She has recently been married and her husband is attending school here. I have talked to her about hours and she is willing to work any time. Because her husband is going the year around to school plus working a bit, she can't see where she would need any time off.

Marv, I really think she is well qualified and her personality is great and would fit in well with everyone. I believe she is the right person for the job and I truly hope you will consider her application.

RYOKO'S RESPONSE

Dear Sir:

I am writing to you concerning Maria Luisa Guion, who is twenty-six years old and single. She graduated from the University of Minnesota four years ago, majoring in Spanish and French with a 3.25 grade average. After graduation, she came to Iowa to develop her language abilities and to get a job. She is a work-study student at the University of Iowa and has been working in the Language Lab for about four years. She has been taking classes in French, Italian, German, Portuguese, and Spanish as a nondegree student. She speaks Portuguese and Spanish like a native speaker.

She has been very curious about studying and teaching English in Japan, because her father has visited Japan many times. Although she has forgotten how to read and write in Japanese since she took one year of Japanese in high school, she speaks a little Japanese. Moreover, she is going to take a class in Japanese next semester.

She has been tutoring foreign students in English for about three years. She also helps them as much as she can to adjust to the American way of living. This is why I know so much about her. She has been taking care of me since I came to Iowa.

She is very active, cheerful, nonjudgmental, and kind. She does not have any prejudice about nations. Actually, she is a very international person. She likes dancing and playing the guitar, especially Spanish dancing and music.

Thank you for taking time to read this letter. If there are any questions, please ask either me or her.

KRIS'S RESPONSE

Dear Ron,

Last week when you asked me if I knew anybody who was looking for a job at a grocery store, and specifically a person who had some type of experience, I thought I was going to have a difficult time finding a person who met those qualifications. Well, I guess I was wrong! I believe I have found you a perfect candidate!

Her name is Tracey Sueppel and she was formerly employed at K-Mart. She left K-Mart last year when she went away to school. She has now decided to come back and attend the University. While employed at K-Mart she ran a register similar to those we run at Eagle's, an asset that would make it much easier to train her. She also was in charge up front, a job much like that of our office workers. She had the power to okay checks and charges, call people up front when extra help was needed, and find things for people to do when it was slow.

I have known Tracey ever since I was in grade school, and have nothing but respect and admiration for her. I believe she meets all the informal qualifications as well as the formal ones. She is always pleasant, wearing a smile on her face, and easy to get along with. She has always considered others before herself, something you must always do when working with a customer!

For formal qualifications, Tracey is nineteen years of age, holds a social security number, can work her schedule around the hours of the store, and always looks respectable. She also holds an added qualification in previous experience, a qualification that would make her an asset to the Eagle corporation.

Situation 16

If you have any further questions, feel free to ask me; I'd be happy to answer them. I think you'd find it hard not to get along with Tracey; make her a member of the working family at Eagle's!

TOM'S RESPONSE

Dear Mr. Jones:

I am writing this letter to recommend Mr. Bruce Breerman for the position of Vice President of Chase Manhattan National Bank. Breerman has a B.A. from the University of Iowa and an M.A. from Harvard. Both degrees are in finance. He was in the top 2 percent of his class at both universities.

In addition to being very intelligent in his area of expertise, he has many excellent personal qualities. He was captain of the University of Iowa swim team and demonstrated a great amount of leadership responsibility above and beyond the call of duty.

In being a teller at my bank for three years, Mr. Breerman was always a responsible young man. His money drawer has never come up short. He has always been very personable to his customers. He has a good sense of how to run a bank. I think the two main reasons that I would hire Mr. Breerman are that he is well educated and that he has the experience that is needed to help run a bank.

ASSESSMENT

Writer _____
Self Assessment _____ Group Assessment _____
Teacher Assessment _____ Other _____
Reader would be influenced in favor of the candidate. _____
or
Writer needs to clarify the letter's purpose. _____
Writer needs work on qualifications. _____
Writer needs work on qualities. _____
Writer needs a more appropriate tone. _____
Other suggestions: _____

Kris and Liz both know the candidate's job history, and they present convincing evidence that the candidate could do the job well. Both writers are strong in enumerating *qualifications:* they not only write about Jane's Big V work and Tracey's K-Mart work with good detail; they also show or imply why that experience is particularly relevant to the job in question. Though Kris and her group found her response successful, I would suggest more attention to *qualities;* "always pleasant and wearing a smile" is too general to be very persuasive for me. Liz does more in this area: I like the story of the attempted robbery become it demonstrates Jane's poise and presence of mind. I also like Liz's observation on Jane's politeness with customers, though this might be further developed and supported with examples. Liz and her group felt that she needed more work on qualities.

One of Ryoko's problems is obvious: she needs to *establish the context.* We don't know what job her candidate is applying for (though we can deduce that it is a position teaching English in Japan), so we find the letter confusing and frustrating. (Although the employer would presumably understand Ryoko's purpose better, this is still a flaw in the letter.) Another problem is the relevance to the job of Ryoko's supporting material; what specifically qualifies Maria for teaching English in Japan? The letter seems to present Maria mainly as a student of European languages. What else can Ryoko tell about Maria as a teacher of English to Japanese students? What would show Maria's suitability for that particular situation? Ryoko and her group both recognized this need. On the other hand, Ryoko deals effectively with qualities: Maria comes across as warm and serious, deeply committed to language study, interested in other cultures, good with people. As Ryoko says, she is an "international" person, and such a quality would be very important for this job.

Is Tom's letter intended as a joke? While Bruce Breerman's education seems appropriate, there appears to be a ludicrous gap between his experience and the position in question: it's a long way from balancing a money drawer to being Vice President of Chase Manhattan. Tom also has a problem with relevance and support in his handling of Bruce's qualities. What does being swim team captain have to do with being bank vice president? If Tom perceives an important connection, he must explain it rather than simply citing "leadership." Also, a banker should certainly be personable with customers and have "a good sense of how to run a bank," but Tom needs to be more specific here and to provide examples. Tom and his group both found the response successful; again, I wonder whether they were putting me on.

17 · A Student Complaint

Persuasive writing is difficult enough when one is dealing with a friend or writing from outside a situation (as you were when you wrote the letter of recommendation to a former employer). When you are inside a situation and writing to someone in a position of authority, the difficulty increases. This assignment presents such a situation.

SITUATION 17

Think about your current classes. Is there something that bothers you about the way one of those classes is conducted? A problem with the teacher's approach or manner? A problem with the organizational set-up? Write a letter to the teacher in which you try to persuade him or her to do something about the problem. (Don't use the teacher's name; call her Professor X. or call him Mr. Y.)

GUIDELINES

1. Establish the basic situation.
2. Make your problem clear and important.
3. Find an acceptable tone. You need to combine respect and urgency.
4. Consider presenting possible solutions.

The main difficulty of writing in this situation is finding an effective tone. Criticism is always hard to take. Because people often react personally to criticism, you must be particularly delicate when pointing out a problem to someone who has immediate authority over you. You must be diplomatic; that is, you should present the problem without giving personal offense. Yet you need to make sure that the teacher perceives the problem as important to students; otherwise, he or she may not be sufficiently motivated to change. The difficulty is ensuring that the problem will be perceived as important, yet maintaining good relations.

Think back on your note to a roommate about a bad habit; that involved a similar dilemma. In that case the solution was *empathy*, showing that you understood the other party's feelings. Empathy might not be exactly the right strategy in this case, however; it might seem presumptuous, as if you knew the teacher personally enough to extend sympathy. Another strategy might work better: concern about a common goal. If you present yourself as concerned primarily with the success of the class, and if you assume that the teacher is also concerned about this, you will establish a common ground that should let you write frankly but without disrespect.

There is another problem with tone: you don't want to sound like a complainer who enjoys making trouble for its own sake. Neither do you want to sound timid and begging, obsequious and servile. You want to impress the reader as a serious and thoughtful person, whose concern goes beyond personalities to what is happening in the class, and who has the best interests of everyone — teacher and students — in mind. One way of indicating this kind of concern is to suggest some possible solutions to the problem. This is dangerous, however; you don't want to sound patronizing, as if you know more about teaching than the teacher and are offering the benefits of your superior insight.

Clarity in presenting the problem is also very important. The teacher must understand what the problem is before he or she can make changes. This may involve a clear general statement of the problem; it may also necessitate raising specific examples of the behavior in question, showing the teacher a particular situation, incident, or moment. All your diplomacy will be wasted if the teacher doesn't understand the problem.

As in Situation 16, you want to establish the basic situation, the context of your complaint. Who are you, and what course are you discussing? The teacher may know, but it is an effective courtesy to supply this information.

LIZ'S RESPONSE

Dear Mrs. X.,

I am writing this letter on behalf of the second-hour French class. We had a small discussion one day before you came to class and we all agreed on one fact: we just aren't learning anything from reading *The Stranger*. It is difficult enough to understand existentialism in English but in French it seems almost impossible. We just don't understand the full concept of existentialism. You just haven't explained this to us, so we don't know what to expect. Could you please sit down and go through each of the definitions? It really helps to understand what to look for, so maybe we could see the meaning to the novel.

The daily assignments are another problem. Twenty pages a night is just too much. It takes most of us two hours to read five pages after looking up all the words and then rereading the work to get the meaning. Eight hours of studying would be extreme even if that was the only subject we had to work on. It is very hard to read quickly when we have to look up every other word, and there are certain little idioms that we have no way of understanding. We would like to make a suggestion: could you please cut the daily assignments? Maybe then we could spend the time to try to really understand *The Stranger*. It would also help if you could tell us the idioms before we read them so that we aren't totally confused. We think the best suggestion is that we have a discussion each day of what we have read. It would also be helpful if the discussion was in English, at least the difficult parts. I know that I have read parts of the novel and thought I understood, only to find out that I had totally missed the point. The discussion would set me and many others straight.

I hope you will take these suggestions and put them to good use. We really want to learn and feel that our suggestions will enable us to do so. Please take this letter into consideration.

RYOKO'S RESPONSE

Dear Professor X.,

I am Ryoko Miyazaki, and I am taking your lecture course this semester. I am writing to tell you how I feel about a problem in your class. I would appreciate it if you would read this letter.

As you know, there are two foreign students in your class who have already learned everything that we are studying now. I am taking your class because my friend suggested that I would learn from your lectures. However, I can hardly listen to your lecture because the two foreigners always want to explain the theorems and questions by writing on the blackboard. This takes up a lot of our class time. They also tend to confuse me in the discussion class by asking questions that do not pertain to the assignment. Since they already know the material, they ask our T.A. to explain much more advanced problems. This is fine for them, but it only frustrates me. In fact, I do not understand what is going on in the class. I am very worried about whether I am comprehending the important points of this class because I am going to take some more advanced courses in this department.

I would appreciate it if I could have some of your comments and if we could talk about this problem.

Thank you for taking time to read this letter.

KRIS'S RESPONSE

Dear Mrs. X.,

Ever since I entered Algebra I, I have had a lot of trouble learning anything from your method of teaching.

I can't seem to comprehend what it is that you're trying to teach me. You throw one example on the board and explain how to work the problem. You never show us how to work the problem, and you never put up more than one example of each type of problem.

Whenever a student asks you a question, you do exactly the same thing as when you are teaching the lesson. This bothers me a great deal because I feel that if I don't learn how to do the work now I will have a difficult time when I get to college.

I think it would benefit all the students in your class as well as yourself if you would slow down and explain things in greater detail. It would also help if you would make sure everybody had understood what you have already taught before you move on to something else.

It also would be a big benefit if you would sit down and take time with students who ask questions. If they don't understand and ask a question, it's a sign they are looking for extra help—help that should come from you instead of from fellow students.

I hope what I have explained to you will be of some value. I consider my learning very important and I believe this problem is hampering me from learning to the full extent.

Situation 17   127

TOM'S RESPONSE

Dear Mr. K.,

Your recent disappointment over our class's low test scores is easy to understand. If I may suggest, the reason why we did not achieve higher test scores is that you have not included time for questions from students about the material covered each day in class. I believe we can solve this important problem together. We can create an effective learning atmosphere that will benefit both the students and yourself. The basic assumptions are that students want to achieve good grades and that teachers like the sense of feeling that they have accomplished a teaching task with students gaining some knowledge. I think you would agree with the basic assumptions as a matter of great importance.

Allow me to suggest a few ideas to conquer this problem. (1) Leave a specific time period for questions about your lecture each day in class. (2) Limit the amount of material covered in one day. Realizing your expertise as a teacher, I know it won't take the class long to conquer this problem. Since this is a large problem, we should get to work on it right away. Your excellent teaching abilities will facilitate our working together to eradicate this important problem.

ASSESSMENT

Writer _____
Self Assessment _____ Group Assessment _____
Teacher Assessment _____ Other _____
Reader would be likely to consider doing something about the problem.
_____
    or
Writer needs to establish the context. _____
Writer needs to clarify the problem. _____
Writer needs to illustrate the problem. _____
Writer needs to make the problem more urgent. _____
Writer needs a better tone. _____
Other suggestions: _____

Liz's letter seems the most successful of the four responses. Liz identifies a specific problem and develops it in detail. In fact, her attention to detail would help convince the reader of her serious concern and her good intentions; someone would have to care about the situation to describe it so precisely. Liz's tone manages to combine respect and urgency; I don't think that the reader would take personal or professional offense. Liz and her group felt that her response was successful.

Though Ryoko seems to have an appropriate and important problem to present to her teacher, her response has a number of flaws. She needs to establish her context better. She needs a clearer presentation of the problem. (Consider the third sentence in the second paragraph: do the foreign students literally take over the blackboard, or do they simply distract the lecturer from his main points?) She needs to give the teacher specific examples—particularly of interruptions and digressions. Ryoko felt the problem needed to be clearer; her group felt it needed to be more urgent.

Kris needs to work on tone. If I were her math teacher, I would be offended by her letter; I would interpret it as an attack and probably react defensively to justify myself. Kris explains the problem clearly, but she could gain vividness and immediacy by citing several specific examples.

Tom's letter demonstrates some interesting problems. Tom has worked out a strategy; he wants to show the teacher how teacher and students share common ground—they both would like test scores to be higher. Fortunately, Tom has a means for achieving this end. Two things go wrong: Tom tends to confuse and obscure the problem while presenting the common ground, and Tom takes a tone that is lofty and presumptuous—he verbally throws his arm around the teacher's shoulders. His inflated diction is particularly noticeable in his last sentence. The teacher might be too put off by Tom's manner to pay attention to what he is saying. Tom and his group found the response successful; I worry about its tone.

18 · Righting a Wrong

If it is difficult to talk to a friend about reforming a habit, and difficult to approach a teacher about changing his or her ways, imagine how much more difficult it is to reason with one's opponent in a conflict. The situation brings out hostility and defensiveness. How, then, can you influence an opponent's thinking? This assignment requires you to deal with that problem.

SITUATION 18

Review your responses to the assignments about an act of injustice. Think back to the time of the incident in which you were unfairly treated, and write a letter to the party responsible for the injustice. Try to persuade the person to correct the situation or in some way to redress your grievance. (Before writing your response, look over Situation 18A as a possible alternative.)

GUIDELINES

1. Identify the situation briefly but clearly, so that the reader is certain what you are talking about.
2. Recognize the other person's viewpoint.
3. Present your viewpoint without giving offense.
4. Suggest a remedial course of action — what you want done now.

People are much more likely to move toward cooperation when they feel understood than when they feel under attack. Make an effort to see the situation through the eyes of the other party. How can you show that you understand his or her viewpoint, that you appreciate how the situation must feel to him or her? Remember to remain honest: don't extend sympathy that you don't feel — that somehow rings false and will probably be perceived as "buttering up." But do the best you can to *recognize* the other viewpoint.

Of course, you must present your viewpoint; otherwise you will only confirm the other party's view of the situation. Present your viewpoint with the idea of making your position understood, in much the same way that you tried to understand the other position. Don't try to prove yourself right; even more important, don't try to prove the other party wrong. This kind of argument tends to drive people deeper into their positions; they will soon be thinking of ways to refute you. You want to draw your opponent closer to your position rather than to drive him or her away.

When you have presented both positions, there remains a final step. What do you want the other party to do now? Is there some way that he or she can correct or make reparation for the injustice? If so, point out that course of action. Your persuasiveness will be in vain unless it brings about a desired change. Be clear about what you would like done. If your opponent is now more sympathetic to your view of the situation, it would be a shame to lose the opportunity for cooperation because he or she doesn't know what you want. There may be situations in which little can be done about correcting or changing what has happened. In such cases, you may simply want an apology, or you may want the person to consider acting differently in the future.

One formal consideration: when you begin your letter, identify the situation you are talking about. As we discussed with regard to Situations 16 and 17, it is always a courtesy and it sometimes saves time and effort for your reader if you briefly identify your subject and purpose. When you do so, describe the incident in neutral terms rather than in a way that reflects your position and arouses the reader's antagonism.

LIZ'S RESPONSE

Dear Officer,

I realize that working as a police officer is one of the most difficult jobs around. You spend long, tedious hours roaming the streets trying to notice even the most minute changes. The worst part is all the flak and harassment you get for doing your job. I can sympathize with you and even understand why you have to get rough with some people, but I just don't feel that it is necessary to treat all those charged as if they were criminals. The fact that you charged us with drag racing is not the point in question here. I thoroughly understand that you were only doing your duty; that is what keeps this town safe. What I don't comprehend is the treatment we received after we were pulled over. Do you realize that you never even told us what you were charging us with? It was left up to us to assume something. Now I know that there are some pretty obnoxious people in the world who deserve to be treated with a little harshness, but I don't think we were like this. From the minute you pulled us over, you began questioning and treating us as if we had already been found guilty. The questions were fired at us so fast that there was hardly time to answer. Questioning is to find out the facts, not to trick people into answering falsely. There is also no need to put a person down by making rash comments. The fact that you said we were hot-shot high school kids trying to see how fast our cars would go really annoyed me. If you really knew me rather than making such a quick character analysis, you would know that in truth I am rather timid. It really took a lot out of me to write this, but I thought maybe then you could see my side of things. You see, I believe that everyone deserves to be treated with kindness and understanding. I realize that this isn't always possible, and that you have to keep your tough image because you are a woman, but remember that everyone is human and deserves to be treated as such.

RYOKO'S RESPONSE

Dear Ryoko,

You might be surprised receiving this letter from me, living under the same roof. However, I thought I should write to you rather than talk to you, since our talks often turn into arguments.

I think you have already guessed what I am going to talk about. Well, as you said the other day, I am an old, conservative, traditional mother whom you do not like. Whatever you said to me made me sad and upset. It was a big shock to me. Being nasty, you didn't feel good either, did you?

You are already fifteen years old, but why do you still try to act like a twelve-year-old boy? You know that I do care about you, so I make lots of claims on you. And you know also that nobody else will tell you the truth. Other people might laugh at you behind your back, not saying anything bad to you.

You often say that you are a human being, but you are neither a female nor a male. Even if that's the way young people think and you agree with them, neither the society nor adults will agree with you and change our ways immediately. You need to know many things to be a responsible person. And if I tell things based on my experience and knowledge, it will be easier for you to understand than by experiencing many things and having a hard time.

I know that you already know what I say here, but you still try to pretend that you don't understand; you pretend that you are perverse, boyish, and delinquent. But I'm afraid that if you keep doing that, you might hurt somebody unconsciously, lose something important— consideration, reliance, or even sensitiveness—and you won't be able to distinguish whether you are pretending or not.

Well, maybe I wrote too much.

Remember that your mind is stronger than your emotion.

KRIS'S RESPONSE

Members of the Selection Committee for the National Honor Society:

For the final two years of high school I have been greatly annoyed with you. It's beyond my comprehension how you select the members of the National Honor Society. I've asked the counselor several times for the reasoning for my not being a member, and since he couldn't seem to find a reason, I'm coming to you hoping for a reply containing the answer.

As far as I know there are three qualifications that must be met for admittance to the National Honor Society: (1) You must have a cumulative grade point of 3.0 or better. (2) You must have been involved in extracurricular activities outside of school. (3) You must be involved in extracurricular activities inside school.

There can be no reasonable doubt that I meet all the specified requirements: (1) My cumulative grade point was 3.472. (2) I was involved in volunteer work for the sick at Mercy Hospital, and I was working with younger children in Religious Education. (3) I was a member of the Student Council for three years, I was a cheerleader for two years, and I was a member of the yearbook and *Spectrum* staff. All of these strongly fulfill the necessary requirements.

Situation 18

Unless there are some other requirements that are unlisted in the student handbook, there can be no reason for my not being admitted to the National Honor Society.

I can think of many people who were sworn into the National Honor Society with less convincing qualifications than mine. I feel very unfairly treated by your method of selection, and would like some convincing and fact-backed reasoning for my being excluded as a member.

I think that every student denied membership should receive a letter of reasoning from the Selection Committee explaining that denial. I know I'm not the only person who has these feelings of unjust treatment, and I'm sure they also would like to know the reasons for their being turned down.

I would appreciate it very much if you would reply to my questions as soon as possible.

TOM'S RESPONSE

Tom elected to respond to Situation 18A; see the next chapter.

ASSESSMENT

Writer _____
Self Assessment _____ Group Assessment _____
Teacher Assessment _____ Other _____
Reader might be persuaded to cooperate. _____
  or
Writer needs to identify the situation. _____
Writer needs to recognize the other viewpoint. _____
Writer needs to clarify his or her case. _____
Writer needs to soften the tone. _____
Writer needs to recommend a clear course of action. _____
Other suggestions: _____

Liz's response seems very much in the spirit of the assignment. Liz tries to see the situation from her opponent's viewpoint; she also presents her viewpoint; she attempts to balance and reconcile, to bring her opponent closer. I am impressed with Liz's perception of the particular kinds of pressure female police officers might feel; perhaps this could be introduced and handled better. I like Liz's description of herself as timid, as opposed to the officer's impression of arrogance and recklessness, and I like Liz's admission of the effort that being honest and self-revealing is costing her. Those things ring true and would have persuasive power. However, Liz badly needs to identify the situation; this might be a confusing letter to receive. Liz also needs to work on organization and paragraphing. Liz and her group found the response successful.

Kris's response suffers from conflicting purposes. Kris is probably not sure what she wants to do to the Committee: (1) criticize it, (2) ask it for information, (3) argue with it. If Kris wants the real story from the Committee, and if Kris wants to move the Committee to change, she must do much more with recognizing their viewpoint and she must soften her righteous and aggressive tone. This was also the advice of Kris's group. Kris doesn't even begin to imagine the Committee's thinking: what could be behind her rejection? In addition to the three formal requirements, is selection also based on intangibles, on teachers' perceptions of a student's character and attitudes? If so, what arguments could justify this part of the selection process? By speculating in an open way, Kris could greatly increase her chances of opening dialogue with the Committee. Perhaps Kris doesn't really want cooperation, however; perhaps she really wants to castigate the Committee. In that case Kris's response might better fit Situation 18A; this was her group's suggestion, so we shall discuss her response in the next chapter also.

Ryoko has turned this situation around: she writes from her mother's viewpoint, perhaps because she feels that in the original incident her mother was mainly the victim of injustice and she (Ryoko) was the perpetrator. First, Ryoko needs to identify the original incident; the remarks in this letter need a focal point, a source, a context. Second, Ryoko's mother (the speaker here) does not try hard enough to see Ryoko's side of the story. This makes the tone too hard and aggressive, closer to attack than to reconciliation. What is impressive is the depth of psychological insight and the emotional honesty of the letter. The speaker's awareness of her willingness to tell her daughter the truth as she sees it (paragraph three), her awareness of Ryoko's behavior as role-playing that could have serious costs (paragraph five) — these notes ring true, and Ryoko as reader would be arrested by their depth and sincerity.

18A · A Tongue-lashing

In certain situations you are not really interested in cooperation; you "would rather be right than president," saying what you think regardless of the consequences. If this is true of the situation in which you were a victim of injustice, you may wish to respond to Situation 18A instead of to Situation 18.

SITUATION 18A

Perhaps reviewing Situations 3, 7, and 11 serves mainly to make you angry all over again. If you would rather vent your feelings than try for redress, write the party responsible for the injustice a letter in which you call him or her to account and express your indignation, pain, and anger.

GUIDELINES

1. Identify the situation briefly but clearly.
2. Find language that makes your anger sound genuine.
3. Show the basis of your negative judgment of the reader's behavior.

What makes a good attack, an effective tongue-lashing? Unfocussed abuse and name-calling make a bad one—any child can do that. Remember that truth is a powerful weapon. If you are going to call your opponent names, call him or her *true* names—use words that accurately describe the way he or she acted in the situation. For example, distinguish folly from dishonesty or carelessness from malice. You may likely find yourself drawing upon figurative language, finding comparisons for your opponent and the situation to express the way you feel. Keep your metaphors and analogies *appropriate*. The better the shoe fits, the more likely your opponent is to put it on, even if he or she doesn't want to. Show your opponent his or her face as you see it, and if there is truth in your portrait, he or she may have the grace to acknowledge it and to blush. The more accurately you can label your reader's behavior, the more effective your attack.

In this situation, let your anger speak. Relive the situation and let your feelings go. It often happens that your anger will help you find the right words. You want your reader to hear the sound of your anger, the real thing. Authentic emotion carries its own force.

Again, when you begin the letter, identify the situation briefly. This time, don't hesitate to present it on your terms. It will reduce your effectiveness if your opponent remembers the occasion only hazily or remembers it the way that he or she wants, rather than the way you experienced it.

KRIS'S RESPONSE

Members of the Selection Committee for the National Honor Society:

For the final two years of high school I have been greatly annoyed with you. It's beyond my comprehension how you select the members of the National Honor Society. I've asked the counselor several times for the reasoning for my not being a member, and since he couldn't seem to find a reason, I'm coming to you hoping for a reply containing the answer.

As far as I know there are three qualifications that must be met for admittance to the National Honor Society: (1) You must have a cumulative grade point of 3.0 or better. (2) You must have been involved in extracurricular activities outside of school. (3) You must be involved in extracurricular activities inside school.

There can be no reasonable doubt that I meet all the specified requirements: (1) My cumulative grade point was 3.472. (2) I was involved in volunteer work for the sick at Mercy Hospital, and I was working with younger children in Religious Education. (3) I was a member of the Student Council for three years, I was a cheerleader for two years, and I was a member of the yearbook and *Spectrum* staff. All of these strongly fulfill the necessary requirements.

Unless there are some other requirements that are unlisted in the student handbook, there can be no reason for my not being admitted to the National Honor Society.

Situation 18A

I can think of many people who were sworn into the National Honor Society with less convincing qualifications than mine. I feel very unfairly treated by your method of selection, and would like some convincing and fact-backed reasoning for my being excluded as a member.

I think that every student denied membership should receive a letter of reasoning from the Selection Committee explaining that denial. I know I'm not the only person who has these feelings of unjust treatment, and I'm sure they also would like to know the reasons for their being turned down.

I would appreciate it very much if you would reply to my questions as soon as possible.

TOM'S RESPONSE

Dear Mr. Greenhead:

Your recent decision about our performance during the tournament was truly an unprofessional call. In review of the judgment you stated that the subject the affirmative brought up (emergency medical care) was not actually refuted by our team. May I remind you that we refuted this subject by support that stated that ambulance and emergency room care has improved.

Ambulance and emergency room improvements are direct refutations of the emergency medical care argument. Since this was not just my thought but the thought of my colleagues also, I believe I am correct in my position. This decision was very disheartening for me because I've worked long, hard hours in building my evidence. It is most disappointing to see my hard work vanish due to a bad call. You should be ashamed of yourself.

ASSESSMENT

Writer _____
Self Assessment _____ Group Assessment _____
Teacher Assessment _____ Other _____

Reader would feel the force of the attack, and might be compelled to recognize its justice. _____
   or
Writer needs to identify the situation. _____
Writer needs to "sound" angry. _____
Writer needs more accuracy in his or her attack. _____
Other suggestions: _____

We see Kris's response in a new light when we consider it as a tongue-lashing. Now the indignation and militancy in her tone are appropriate; now there is no need to try to present the other side. Kris states very clearly what the Committee has done (or rather, declined to do). If Kris really wants to sting the Committee, however, she needs to lay her real charges on the table. Kris seems to wish to charge the Committee with favoritism and hypocrisy — with stating one set of rules and standards and then acting by another. To make this the best possible tongue-lashing, Kris should realize that there is nothing to lose; she should make her accusations boldly and bluntly.

Tom needs to identify the particular debate more clearly so that the judge can immediately recall it. But the interesting issue about Tom's response is focus. In one way Tom's focus is good: he states a specific complaint — the judge's disregard of a particular line of argument. In another way Tom's focus is fuzzy: what does he mean by "unprofessional conduct"? Does he mean that the judge did not hear the particular line of argument? Or that the judge made a mistake in judgment — that the judge found a solid position (according to Tom and his colleagues) to be unconvincing? The first charge would be more serious because such a lapse of attention would be clearly unprofessional, but the second charge would put us into the realm of opinion. Tom needs to clarify his charge. Tom's group thought he needed more focus; Tom disagreed.

19 · Concerned Citizen

Letters to the editor are a form of writing that you are probably familiar with. Perhaps you read the letters in your college newspaper. Many people on college campuses read the letters column regularly because it is one way to find out what is going on, what people around them think and feel. They enjoy hearing amusing voices, finding out current issues and problems, listening to passionate rhetoric. It is like tuning in on a town meeting; it fulfills part of the need for gossip, discussion, debate, interchange; it is a way of participating in a group.

The quality of the letters is usually uneven. What makes a good letter to the editor? Think about this question while you prepare for this assignment.

SITUATION 19

Think over your college experience so far. Can you identify any institutional problems that are hindering your pursuit of an education—problems with regulations, student behavior? Try to single out one problem common enough that you could call it to the attention of your college community. (Review your responses to Situations 12 and 17 to see if they give you a suitable topic.) Write a letter to your school newspaper calling attention to the problem. (Before writing your response, read Situation 19A as a possible alternative.)

GUIDELINES

1. Establish the context of the problem.
2. Make the problem clear and vivid.
3. Address the college community. Show why your problem should matter to the community as a whole.

4. Sound concerned and responsible.
5. Consider offering possible solutions.

Letters to the editor are usually written to bring a particular problem to the attention of the community. What matters most in writing such a letter is *taking the right stance,* showing that you are aware of your audience, sounding as though you are speaking to the college community. Although you address one community, within that community there are many different kinds of people—students, teachers, administrators, staff. To address this varied audience successfully is not easy. Often, responses to this assignment sound like personal gripes without any particular audience in mind, or like imitations of letters to the editor that are really written to the teacher. To judge how well you are handling this difficulty, ask yourself whether you would actually be willing to send your letter to the paper. If you draw back from that possibility, your intuition may be telling you that you haven't solved the matter of stance and address.

A letter to the editor requires great care in establishing context. Remember that members of this audience don't know what you are talking about until you tell them. Context has come up again and again in our discussion of explanatory and persuasive assignments, but in some of those cases you were reminding a reader of a familiar situation. In this case the situation is unfamiliar; as far as the reader knows, your letter could literally be about anything. Try to move the reader inside your frame of reference as quickly as possible. Identify your problem quickly and clearly, at the same time as you engage the reader's interest and sympathetic attention. Simultaneously informing and engaging the reader is hard but important. You will probably spend a lot of time trying to get your beginning right.

Another key requirement is presenting your problem as a *public concern* rather than a personal difficulty. The letters column is a place for discussing common problems and concerns, rather than for airing personal problems that affect only you. The difference may not be clear: something that seems to be your problem may really be a problem that others face also. But in most cases, you should be able to decide whether the problem is closer to the private or the public domain. For example, assume that a particular teacher has a habit of lecturing overtime and making his or her students late for their next classes. In such a case, a student would want to raise the problem with the teacher himself or herself. If this habit were becoming widespread, however—if many teachers were lecturing overtime—writing a letter to the editor would seem like a good course of action.

Another problem of address is, what kind of person do you want to sound like? If you are presenting your problem in a straightforward way (for other approaches, look ahead to Situation 19A), you probably want to sound like a concerned citizen, a responsible member of the community who is interested in the common good. Taking this stance is not a matter of playing a role in the sense of playing a false part; you wouldn't be writing if you weren't concerned about a public problem. Since you want people to take you seriously, however, you need to sound like someone worth listening to. Define your problem well so that you sound knowledgeable about the problem and careful about the reader; work on your tone so that you strike a note of genuine concern. One way to obtain serious attention is to sound earnest, sincere, and responsible.

It may be enough to call attention to a problem; you are not necessarily responsible for its solution. However, if you have ideas about a solution, you might advance them. Not only may your proposed solution have merit, but it will also show the sincerity of your concern with the problem; it may add to your credibility.

LIZ'S RESPONSE

Liz responded to Situation 19A; see the next chapter.

RYOKO'S RESPONSE

To the Editor:

Two weeks ago a freshman left her room, leaving a message on our dorm's message board: "Hi, everybody! I am leaving here. It seems to me I cannot keep up in my studying. Good luck to all of you. (Signed) Wendy."

She was a newcomer here, living next door to us. Her room was the same size as ours, a big triple room. But her roommates never showed up. We talked to her and ate with her in the cafeteria whenever we saw her there. But none of us knew how lonely she was and what problems she had. She was always quiet. We'd never heard her phone ring, either. Actually, we could never tell whether she was in her room or not.

What could we have done for her?

The same thing happened to me last summer, though I did not leave school. Everything was new to me. No friends. No place to go. No ideas about the university. And always worried about how I was doing. Living in a big, empty room in a dorm, I was too lonely to stop crying and asking myself, "Who cares? Everyone has forgotten about me. Why am I studying and putting up with this situation?"

There are advisors, counselors, teachers, and classmates. However, none of them knows you well enough to talk about your personal feelings, especially when you are stuck and confused. Making an appointment to talk to one of them, you have to wait for a long time; then can you say, "I am too lonely. What shall I do?" or "I don't have any desires. Why am I studying?" In a large university, it is so easy for a student to lose his or her way and to be isolated.

So we should open our eyes and keep trying to care about others, classmates or neighbors. We may notice who needs our little help and be able to do something for her or him. In fact, if my two roommates and I had cared much about Wendy, she might not have had to leave here.

KRIS'S RESPONSE

To the Editor:

I'm writing out of concern with the teaching in the math department. I'm currently enrolled in Algebra I taught by Mrs. M., and from all the work I can honestly say that I haven't learned a thing!

I have talked to several other people in my class, and they feel the same way. We find it very difficult to learn anything from Mrs. M.'s method of teaching.

She throws an example on the board and explains how to do it, but she never shows how to do it. She never shows you more than one example of each different type of problem. When you ask for extra help, she fails to help you; she just confuses you more.

We all consider our education a very important part of our lives, and we can't develop our learning to the fullest if we don't have the right educator. We're not saying Mrs. M. isn't a good teacher; we're just saying that the way she is teaching us just isn't right.

We believe Mrs. M. could go a little slower when teaching daily lessons. She could also develop each daily lesson to a greater extent so that students do understand it. She also could spend more time with students who ask for help, instead of pushing them away. When a student asks for extra help, it means he doesn't understand and wants to try to understand.

All of us who consider our education a very serious matter find this a very frightening problem. We would appreciate it very much if the persons with the correct authority would look into this situation and try to come up with some sort of solution. When you come up with a solution, we would appreciate it a great deal if you would give us a reply.

We as students hope you understand our position and what we are trying to say. We aren't trying to put down Mrs. M. or the teaching staff at Regina; we are just trying to express our concern about our education!

TOM'S RESPONSE

Tom also responded to Situation 19A; see the next chapter.

ASSESSMENT

Writer _____
Self Assessment _____ Group Assessment _____
Teacher Assessment _____ Other _____
The casual newspaper reader would pay attention. _____
   or
Writer needs to establish the problem's context. _____
Writer needs to explain the problem more clearly. _____
Writer must make it an important public problem. _____
Writer must sound more like a concerned citizen. _____
Other suggestions: _____

I find Ryoko's letter moving, appropriate, and skillful. Writing about a genuine community problem, she is more than a concerned citizen — she is a compassionate citizen. By opening with Wendy's note, Ryoko catches our interest and dramatizes the problem. By revealing how she has been in Wendy's hopeless and isolated position, Ryoko indicates that Wendy is not an unusual case. By admitting how she and her roommates "failed" with Wendy, Ryoko can bring the problem to our attention without being moralistic, because she recognizes herself as part of the problem. While the beginning of Ryoko's letter is excellent in many ways, she needs to establish the context more clearly, particularly who the writer is and where the action is taking place. Though these matters sort out later on, the reader initially experiences some unnecessary confusion.

Kris has misjudged the rhetorical situation. In her second-to-last paragraph she indicates what she really wants — to obtain the attention of "persons with the correct authority." Kris wants a change in Mrs. M.'s teaching methods. To achieve this it would be better to address Mrs. M. herself (as Kris did in Situation 17) or to write to Mrs. M.'s supervisors. Public criticism is not appropriate and would probably have a destructive effect. Kris is confused about purpose.

19A · Madman or Fool

Difficult as writing is, it does offer freedom and latitude in one respect: there are usually a number of ways of solving a particular writing problem, a number of stances the writer can adopt. In approaching a letter to the editor, you need not necessarily adopt the concerned citizen's role.

SITUATION 19A

You wish to bring an institutional problem to the attention of your college community by writing a letter to the editor of your school paper. But perhaps you feel that the role of concerned citizen is too serious for presenting your problem. Write a free-swinging letter in which you exaggerate your feelings, in which you play the outraged victim. Or write a satiric letter in which you *say what you don't mean,* in which you take the opposite position in a deliberately wrong-headed way. These kinds of social criticism can have the advantage of amusing your reader, but they are not easy to write.

GUIDELINES

1. Create a speaker who is entertaining and consistent.
2. Make sure that your point about the problem comes through.

If you are a regular reader of your campus paper's letters column, you have probably noticed that a sizable proportion of the letters are far from "straight." Many people enjoy clowning in print, sometimes playing exaggerated and amusing roles, sometimes using irony — undercutting the opposition by presenting its points in an absurd and ridiculous way. It is possible to be playful and to make a point at the same time; a playful approach often makes its point more effectively than a straight argument because it disarms and entertains the reader. A fantasy portrait of Starch

Woman might be more effective than a reasoned attack on a dormitory menu. A parody of the violent passion of the critics of the football coach might be more effective than a reasoned defense of his strategy and character.

If you choose to play with your subject and your readers, it is important to *keep your speaker under control.* One aspect of control is consistency: a letter that is half straight and half put-on cannot stand. If you are impersonating a wild-eyed and crazy critic of the football coach, don't inject a sincere endorsement of his player relations into your parody. When you create a "strange" speaker, your speaker needs to be consistently strange throughout.

Another kind of control is also necessary: it is important not to lose your point amid the highjinks of creating an amusing speaker. Make sure that your reader can figure out that you are against the making of a scapegoat or that you are for protein on the table. The entertainment will be wasted if it doesn't advance your view of the problem.

LIZ'S RESPONSE

To the Editor:

The relationship between the students and teachers has gone through a drastic change over the past ten years. No longer does the teacher have a personal interest in each student. Instead of being concerned with the learning capabilities of all students, teachers merely present the information they see as valuable and if you learn, that's okay, and if you don't learn, that's okay too.

Since this is the day of the dollar I have a suggestion on how the school system can save some money. The teachers and students no longer have an emotional feeling for each other, so why do we need them? Their usefulness has been greatly depleted. Why not replace each instructor with a tape recorder? The advantages of this system greatly outweigh the feelings of tradition. It has been questioned whether all students are receiving the same well-balanced education. With the tapes the government could be assured that there is no discrimination. No longer would we have to worry about bussing. The Boston school system could return to the happy world with the thought that there is no discrimination in taping.

Situation 19A

There would be an increase in extracurricular activities with extra money available through the absence of faculty salaries. Consequently, the taxes would decrease because we would no longer have to pay for teacher vacations, maternity leaves, gas for buses, and substitute teachers, and there would no longer be fear of a strike—unless of course the tape recorders form a union.

For those of you who are worried about the possibility that the student would suffer from a lack of attention, we have fixed that. They will be automatically strapped to their chairs with mind stimulators placed on them. That way the student is never allowed to daydream.

If you look at this situation clearly, I know that you will see that it is time to modernize the educational system. A failure to do so would mean the deterioration of the human mind.

TOM'S RESPONSE

To the Editor:

If the University is truly concerned about the health of students, I think they should include all the other personnel in this concern. I would strongly suggest that it be required of all teaching personnel to do 200 push-ups in front of class each day. If they fail to do this, they should be suspended from the University until they are able to fulfill this requirement. Another physical requirement I would recommend is that no teaching personnel be overweight. If they are overweight, I would recommend a fine of $1,000 for each extra pound.

I think that before the University requires liberal arts students to complete a physical education requirement, it should firm up all the soft brains and bellies of all overweight teaching personnel and administrators who suggested this idea.

ASSESSMENT

Writer _____
Self Assessment _____ Group Assessment _____
Teacher Assessment _____ Other _____

Writer catches and keeps the reader's attention and makes a point. _____

   or
Writer must establish the context. _____
Writer needs more control of his or her speaker. _____
Writer loses the point of the problem. _____
Other suggestions: _____

Liz's response and Tom's response make clear some of the technical difficulties in writing successfully from an ironic stance, in playing the role of madman or fool. Both Liz and Tom have a good strategy, an imaginative idea for a satirical treatment of an issue, but both run into problems of execution.

Liz's problem is consistency. Her first paragraph presents a straightforward concern with the depersonalization of education; the rest of her letter is an absurd and ironic proposal for mechanization. The mixed signals trouble the reader. My advice would be to turn the whole letter over to the tape recorder advocate; I think Liz could be consistently ironic while still establishing her real point.

The glaring problem with Tom's letter is context. The reader is immediately disconcerted and annoyed because it is not sufficiently clear what the letter is about. Tom's last sentence reveals that he is addressing the physical education requirement for liberal arts majors, but this comes too late. Like Liz, Tom successfully finds a vivid way to extend a position to a ridiculous extreme. His phrase about firming up "the soft brains and bellies" is a witty use of language; he combines in a phrase his feeling that the requirement rests on hypocrisy and poor judgment. Someone in the class made the point that if Tom reduced his proposed regimen of exercise and fines, the proposal would become both sharper and crazier as it became more seemingly realistic. This seems both paradoxical and true.

Liz and Tom and their groups found these responses successful; I think they have the potential to become so.

20 · Peering into the Future

Although the writing teacher's most frequent advice is to "be more specific," there are writing situations that require the opposite — generality and abstraction. Good writing at a high level of generality and abstraction is difficult for several reasons: because it is easy to lapse into vagueness, to become cloudy, hazy, foggy; and because everyday life only rarely requires us to use language at a high level of abstraction. For many people, working with abstraction requires the acquisition of a new vocabulary, and their writing may tend to be awkward and imprecise until that vocabulary is under control. It is important, however, to learn to write well on an abstract and general level. If you are bound to concrete and specific situations and circumstances, you can never rise to general laws and principles; you are kept from coming to the heart of the matter. Obviously, college demands the development of these powers: academic disciplines are *systems* of generalizations at a high level of abstraction. In academic writing, you must frequently move back and forth between the specific and the general, the concrete and the abstract — from the specific case to the principle, from the principle to its application.

This assignment asks you to write on a general and abstract level about two subjects you have probably spent some time contemplating: yourself and your future work.

SITUATION 20

You have made an appointment with your advisor to talk about your long-term plans and goals. In preparation for this meeting, write a paper in which you assess your suitability for the field you are considering. What does your field require? What signs indicate that you may be right for the field? (Think back to Situation 16, when you were recommending a candidate for a job. Then you had to anticipate what qualities the employer was looking for. This situation requires the same kind of thinking, except on a more general level, and with yourself as subject.)

GUIDELINES

1. Identify the qualities that your field requires.
2. Present the evidence that leads you to think you have those qualities.

This writing task requires an analysis and then an application of that analysis to a particular case. First, what qualities does your field require? What makes a good mathematician or football coach or social worker or pharmacist? You may find it helpful to think comparatively: what qualities distinguish this work from other kinds of work?

Second, why do you think you fit the field? Why do you suspect that you have the right qualities? On what occasions, in what situations did you discover these qualities in yourself? Did you find that you had the necessary patience for teaching when you were teaching your little sister to ride a bike? Did you discover that you had a nose for errors in calculation when you were learning how to balance a checkbook? What evidence leads you to think that you have the qualities necessary for your field?

The success of your response depends on your thoughtfulness in analyzing the requirements of your field. Do your qualities seem *field-specific*, that is, do they particularly apply to your field rather than to all fields? Qualities like willingness to work hard seem to be required for success in most fields. Second, do you make a convincing case for yourself as possessor of those qualities?

LIZ'S RESPONSE

During my junior and senior years in high school I began taking a deep look into what I wanted my future to hold. I always knew I wanted to be involved in science in some way and I truly feel that being in Medical Technology is for me. It will supply me with the excitement of discovery. The job would be eight-to-five so that it wouldn't disturb any family that I might have. Also there will always be a need to read and study new methods so my brain will not get stale. I worry about being in a job where every day is the same routine. In Med Tech you do all kinds of testing so each day brings a different set of problems. I like the fact that I will be working with people who need help. I like dealing with people, and by showing kindness and strength I hope that I can spread a little sunshine into their lives. Although I like dealing with people, I also like being left to myself in my work. The lab work will give me this. I have done a lot of thinking on my career and have found Medical Technology is for me.

RYOKO'S RESPONSE

I want to be a speech therapist. My father is a dental surgeon who works especially for handicapped children. Since I look up to him and his great job, I am interested in working in the same area as he does. And also I like children. That's why I am interested in studying speech pathology.

When I was a high school student, I started working with hard-of-hearing children. I enjoyed working with hard-of-hearing children and with harelip children, and I learned so many things from them. Harelip is a deformity whose occurrence rate is pretty high. The harelip baby has to be operated upon and has to practice how to make sounds and how to speak for a long time. What attracts me is that these babies need help to live with their handicaps.

In Japan, a speech therapist is not accepted as an important worker. Therefore, there is no special license or degree. That's why I came to the United States to study, since here a speech therapist is considered a special worker for handicapped people. Besides, the difference of languages does not matter in being a speech therapist. So I'm planning to get the B.A. at the University of Iowa and to go back to Japan.

KRIS'S RESPONSE

Here at Iowa I'm majoring in business education, namely accounting. I've known for several years that I want to try accounting for my career. I took accounting when I was a junior in high school and it really captured my attention.

During my course in accounting I really had a lot of fun. I really enjoyed figuring out the balance of certain accounts, whether they were a debit or a credit. I enjoyed doing the work a lot, and really didn't have much problem learning how to do it.

I know that the accounting course I took in high school covered just general areas, but I think I would also be able to understand harder accounting and business courses.

From the accounting courses I took in high school I know it takes a lot of time and effort. I do believe I can handle it because of my great interest in the subject, and when I enjoy something I dedicate a lot of time to being a success at it.

I think what attracted me most to a career in accounting was my experience with it in high school. The thing I think will carry me a long way to becoming an accountant is my interest, enjoyment, and dedication to the subject. I'm anxiously awaiting the first day on the job of being an accountant!

TOM'S RESPONSE

Being an agent for the Central Intelligence Agency has two distinct qualities: (1) You are always on some kind of adventure. (2) You get to travel around the world a lot.

The extra adventure you get from the job stands out far from any ordinary work, because the main thing is that each job you take on is so important, such as gaining access to secrets in the Kremlin. The traveling is great because you get to see such famous cities as Hong Kong, Moscow, and Peking. These two elements are the biggest reasons why I would like this job.

ASSESSMENT

Writer _____
Self Assessment _____ Group Assessment _____
Teacher Assessment _____ Other _____
The advisor would feel that you understand the requirements of your field and have thought about your suitability. _____
   or
Writer needs a better analysis of the field. _____
Writer needs better evidence of suitability. _____
Other suggestions: _____

Kris's response is a good starting place for discussion because Kris so clearly misses on this one. The content of Kris's response can be simply paraphrased: she liked her high school accounting courses. She doesn't analyze herself or the occupation, a failure that was pointed out by her group. Kris mentions that she can't write more about the occupation without job experience, but this might be an evasion. If her attraction to the field is a fact, *something* must be behind that attraction; Kris could try harder to name and explain that something.

Ryoko and Tom are not in tune with the rhetorical situation. Ryoko has the right idea when she writes about her attraction to children and her impulse to help the handicapped. But most of her response seems directed toward explaining her educational and occupational situation to the advisor — her reasons for studying in America, the low status of speech therapists in Japan, and so on. The purpose of these notes should be self-exploration in the context of occupation, including the advisor in the process. Ryoko seems primarily to be explaining the status quo rather than exploring. Ryoko's group wanted to see a stronger connection between Ryoko and the work; Ryoko saw a need for this and for a better self-analysis. She also suggested an interesting question to explore: of all the kinds of work with the handicapped, why did I pick speech therapy?

Tom still seems under the spell of Situation 19A. I don't think that an advisor would be willing to devote much time to a James Bond fantasy, but if Tom is going to write a Bond fantasy, he should give us the full treatment. Where are the women, the cars, the casinos, the caviar, and the martinis (shaken, not stirred)?

Liz is in the spirit of the assignment, but some of her points seem unclear to me and others call for more exploration. Would Med Tech really provide the excitement of discovery, or is the analysis of samples a routine business? What does Liz mean by discovery? Do Med Techs work with patients? In what capacity? I understood that they were confined to the laboratory. Does the job require the kind of rapport that is required from nurses? Liz could go deeper and further in her analysis. Liz's group felt the response was successful; Liz wanted a stronger connection between herself and the work.

21 · A Particular Kind of Excellence

Though you are most likely to make generalizations at a high level of abstraction in school, in an academic context, there are no barriers to theorizing in other areas of your life, and undoubtedly you sometimes do so. If you have ever speculated about what makes your father a good cook or what accounts for a friend's popularity, you have indulged in an informal kind of theorizing. This assignment asks you to treat a familiar subject in a speculative way, to advance some hypotheses about it.

SITUATION 21

Think again of the sport or activity you wrote about in Situation 2 (and possibly in Situations 8 and 14). You are talking with some people who also love the activity. Talk turns to what makes a great performer, a champion, a master, an award winner. After the conversation, you write down your speculations about excellence in this activity. Try to identify and explain several of the key qualities that lead to excellence.

GUIDELINES

1. Identify qualities that are specific to your activity.
2. Single out qualities that would inform and convince, qualities that are *original* and *basic*.
3. Develop those qualities at length.

What matters most in performing your activity? What particular gifts or skills account for excellence? In approaching these questions, you must above all *be specific to your activity*. If you write about qualities like the will to win or excellent physical conditioning, you will miss the point of this assignment; such qualities are necessary for many sports and therefore do not tell us much. If you write about shortstops, try to show how a

154

great shortstop differs from a great second baseman or a great free safety. You can't point out the essence of your activity by writing in terms that might apply to sports and activities in general.

When you analyze your activity, brainstorming for qualities, remember that your reader will want an analysis of the sport that is both *insightful and fresh* and *fundamental and basic*. That makes your task difficult: saying something that seems both original and basic is never easy. For example, suppose that in writing about trap-shooting you state that sharp distance vision is a prime requisite. Your reader will not argue with you, but neither will your reader feel very enlightened. On the other hand, suppose you propose that a football quarterback must have superior peripheral vision. This may be a new idea to the reader, but it may also be difficult to convince him or her that the quality is essential and basic. I once read that the secret of Muhammed Ali's success as a boxer was his eyes—that he was able to hold them open more consistently than any opponent, to keep from blinking and flinching, and thus he stayed on top of the action and could hit without being hit. That speculation is strong on originality, but the writer might have to work hard to convince a skeptical reader that the quality was basic to Ali's excellence.

The Ali example brings up another requirement of the assignment: it will probably be necessary to do more than mention your qualities. To establish them as both original and basic, you will probably need to explain and develop. I believe, for example, that a primary quality for success in crew is strong thigh muscles, but to convince a reader I would probably need to explain the construction of a shell, so that the reader could understand why the thighs provide the most important source of thrust.

LIZ'S RESPONSE

Anyone can play basketball but it takes a person with special attributes to become a great forward. Being a forward is not just running down the court and throwing the ball at a metal hoop; there is much more to the sport. There are not many people in the world who can be labeled as great forwards, but those who are possess certain skills.

One of the best attributes is the person's ability to make quick jabbing movements without losing control of her body. To be an effective forward you must be able to get rid of your defensive opponent by making quick movements from side to side to catch your guard off balance. If a forward can start and stop with speed and not lose control, he/she can catch the defense in an awkward position and thus become free for an assist.

All great forwards have a keen sense for the ball. They know how to handle the ball with their hand-eye coordination. Thus they are able to make crisp passes between defensive players and to keep the ball under control while dribbling. Many games have been saved by the forward's ability to save a bad pass or recover a lost ball.

Each great forward also has a keen perception of the dimensions of the floor, the hoop, and the ball. He or she is thus able to tell the distances for passes and the pressure needed on the ball.

If the forward can anticipate a pass or a break, he or she can catch the defense. A person who waits till the opening has been made before passing runs the risk of giving the opposition time to recover and steal the pass. To summarize the floor work, I believe you must have a keen perception of dimensions, move in quick jabbing motions to lose the defense, and move the ball with speed and accuracy.

Although each forward has his or her own style for shooting, I think the best form for accuracy is: (1) a high horizontal jump, (2) slight hesitation before shooting, (3) forearm of the shooting arm perpendicular to the floor, (4) the ball placed in the middle of the forehead, and (5) the wrist cocked back for a smooth-flowing extension to the basket, thus placing a lot of spin on the ball.

Each person perceives a great forward differently, but I think you'll find mutual agreement on these attributes.

RYOKO'S RESPONSE

He wears a white traditional overwear and a navy-blue *Hakama*, which is like a long skirt. His *Hakama's* folds are straight and tidy. His mask's long strings are neatly tied behind his head and are swinging with a long red ribbon, which helps to identify him. An opponent and he stand on the edge of the court and look at each other. They make a special bow in the center of the court.

When the judge says, "Start," he shouts loudly with his shrill voice to threaten the opponent and to cheer himself up. The high-pitched shout resounds in the silent gym. His bamboo sword aims at the opponent's head. He walks step by step without changing his posture. His quick decision elects a little moment of the opponent's unguarded point and all his well-disciplined muscles obey his decision to make an attack. While his eyes in the dark mask blaze at the opponent, his left foot quickly comes close to his right foot in a long, strong hop. At the same time, he raises his sword promptly and lightly. Before the opponent gets ready to protect himself, he must make an unexpected and exact attack. Otherwise, the opponent will get a chance to make a much easier attack. As he shouts and hops, he hits the opponent's front helmet with the front part of the bamboo sword. His arm muscles tense to wring the sword to make a strong hit; the opponent cannot avoid the strong hit and he can remove the opponent's immediate protection.

The high-pitched metallic sound echoes in the gym, as three judges raise their red flags in recognition of his correct attack on the head. He runs through the opponent to emphasize his exact attack.

Right after this attack, he has to get ready to make a next attack and to protect himself. He approaches the opponent to drive the opponent into the corner. His mind is in the nothingness and very calm. He concentrates on reading the opponent's mind. He gives the opponent a chance to make an attack. When the opponent seizes this chance, he immediately looks for an unguarded point and makes a much more prompt and exact attack. His decisiveness, concentration, and quick movements of his well-disciplined muscles and nerves make this attack exact and strong.

After he gets two correct attacks, they make a bow again to appreciate each other and the judges. His sweat is glittering on the mask and he smiles.

KRIS'S RESPONSE

When you're looking for a champion in swimming, you're looking for a lot of things. The most important thing to look for, as you do in any sport, is a person who you can tell is really enjoying what he or she is doing. After you've found this, you start looking for the little things that might make that person the champion of the swimming pool.

First watch how effective their racing dive is when they jump off the starting block. When they dive from the block, their fingers should be the first thing to touch the water with the rest of the body gently following. The head should just glaze under the water, with a very thin layer of water covering the rest of the body. There also should be no large splash, and the strength of the dive should glide them close to a quarter of the way down the racing lane.

After their entrance to the water you should watch their specialized stroke. Since I was a freestyle swimmer, that is the stroke I shall describe. The hands should be held in a half-cupped form so that they can grasp the water and pull you through.

The stroke starts with both hands on top of the water with the hands in the cupped position. Your body should be held straight and taut on top of the water with your head face down in the water. The legs should be flexed with the toes of the feet turned slightly upward toward the top of the water. The legs should be allowed to dangle beneath the water at the knee.

With your body in correct position, you're ready to start on your way to the finish. You should begin with your feet kicking what is known as a flutter kick. Your feet should kick at the angle not allowing your feet to break through the surface of the water. Your feet should act as a propeller to push you through the water, and your feet should be kept in constant motion.

After your feet are in working motion, your arms begin. You should start with your right hand pulling straight down through the water, along your side, up over your head, and back to the resting position on top of the water. When your right arm reaches the side of your body, your left arm should begin in the same fashion as the right. When your arms are on time they will create what looks like a pinwheel.

When your arms are timed right you should begin your breathing. An excellent swimmer usually breathes about every three strokes, a stroke being when both arms have made a complete revolution. When you take a breath your head should turn to the side, allowing only the nose and mouth to come out of the water.

An excellent swimmer will then use a flip turn when he reaches the wall. About five inches before he reaches the wall he will roll his body up into a ball and turn a complete somersault, pushing off the wall with his feet.

With all these things perfectly timed together and speed, strength, and stamina thrown in, you're on your way to becoming a champion swimmer.

TOM'S RESPONSE

To be a good public speaker you must be interesting, knowledgeable, organized, and receptive to your audience. To win a debate you must be interesting enough to capture the judge's attention, knowledgeable enough to convince the judge you know what you are talking about. You must be organized because you have very little time to say a number of facts and concepts. One must always be receptive to the judge as he or she is that person who holds your destiny.

The basic thing you must do in a debate is show the judge that your position is acceptable by using the techniques of good public speaking; once you have gained this confidence you will be able to command the debate. This is the main key to winning a debate: being a good public speaker.

ASSESSMENT

Writer _____
Self Assessment _____ Group Assessment _____
Teacher Assessment _____ Other _____
Reader is given convincing new insight into the activity. _____
    or
Writer needs more activity-specific generalizations. _____
Writer needs to be more original. _____
Writer needs to be more basic. _____
Writer must discuss and extend generalizations. _____
Other suggestions: _____

Ryoko and Kris misjudge this rhetorical situation. Instead of analyzing her martial art, Ryoko re-creates a match, showing her expert in combat. Her scene is vivid and engaging (though sometimes confusing), but we have to draw our own conclusions and generalizations about excellence in this activity; Ryoko provides the raw material but not the analysis. Ryoko needs to state explicitly a number of points that are implicit in her description; she could make some strong points about the attitude and psychological state of the excellent performer. Ryoko's response seems to fit Situation 2 (describing a moment of high involvement) better than Situation 21, except that Ryoko writes here as a spectator rather than a participant.

Kris also writes for a purpose that doesn't fit the assignment; she seems to be writing Instructions to a Beginner for Swimming the Crawl (most of which would be appropriate for Situation 8), rather than analyzing excellence in this activity. Kris's response was convincing to her group and to herself, probably because Kris was willing to develop in detail (and even though the writing often seems careless, wordy, and difficult to follow). That her group was convinced shows the power of development to create credibility, even when the writer is off-center in terms of purpose.

Tom analyzes his activity and his points are undeniably basic to excellence in public speaking and debate. But the element of originality and fresh insight seems lacking; the reader has not learned much about public speaking by the end of the piece. Also, the development that might give these generalizations greater force and meaning is missing. Tom and his group recognized these problems.

Liz seems to have the idea of the assignment. Her generalizations about playing forward read like basic observations *and* fresh observations. The reader of a good response to this situation should say, "Yes, I bet that's true" and "I never thought of it quite that way before," and many readers would have that double reaction to Liz's response. Liz does have a problem with readability; she sometimes fails to say what she means cleanly and clearly. Liz's group was affected by this; they found the response difficult to understand.

22 · A Definition of Justice

You know much more than you can say. You understand more about the world than you can put into words. For example, you probably know how to ride a bicycle, but think about explaining to someone else how to ride. Finding the right words would be complicated and intimidating. Nevertheless, putting knowledge into words is one basic way of learning. If you can put an idea into words, you can examine it from all sides and come to a clearer and sharper understanding of it. It might be argued that you don't really know something until you can verbalize it.

In the situation that we have been calling an act of injustice (Situations 3, 7, 11, 18, or 18A), you have been operating on the basis of an intuitive idea of justice. If you had no idea of justice, you would not be feeling indignation and outrage; nothing would be wrong because no standard would have been violated. This assignment asks you to put your intuitive idea of justice into words. While it is difficult to define a general and abstract idea like justice, remember that justice is something you know and feel and operate with. Now it is a question of finding the words.

SITUATION 22

Return once more to the situation in which you felt unfairly treated (Situations 3, 7, 11, 18 or 18A). If your treatment struck you as unjust, you must have some inherent idea of what justice is. Try to state explicitly the idea behind your feeling. Imagine that you have taken the injustice to court; your complaint has come to trial. Acting as your own lawyer, you make a summation to the jury. You must convince the jury that you were the victim of injustice. Explain again what happened; then establish a definition of justice; then show how your definition applies to the incident. Good luck with prosecuting your case. (If you are no longer clear about *what justice is* in this situation, write a response about the difficulty of finding and applying a definition.)

GUIDELINES

1. Restate the essentials of the incident.
2. Compose and discuss a persuasive definition.
3. Make a clear connection between the definition and the situation.

What will make a suitable definition for this assignment? You must offer a statement that says something, that has some content. For example, if you define justice as a fair deal, you haven't really said anything; you are essentially offering a *synonym* for justice: justice equals fairness. Now the reader wonders, "What is fairness?" (This problem is typical of dictionary definitions.)

On the other hand, don't define justice by giving an example, such as, justice is returning the wallet you found at the bus stop. Examples illustrate what you mean, but in this case we have the example (your experience of injustice); what we need is a statement of a general principle. You must turn your example into an abstraction.

When evaluating your definition, consider whether a reader would find it a credible account of justice, a position deserving serious consideration. For example, many arguments have been waged over the Old Testament "eye for an eye" concept of justice, but no one denies that it is a credible definition, expressive of a deep human attitude. The debates focus on whether it is the right definition. Search for a definition that will strike readers in the same way as comprehensive, convincing, and rooted in human nature.

Simply stating a definition in a sentence or two is not enough. Expand on your idea, discuss its implications, show how it works. Consider the pattern of this textbook. In every chapter, the Guidelines are followed by a section of discussion. The Guidelines *compress* ideas into compact statements; the discussions *unfold* those ideas, offer alternative ways of executing them, and present complications, implications, and subpoints of the ideas in detail. Your definition requires this kind of clarifying discussion to be complete.

Once you have formulated a definition, determine whether it *applies* to your incident. Is it clear how your definition fits? What else do you need to do to establish the connection in your reader's mind? Your definition of justice may be a good one, but unless it fits your experience it will not explain your experience and justify your position. Without a convincing correspondence between your definition and the incident, your summation will fail.

A reminder: summarize what happened before giving your definition. The reader must know what you are talking about, to make sense of your definition and its application.

LIZ'S RESPONSE

Justice for all is what the Bill of Rights guaranteed to each person in the United States. The only problem with the Bill of Rights is that it is only a piece of paper, and there are some people in this world who find it very easy to ignore, especially the Iowa City Police Department.

As a child I had always put my trust in the police, thinking of them as more than human. Last summer I found that my childhood fantasy was just that, a fantasy. On July 26 while riding down Riverside Drive, we noticed red flashing lights behind us and then finally the siren. Immediately we pulled over to the side and got out of the car. The cop jumped out of the car and ran over. At once she began scolding us like little kids, calling us big-shot high schoolers while at the same time writing out a ticket. Not once did she tell us what the charges were. Only after the bombardment of questions did we get any notion of what we were being charged with. Another scolding and we were told to be on our way and she would see us in court in two weeks. After five and one-half months of continual court delays (all the delays were caused by the police officer), we finally made it to court on a drag racing charge. While the prosecutor was questioning the police officer, she proceeded to tell him that we had pleaded guilty at the site of the crime and a whole bunch of other lies. It wasn't until the defense lawyer questioned the officer that her lies were brought out into the open.

This is not justice. By the Bill of Rights a person is innocent until proven guilty. That was not the case in our incident. As soon as we were pulled over we were marked as criminals. We were continually lectured on what bad kids like us were like and what our punishment should be. The way in which our situation was handled was unfair.

1. When the officer first came to the car we should have been told the charges, so we could bring the entire incident out into the open. I believe people should know right off what they are being charged with, and not have to guess as we did.

2. I don't believe it was the policewoman's duty to scold us like little children. She should have told us the charge, explained it, and written out the ticket. The sarcasm should have been left out.

3. The Bill of Rights also states that each person has the right to a speedy trial. Five and a half months is not a speedy trial. I believe the policewoman should have found time for the trial instead of having continual delays put on it.

4. Probably the most unjust part of the situation deals with honesty. I believe that if a person is truly guilty then he should pay the consequences. But in this case the officer must have realized that she had no case, so she tried to use lies to cover up. If the world cannot live without lies and deceit, then justice has no meaning; it becomes only a seven-letter filler.

RYOKO'S RESPONSE

What is fair and what is not?

In my mind, fairness and unfairness are struggling and putting me into a deep, inconsistent hole. It takes me so long to climb up the hole that I probably can't creep out of it, going up and down inside the darkness.

A long time ago, I had a big argument with my mother. I thought that I was treated unfairly by her. But my judgment turned out to be unfair. I often made this kind of mistake when I was a little younger than now. And still my emotional judgments beat my logical reasons and make me feel guilty and inferior.

When I had the argument with my mother, she criticized my behavior; she said that I had displayed bad manners and that I was acting like a spoiled little boy. So she said to stop this because I was a girl and that I should help her cook and be more feminine. (Women's liberation was just getting popular in those days.)

Without knowing much about human rights and duties, I often emphasized women's rights as those of all human beings. But it wasn't fair for me to cry for the rights, because I wasn't doing my duties, either. It was my duty to do some work—helping my mom cook and doing a little housework—in my house, not because I was a little girl and therefore had to do it, but because I was a member of the family and sharing our work was a little, simple law in the family.

So, fairness or justice means that I should see the fact from both sides' viewpoints and clarify what is really happening deeply and logically so that the situation of both parties is equalized as much as possible.

This is still too ambiguous to define my thoughts about justice. However, if I think about my experiences, being treated unfairly and treating somebody else unfairly, I will be more careful in an emotional situation.

KRIS'S RESPONSE

I come from a very small family, only four members. In the past I have heard my friends say that they wished their families were as small as mine. I've heard them say things about how they were treated unfairly because of having a large family. Well, believe me, those feelings of being treated unfairly also happen in small families. I know because those feelings have at times been felt by me.

I am the younger of two children, both girls. There is only a year's difference between my sister, Kim, and myself. At times I wish that difference could be six or seven years so that my parents could forget what Kim had done in certain situations. Because of my sister's behavior I have been told I couldn't do the things I wanted to do.

One time Kim had ridden to a boys' basketball game with a few of her friends. She was a sophomore in high school and my parents thought she knew by now what she could do and couldn't do. Well, as it happened my sister got in trouble on the way and never showed up.

It seems that one of her friends had brought some beer and was drinking it on the way up. After a few of those beers it seems that that friend became a little crazy and started throwing the cans out the window. But not for long! They were caught by the local authorities and were taken to the local police station.

They were later sent home, having been told that they must tell their parents. The police later checked with the parents, and a letter was also sent home.

Finally a year later it was I who became a sophomore and I thought it was my turn to ride to the games with my friends instead of my parents. I guess I was wrong! Because of what my sister had done, I was not allowed to ride with my friends.

I was totally upset when my parents said no. I felt as if I had been treated unfairly. After all, I was not Kim; I was me, but I was treated as if I were my sister. I was afraid that every time I wanted to do something, I was first going to be compared to Kim. I didn't want to be compared to my sister; I just wanted to be me.

Justice to me means many things. It means being innocent until proven guilty; it allows every person to be himself or herself; but most of all it means that every person is allowed to prove himself or herself with his or her own credentials (individuality).

I think that my definition of what justice means to me shows why I felt I was treated unjustly. I felt denied the chance to prove myself on my own credentials; I was already tagged with the credentials of my sister. I wasn't allowed the chance to prove that I was innocent. It was already presumed that I would be guilty of the same thing that Kim was.

I strongly feel that my definition applies to this certain situation. Everything that I believed to be justice was overruled because of a situation in which my sister was guilty. My parents didn't give me a chance to prove myself in a similar situation, and because of this I felt I had been unjustly treated. Had I been given a chance to prove myself, I think my parents would have seen that I am not my sister.

My parents now see that I am capable of handling myself, and of proving myself on my own account. But this one instance in which I felt injustice will never be erased from my mind.

TOM'S RESPONSE

Last year, I was cheated out of a possible chance of winning a debate tournament. During the second round of the tournament, we faced a very inexperienced affirmative team. They did not present a well-planned argument. We presented a number of strong counterarguments that startled the young affirmative team. After the round it was generally assumed that we had won. But before that round of debating, the judge who was

Situation 22 167

about to judge our second round of debating was conversing with the eventual winning team of the tournament about "helping them any way he can." It seems natural to assume that the judge unfairly judged our round of debating. All the evidence seems to back up this assumption. There are two reasons why he cheated us: the first and most important was the flow sheet, which proved that we had won the debate, and the second was that conversation with the eventual winning team of the tournament. A strong definition of justice would be to give the parties involved an even break. This bad call by the judge who was working our debate was not giving us an even break.

ASSESSMENT

Writer _____
Self Assessment _____ Group Assessment _____
Teacher Assessment _____ Other _____
Reader finds the definition persuasive, and would agree that it applies to the particular case. _____
  or
Writer needs a better summary of the incident. _____
Writer needs a clearer definition. _____
Writer needs a definition with more substance. _____
Writer needs more discussion of the definition._____
Writer needs a stronger connection between definition and incident. _____

Other suggestions: _____

Tom has made progress in writing about the debate tournament; in this response he shows signs of pulling together his judgment of the debate judge. He accuses the judge of erring in two ways: socializing with competitors in the tournament and misjudging a competition. Taken together, these charges lead Tom to the accusation that the judge deliberately falsified his decision. Tom's view of the situation is more clear than ever before.

However, Tom does not even begin to define justice; calling it "an even break for all" is circular, tautological. Tom's piece doesn't deal with justice as an abstraction. One interesting direction he could explore is that justice is not only impartiality in decision making; it also entails avoiding any *appearance* of taking sides. Perhaps the judge's real offense against justice was that he undermined the system by causing Tom (and others) to doubt its fairness. In any event, Tom does not discuss principles and ideas—but he does clarify his understanding of the situation.

I like a number of things about Kris's response: I understand her incident; I follow the application of her definition to the incident; I think that her definition itself is striking and forceful. Kris presents justice as protection of the flowering of the individual—starting with the presumption of innocence, but extending to the freedom to determine and to demonstrate one's nature. Kris stakes a striking philosophical claim. However, she needs to expand and develop her definition; the core idea is stimulating but she furnishes only the backbone of the skeleton of the concept. (Kris could consider these points: how does society fit in? Do teenagers themselves need rules? Is justice simply the absence of controls, until it is shown that controls are needed?) Another improvement: Kris should condense the contents of her last three paragraphs; she unnecessarily repeats herself.

I would give Liz some of the same praise I gave Tom. We come closer here to seeing her incident whole than anywhere else in the sequence of assignments. I also like her analysis of the officer's four misdeeds. She is on the verge of writing about justice on an abstract level. Liz's response locates justice in two forms: common courtesy and civility; public truth-telling and forthrightness. She begins abstract discussion in her last paragraph (point four), suggesting that direct dealing is what holds the social fabric together. This could legitimately move a jury. Liz should build on this start; she should leap from her incident into social philosophy.

Ryoko states that she doesn't know what justice is, that even thinking about it throws her into a dark hole. But Ryoko writes deeply and movingly about justice both in her particular situation and in general. In terms of the domestic quarrel with her mother, when Ryoko decides that she was using feminist philosophy as a smokescreen to avoid general human duties, she demonstrates human insight and the ability to handle ideas in language, both of which reinforce each other. When she writes about justice in general, her idea that justice is connected with a deep understanding of both sides of an issue strikes me as powerful and profound. To illustrate her general idea of justice, Ryoko should show the second side of her quarrel; she should see whether her particular incident conforms to her tentative definition. Another suggestion: Ryoko should sketch the basic facts of her quarrel (as Liz does with her run-in with the police), so that the reader has fresh in mind the particular occasion that gave rise to these reflections.

23 · The Good Teacher (Or, The Good Student)

Generalizing and theorizing can give you the sense of penetrating to the core of the matter, of generating thoughts that cover a number of specific situations. When you are generalizing or theorizing well, you sense that you are going behind specifics and particular situations to arrive at the truth or the essence of something. This assignment asks you to convert a rich store of specific experience (you have all known many teachers and many students) into an ideal type, model, or form.

SITUATION 23

In Situation 5 you drew a portrait of a teacher of yours for a friend who wants to become a teacher. You continue the discussion with your friend, talking about what makes a good teacher *in general*. Write your speculations about the qualities of a good teacher. (If you wish, take up a closely related subject instead; write your speculations about a good student.)

GUIDELINES

1. Come up with fresh and basic insights about teaching.
2. Develop and extend those insights.

In this assignment you will work with the same basic guidelines as in Situation 21, when you described excellence in another activity. The challenge again is to make points that are both basic and fresh, points that your reader will recognize as true, and points that make the reader feel enlightened, as if he or she has learned something new. The task is not easy. For example, the idea that a good teacher can communicate with his or her students is basic but not very fresh, at least not until the writer does something with it. The idea that the good teacher is a role model for students is fresh, but is it basic? While it is obvious that coming up with the right sort of insight is not easy, it is equally obvious that *only* fresh and basic insight will be of value to a friend who is seriously considering teaching as a profession.

Achieving fresh and basic insight in this situation is not simply a matter of the quality of your raw ideas; your treatment and development of the ideas are at least as important as the ideas themselves. For example, a reader would probably regard punctuality as a desirable quality in a teacher but nothing basic. But if a writer showed how being on time can symbolize a teacher's respect for his or her students and for the profession of teaching, the reader might come to see that quality as basic. Remember that your success with the situation likely depends on the quality of your development.

LIZ'S RESPONSE

I have experienced many different types of teachers and from each of them I have drawn out characteristics to form the ideal teacher. The person has no age or sex requirements but this person must be pleasant to look at. I don't believe teachers have to be beautiful, but they have to keep themselves well groomed. I have had a teacher who didn't keep herself well groomed; the other students and I found her appearance quite distracting. I believe that a teacher should wear the clothes he or she likes, but not things that are shocking or totally strange. I find that students spend more time staring than they do listening.

This person should know his or her subject in detail. He or she must also possess a certain love for it to get the students excited to learn. If a teacher is excited then he or she is better able to make the students enthusiastic. She/he must be able to make lessons humorous and pick out little details that relate it to the students. A teacher who just relays facts tends to be boring. A student can pick out facts from a textbook; it is the teacher who is to tie the subject together in an interesting fashion.

To have an interesting subject the teacher must be well prepared for class. I find it very difficult to have respect for a teacher who fails to have his/her homework done. Students are punished for not having done their studies, and so it should be for the teacher. In the same fashion the teacher should be prompt. One duty instructors must fill is to set a good example, and nothing is worse than having a teacher who is lacking in that responsibility.

This "great" instructor would also be fair and able to relate to the students. Growing up is one of the most difficult experiences; it can be made almost impossible by a teacher with a hard heart. The best teacher is one whom you can talk to and who will understand when life gets you down. I can only hope that someday I'll meet a teacher such as this. It should be my best class.

RYOKO'S RESPONSE

What makes a good teacher?

I don't know. But who was a good teacher to me?

I had good teachers who were unique. Especially the one who was my classroom teacher when I was a freshman in high school; he was a very energetic, attractive teacher.

He didn't seem like a very exciting, unique person when we first saw him. Moreover, it looked like he would never care about us and would make us study hard. But the more time we spent with him, the more we liked him.

He was our math teacher and we had his math class every day, besides our daily class meeting. He was the one who knew when he should talk to whom. He must have had a special kind of intuition about who needed help and when he should give his help. And he must have been observing us very well, even though he never looked as if he had been paying special attention to us individually. Or could he read our minds?

As you know, even if I had trouble, sometimes I wouldn't tell anybody about it, not even my mom or my best friend. So when I felt like that, I would never have gone to talk to my teacher about my trouble. It would have sounded like making my trouble much bigger than it was, if I had done so. But he was different. He was very patient and waited for me until I felt like telling him my problems. We knew that he would never tell anybody about our problems and would give us a little hint or advice. If he didn't know, he would say that he had no idea but could think about it with us, instead of pretending to be an authority.

We had lots of fun doing something with him, too—going hiking, watching baseball games, going to movies, and so on. He was just like one of our friends and, at the same time, he was a very smart, respectable teacher.

When I think of my teachers, if I can remember strong impressions I had of them, they must have been either very good or very bad teachers for me. That's why I remember them vividly.

KRIS'S RESPONSE

When I was in high school, I ran into many teachers who I felt were exceptionally good. Along with the good teachers there were a few bad ones, but I found it much easier to distinguish a good teacher from a bad teacher.

I think the most important quality a good teacher should possess is the ability to relate to the students on their level. I found many times that teachers were way above the heads of their students. Many times this caused the students to lose interest in the class, and in turn the teacher earned the reputation of being a bad teacher.

Along with the specific quality of relationship, I believe there are many more things that tie together to make a good teacher. (1) I think that teachers need to be well educated in all areas, but it may not be necessary for them to use all that education. (2) Teachers need to have exceptionally long patience; they really need to control their emotions in front of their class. (3) They need to get involved and help *all* their students, not just a few favorites. (4) A good teacher also needs to be able to listen to the students as well as to teach them. (5) I believe a teacher needs to fit into the atmosphere of the school he or she teaches in.

Along with specific qualities I also believe teachers need to possess a few general qualities, such as being able to understand students, and being able to cope with the students' problems. Just letting the students know that they are there for the students' needs is a big help. They really have to get to know their students, not just as members of a class, but as persons!

All the specific qualities tied together with the general qualities make up my idea of what a good teacher is. Although I believe there are no teachers who possess all the qualities, I do believe there are teachers who possess more than others.

I don't believe there are any exceptionally great teachers, but I do believe there are teachers who are exceptionally good. I believe that some teachers are more qualified for their jobs than others.

Many people may not have the same idea of a good teacher as I do, but then all people aren't exactly alike. We are all different, and all have different likes and dislikes. I guess that's what makes up people.

TOM'S RESPONSE

To be a good teacher, you must be compromising, kind, firm but not strict, and very receptive to the needs of the class as a whole, because most of the time you will be dealing with the class as one large group of individuals.

Basically speaking, when in a teaching situation you must be an easy-going type of person because you deal with a variety of people—a jack of all trades but a master of none.

When you begin to become a teacher, you must be able to conduct a classroom with authority but still be able to know the needs of the students. As a teacher you are always looking for this perfect middle position.

ASSESSMENT

Writer _____
Self Assessment _____ Group Assessment _____
Teacher Assessment _____ Other _____
Reader is given insight into teaching. _____
   or
Writer needs to be more basic. _____
Writer needs to be more original. _____
Writer must develop and expand his or her points. _____
Other suggestions: _____

Tom makes an interesting point: his idea of the teacher as compromiser—the person in search of "this perfect middle ground"—balancing discipline and sympathy, individual needs and group needs, control and responsiveness. Tom suggests that there is no room for purists and "true believers" in teaching; one must have the flexibility to respond to the demands of different situations in different ways. A promising line of thought, but Tom must develop it to realize its potential.

Kris seems to be listing rather than developing; while some of her points seem basic, none strike me as fresh. Kris writes with most conviction and persuasive energy about the need for teachers to provide personal understanding and empathy.

Liz is at her best when writing about the need for the teacher to love his or her subject and to convey that enthusiasm. Although this point is not exactly fresh, the sincerity of Liz's treatment gives it force. She also writes movingly about the difficulty of growing up and the need for teachers who can provide understanding. (On this point Kris and Liz seem to be in close agreement.) Liz persuades the reader that she is developing some basic issues.

Ryoko seems to have a high resistance to generalization and abstraction. What she does in this assignment is really another version of Situation 5, I Knew a Teacher — another specific case, an individual portrait. However, Ryoko has the basis here for writing a response that fits Situation 23. In her third paragraph she mentions the intuition that tells a teacher when to offer individual attention. This is a fresh and basic generalization about teaching. It requires discussion, development, elaboration, and extension. Ryoko is good at illustrating through examples; she needs to practice another kind of development — discussion at a general and abstract level.

24 · Self-portrait of a Writer

Another subject about which you should be able to generalize at this point in the course is *yourself as a writer*. This assignment asks you to move between the general (your characteristics as a writer) and the specific (evidence and examples of those characteristics), at the same time expressing your feelings about the activity of writing.

SITUATION 24

Your teacher is interested in how you see yourself as a writer at this point. Think about your writing in this course and other writing experiences. What kinds of writing and kinds of assignments can you do well? What kinds give you trouble? Do any problems occur regularly? Have you any thoughts about your style? About your writing habits? About the way other people respond to your writing? About your feelings about writing? Draw a portrait of yourself as a writer.

GUIDELINES

1. Search for informative generalizations; search out your strongest and sharpest impressions about you and writing.
2. Support your generalizations with illustrations and examples.
3. Create a voice that expresses how you feel about writing.

As in the other "theory" assignments (Situations 20–23), you want to produce generalizations or hypotheses with a lot of content. The writing situation in this case makes this requirement very clear. Your teacher wants to see into the heart of your nature as a writer, so that both of you can understand your strengths and needs. It is time for assessment, for making statements that will help you know where you stand and where to go from here. You are in the best position to generalize about yourself as a writer; you are the expert with the inside experience. Your teacher is also in a good position, with the products of twenty-three situations to analyze. What insights can you offer?

Unlike some of the other "theory" situations, this assignment requires you to bounce back and forth between the general and the specific. Assume that you have identified one of your characteristics as a writer. Perhaps, for example, you have difficulty recognizing and acknowledging the other person's viewpoint in persuasive writing. How do you know that this is so? Show the basis for your generalization; refer briefly to the situations or assignments in which this happened. Or perhaps you tend to use only one sentence pattern, to keep writing the same kind of sentence without variation. Quote a passage that illustrates the problem. Support your generalizations; make them real for your reader.

So far, this assignment may seem more like an X ray than a portrait. But beyond generalizations and support, it also calls for your feelings about writing. (Don't feel coerced to praise writing; many professional writers find it a kind of self-inflicted torture. On the other hand, if you do like it, don't be afraid to say so. Perhaps you will find that your attitude is mixed.) If you successfully incorporate your feeling into your portrait, your analysis will take on a personal sound. Your reader will hear a version of you behind your words; your teacher will hear a *voice* expressing a personal and authentic opinion.

Let me offer a few hints about creating voice in this situation. You are trying to go beneath the surface to uncover what is essential about you as a writer. But to capture the flavor and feeling of your relationship with writing, you may need to return to the surface. Is it true that through some quirk of your nervous system you can compose only when the radio is playing? Do you talk your papers through to your roommate before you write them? Do you read the first draft to your roommate? Perhaps you can never make yourself settle down to write until 2 A.M., when other distractions are gone, everyone else is in bed, and there is nothing to do but face the blank page. Surface detail may make your portrait personal and individual.

Don't forget figurative language. What is writing like for you? What would you compare it with? While analogies can make points about you as a writer, they also give your self-portrait a personal dimension because they characterize you at the same time.

LIZ'S RESPONSE

At this point I see myself as a growing writer, and as in life I have a lot to learn and have made a lot of mistakes in the past. When I entered rhetoric this past summer I was as an infant at birth, given all the utensils to be successful but needing the knowledge of how to use them to my advantage. I left that protective little world of high school where writing wasn't really a requirement. I grew up in the day where people felt that learning grammar and writing skills was a waste of time; if you could communicate by mouth that was good enough. Consequently the only exposure to writing I received was by an Advanced Placement English course. This class dealt mainly with the reading and analysis of famous novels, essays, and poetry, but did require essay tests and term papers. After a year of A.P. I no longer had a fear of essay tests but I still lacked exposure to different types of writing (we dealt with analysis only).

The first day of rhetoric I entered class feeling that A.P. had prepared me for any type of writing assignment; little did I know. The first assignment took me four hours to write, not necessarily because the assignment was difficult, but because I just didn't know how to express myself. Expressive, persuasive, and explanatory writing was something I read but never thought of writing. Here are some of the problems I ran into:

1. I didn't know how to make a thesis statement from something so infinite as an expression. Before, I had a definite opinion or analysis, and was able to supply facts from a solid source. I found it very difficult to back up my thoughts with solid evidence.

2. My organization of facts has left a lot to be desired, too. I seem to jumble my statements around, as can be seen in Situation 6. I take people from room to room but jumble the facts so much that the reader has no sense of orientation within the story. My supporting evidence also jumps around in Situation 10, where I describe a person's appearance with no organization. I move from shoes to makeup to scars with amazing speed.

3. I lack a vocabulary of descriptive words. If I had a wider knowledge of words, I could make my papers more interesting.

For me, writing essays analyzing poetry or essays is much easier than expressive or persuasive writing. I find it very difficult to express my feelings in speech and it is doubly difficult to find the words to write down. It takes a much deeper thought into my feelings than I would like to look at. Although I don't exactly like these types of writing, I think I have learned a lot and need this type of exposure.

I hope in the future to improve my grammar, style, and vocabulary. Also I hope to write on a regular basis, not just because I have to. It is a type of communication that is overlooked too much.

RYOKO'S RESPONSE

Writing something in English takes a really long time and depends on my feelings. When I am fine, I can write better, but when I am not fine or am worrying about something, I cannot write anything good, making a lot of mistakes and misunderstandings.

I like writing, especially when I describe my specific feelings, as if I were on the beach, or as if I were in the temples. I write many scenes passing through my head as if I were daydreaming.

There is a big cultural difference when I write argumentation or persuasion. In Japan, we don't show our strong opinions exactly and make ironic sentences. Of course, this is not always true though; since I don't have strong or specific enough opinions to write these kinds of papers, I tend to be sarcastic. I am not good at organizing structures, so my papers are weak and sometimes don't make sense.

I know that I like writing but there are no readers in my writing; I am just writing for myself—entertainment.

KRIS'S RESPONSE

I believe my writing has improved a great deal since I have been taking this course! It has helped me a lot to see how others view my writing, and it has also allowed me to see my writing in the right perspective. It has also helped me to learn where my strengths and weaknesses are in writing.

For the most part I think my writing is quite good. I've never had much trouble trying to write, but this course did present me with many challenges, challenges I think I have met. Having to write every day on certain topics is one of those challenges. Having to write every day on a certain thing made me really stop and think before I wrote my thoughts down on paper.

There were also other challenges such as having to write every day, getting up early enough to make it to class on time, and having to adjust to putting some work into what I was trying to accomplish. These challenges are the things that I believe have helped me improve my writing.

It seems that most of my classmates view my writing in much the same way. Out of the papers we have done so far, sixteen of mine have received passing marks from my classmates. I don't think that's too bad for my first-year writing course.

Of the papers I have written, ones that use feeling and expression seem to be the easiest for me to write—ones such as Situation 13, in which you had to find a habit of someone close to you that bothered you. I think that paper was one of the best ones I've written.

Ones that seem to pose a problem for me are ones that are supposed to contain a lot of detail. I've never been able to write down just what I'm thinking.

I think all my papers are written in the same style. They start with an introduction, move to a body, and end with a conclusion. I believe they follow this pattern because that was the way I was taught to write in high school.

All in all, I think my writing is quite good, but there is always room for improvement.

TOM'S RESPONSE

My style is the best quality of my writing. I think I do editorial and position papers the best because I can build my position with much more ease than other types of papers. My creativity is the weakest part of my writing because I am too much of a restricted writer, sort of a (Mark Twain) country lawyer type of writer. My descriptive writing is fairly average, maybe because I can get certain facts and details across.

Probably the best examples of these three types of writing are shown in Situations 19A for editorial writing, 6 for creative writing, and 10 for descriptive writing.

Looking at all these types of writing as a whole, I would say that I am a type of writer who doesn't like to write. But when there is a cause to write about I don't mind.

ASSESSMENT

Writer _____
Self Assessment _____ Group Assessment _____
Teacher Assessment _____ Other _____
Reader could distinguish this writer from other writers, and knows how
   the writer feels about writing. _____
   or
Writer needs generalizations that individualize the portrait. _____
Writer needs more supporting material. _____
Writer needs to project a stronger and clearer attitude. _____
Other suggestions: _____
_____

I am in a good position to comment on the responses to Situation 24, for I am the "designated reader" — the intended audience. Tom's and Ryoko's responses are valuable because they are working toward large, interesting generalizations about their identities as writers. Tom and Ryoko present themselves as opposite types of writers. Ryoko enjoys writing as a form of meditation and self-expression, a way of re-creating scenes and experience. She says that "there are no readers in my writing"; Ryoko is writing for herself, and she is thrown off-stride by assignments that stress communication and audience — persuasive writing in particular. Tom, on the other hand, is interested in writing only as a tool for social interaction: he likes editorial writing and other situations in which there are "causes" at stake. This seems like a classic introvert/extrovert contrast, with Ryoko interested in writing as interior exploration and Tom interested in writing as a connection to the world and to people, in writing as social dialogue. Tom and Ryoko both could use more supporting material; their generalizations would gain force and clarity through illustration. And much of what Tom says is confusing: a Mark Twain who is restricted? What does Tom mean by style? By his distinction between creative and descriptive writing?

Kris seems to write for a political purpose: to convince me that she did pretty well in the course. She tells me very little about her writing otherwise. She mentions feelings, detail, and form, but none of these points is really developed or supported. Kris gives me no general leads about her identity as a writer of the sort that Tom and Ryoko provide.

Liz develops her response in much more detail than the other writers, though it lacks the large clues of Tom and Ryoko. From her explanation of her writing background, from her effort to specify her problems, she produces a strongly individual portrait. Though this response illustrates Liz's complaint about working with a limiting vocabulary, I concur with the judgment of Liz and her group that her response is successful.

II · TIME OUT

If you have written responses to all twenty-four situations, you may now be saying to yourself, "Well, okay, I've done it, but what does it all mean?" I hope that the meaning is mainly *in the doing*, that you have learned not a *what* but a *how* — a method and an attitude for approaching writing situations. And I hope that you feel more confident of your writing ability; Situational Writing gains its meaning from your sense of increased writing competence. For the sake of rounding up and rounding off, let's review some of the main ideas that surfaced in our discussions of the situations.

Writing is always a personal action. You make up and project a personality every time you write. In some writing situations your success depends largely on how real you make your speaker, how well you express your unique way of organizing and experiencing the world, how well you capture the force of your living personality in the written words. Your responses to the first assignments about a sport (Situation 2), a job (4), a teacher (5), and an instance of injustice (3) stand or fall on your presence or absence in the piece.

How does one project personality into written language? This is a mysterious process, and much goes into it; your characteristic word choice, your general level of diction, the characteristic syntax of your sentences, your unstated attitudes toward your subject and your reader — all these affect your presentation of self upon the page. There are two particularly powerful means of characterization: *specific detail* and *figurative language*. Perhaps specific detail is so important because it provides direct evidence of the world that the writer experiences. When you *show* readers the world through your eyes, you give them a pattern of evidence that reveals what matters to you, what you value, how you organize and react to experience. The sharper your world comes into focus, the more you are present as the organizer of that world. Figurative language is a different means for expressing self on the page. As elusive as feeling is, we often find ourselves expressing it indirectly, through comparisons. Your comparisons say a great deal about the quality and nature of your feeling; you dramatize and demonstrate your way of seeing and feeling through your metaphors and analogies.

The topic of specific detail brings us to the principles of *selection* and *focus*. What specifics do you decide to include in a piece, and which do you exclude? The answer lies in your *purpose* — what are you trying to do? What details will serve that purpose? Your effectiveness as a writer in any situation depends upon the sureness of your grasp on your purpose. Focus refers to the way writers use their sense of purpose in structuring discourse. Most writing requires a core, a complex of idea and feeling at the center, and everything in the piece should circle around that core, as the other atomic particles circle the nucleus of an atom. When a piece of writing hangs together in this way, it has focus.

We have talked about writing as a way of putting one's interior world into language, a way of capturing and expressing personality and individuality. The nature of things seems to bear out this approach: we each inhabit unique worlds; no one else sees the world exactly the same as you do; therefore, all writing is a personal action, an attempt to present your way of seeing.

Another way of thinking about writing, however, is to consider the world as a buzzing, changing, confusing field of forces and objects in motion and collision. People make sense of the chaos of experience by *imposing structure* upon it: experience must be analyzed, defined, classified, divided into categories before we can deal with it. From this perspective, the writer emerges as someone who brings order to experience. The writer divides, defines, analyzes, and classifies so that the reader can understand and act. This view of writing shapes Situations 8–12 and 20–24; you can probably see it most clearly in Situations 8 and 9, where you explained a process in a sport and analyzed a job problem. When you write to explain, you construct a frame for seeing the world. What matters in this kind of writing is *order* and *clarity*. You are concerned primarily with being clear, both in terms of sentences, paragraphs, and sections, and in terms of the basic analysis and classification at the core of your paper.

A major device for achieving clarity is *establishing context*. Because writing situations are complex (many variables operate at once), writers must always make sure that their readers understand the situation — what the writer is writing about, what the writer wishes to accomplish, to whom he or she is writing. Facing a piece of writing, readers automatically and half-consciously ask, "What is the basic situation here?" In all writing, quick and clear orientation of the reader is essential. The guidelines to the situations again and again stress establishing the context. There is an interesting complication, however: different kinds of situations require different treatments of context. Beginning with Situation 8, our writing situations are predominantly explanatory and persuasive; they seem to call for direct, explicit statement of context. For example, in the letter of recommendation (Situation 16), the writer should come directly to the point with the employer:

I understand that you are now looking for a waitress, and I would like to recommend Sally Jones.

In expressive writing (such as that called for in Situations 2–7), writers as a rule should try to establish context indirectly while jumping into action or description. Rather than starting a description of a teacher (Situation 5) like this:

I am now going to tell you why I liked my fifth grade teacher.

a writer would do much better to put the reader into the middle of a scene, establishing context as the action or description advances:

Mrs. B. was never late to class, and she always started speaking in a soft voice the moment the bell died away.

Context is always important, but different purposes call for different ways of handling it.

There is yet another way of looking at writing: rather than the expression of one's interior world, rather than the ordering and definition of *the* world, writing is an attempt to reshape the reader's world, to change the reader's understanding and behavior. From this perspective, writing becomes a social force, a means for people to secure cooperation and to pursue mutual goals. Such writing requires writers to transcend their limited perspectives, to grasp how others see the world. Considered in this way, writing is a potential means of manipulation (unscrupulous and cynical use of the reader), but it is also a potential source of positive social change—conferring benefits on writer, readers, and society at large (mightier than the sword, as the adage has it).

From this reader-centered view of writing, what matters most is *tone*, the relationship the writer establishes with the reader. How well can you imagine what goes on in your readers' minds? What arguments will appeal to their reason? To their emotion? How should you present yourself to gain their trust, their belief in you, and therefore their belief in your proposition? Where will they most need evidence, and what kind of evidence, to accept your arguments? When you consider writing as primarily persuasive, you focus upon the reader and the strategies that will move him or her.

Let me offer one other perspective on writing: we write to explore the world. This is *speculative* or *theoretical writing*, writing that treats *not* what happened on one occasion, or what happens most of the time, but what principles underlie what happens — in other words, how the world seems to work and why. Such writing is at a high level of abstraction and generalization; it is "academic" writing, the kind often called for in college because it serves as the vehicle of intellectual curiosity. Situations 20 – 23 asked you to try some theoretical writing.

Theoretical writing requires development and expansion of ideas, and this is not easy. Few ideas can be captured in a sentence; when you are presenting a speculation or hypothesis about how the world works, you usually find that your idea has complications, implications, and subpoints that call for elaboration and connection. Presenting an idea is like spinning a web. Presenting an idea is also like showing your readers a piece of sculpture; you must let them see it from a number of angles. Ideas require discussion; discussion in theoretical writing might be compared with specific detail in expressive writing: it is a major means of development.

A main objective of theoretical writing is to be basic and original at the same time. You want your reader to be surprised and convinced simultaneously. Such a response shows that you have succeeded with your interpretation of the world.

Writing does so many things that generalizing about it is difficult and dangerous. Think of writing as a flexible medium used for many purposes; keep in mind its *situational nature:* every writing situation is a new and complex problem to solve.

III · TWENTY-FOUR MORE WRITING SITUATIONS

25 · Meeting an Old Friend

SITUATION 25

On the street, you meet an old friend you haven't seen for years. The two of you stop for coffee. Your friend asks, "How are things?" What your friend wants to know, really, is what life feels like to you at this particular time. Your friend is asking about your sense of yourself, your sense of your relationship to the world and to life. Write down the thoughts you would share with your friend.[4]

GUIDELINES

1. Try to characterize your general sense of yourself and things. You may find that you can do this best by making a comparison, by using a metaphor or an analogy. ("I feel as if I'm on a rollercoaster." Or, "I feel as if I'm in a foreign country and don't know the language.")
2. Bring up specific events and situations that illustrate your general feeling.
3. Capture your feeling in your tone.

ASSESSMENT

Writer _____
Self Assessment _____ Group Assessment _____
Teacher Assessment _____ Other _____
Reader gains a vivid idea of how life feels to you now. _____
    or
Writer must more clearly establish his or her central feeling. _____

---

[4]This situation and the seven following situations are modifications of suggestions for writing presented in Ira Progoff, *At a Journal Workshop* (New York: Dialogue House, 1975).

Situation 25

Writer needs more examples of specific events and situations. _____

Writer needs a stronger connection between feeling and examples. _____

Writer needs a more appropriate tone. _____
Other suggestions: _____
_____

26 · A Way You Were

SITUATION 26

Reminiscing with an old friend starts you thinking about a particular period in your past: a time when you were adjusting to a move, a period when you were getting into trouble at school, or a time when you were in love, for example. Write your thoughts about this period, as if you were trying to make clear to a friend what living through this period was like.

GUIDELINES

1. Establish boundaries for the period. Can you say what began it? What ended it? What event was the center of the period?
2. As you did in Situation 25, try to characterize your general sense of the period. What was your central feeling? An analogy or a metaphor may help you express and focus the feeling.
3. Bring up specific situations and events that illustrate the feeling and characterize the period.

ASSESSMENT

Writer _____
Self Assessment _____ Group Assessment _____
Teacher Assessment _____ Other _____
Reader understands how you felt during this period. _____
   or
Writer needs sharper boundaries. _____
Writer needs a clearer central feeling. _____
Writer needs more examples of specific events and situations. _____

Writer needs a better connection between feelings and examples.
_____

Other suggestions: _____
_____

27 · A Major Change

SITUATION 27

Continuing your reminiscing with an old friend, you recall something that happened to you that changed your life. Maybe it was a death in your family or the separation of your parents. Maybe it was making an important friendship, or an achievement or a setback in school or in sports, or a serious illness. Maybe it was breaking with an old circle of friends and making new ones. Write an account of what happened and how it changed your life.

GUIDELINES

1. What happened? Tell clearly the story of the event that caused the change. Make sure the reader has the necessary background information to understand what happened.
2. Make clear what the change was. In other words, make the reader understand what your life was like before and after.
3. Make sure that the connection between event and change is clear.

ASSESSMENT

Writer _____
Self Assessment _____ Group Assessment _____
Teacher Assessment _____ Other _____
Reader understands the change and how the event caused it. _____
  or
Writer must tell more clearly what happened. _____
Writer needs more background to set up the event. _____
Writer must make the nature of the change clearer. _____

Situation 27 195

Writer must make the connection between event and change clearer.
_____

Other suggestions: _____

_____

28 · At a Crossroads

SITUATION 28

Your conversation with an old friend has turned to "what might have been." You are talking about crossroads, turning points, times when your life might have gone in two or more different directions. Did you reject a good job opportunity to come to college? Did you break off an engagement to be married? Did you move from the city to the country at an early age? What would your life be like if you had gone down the other road? Write about one crossroads when your life would have gone in several directions. Explain what happened, and speculate about what might have been.

GUIDELINES

1. Make the crossroads clear. Make sure that the reader understands what the alternative directions were—both what *did* happen and what *might* have happened. Make sure that the reader has enough background information about your life so that the crossroads makes sense.
2. Imagine "the road not taken" in some detail. Give some images showing who you would be and what you would be doing if your life had turned this way. The images should express your feeling about the road not taken.

ASSESSMENT

Writer _____
Self Assessment _____ Group Assessment _____
Teacher Assessment _____ Other _____

Reader understands the crossroads and your feelings about it. ‒‒‒‒‒‒
  or
Writer must explain the crossroads more clearly. ‒‒‒‒‒‒
Writer needs to give more background. ‒‒‒‒‒‒
Writer needs to give more vivid images of the road not taken.
‒‒‒‒‒‒

Other suggestions: ‒‒‒‒‒‒‒‒‒‒‒‒‒‒‒‒‒‒‒‒‒‒‒‒‒‒‒‒‒‒‒‒‒‒
‒‒‒

29 · A Formative Influence

SITUATION 29

You and your old friend start thinking about people who have had an impact on your lives, who have changed you for better or worse. Jot down a list of people who have had this kind of major influence on your identity and your life. Choose one person from the list and write an account of what he or she has meant to you, what effect he or she has had on your life.

GUIDELINES

1. Focus on the aspect of the person's personality that has affected you.
2. Be clear about the change this person has caused. In what particular way were you changed by the relationship?
3. Show the interaction between the person and your life. How did the key aspect of the person's personality cause the particular change in you?
4. Give examples of both of you in action. Re-create some scenes and situations in which you both were involved, so that your relationship becomes real for us.

ASSESSMENT

Writer _____
Self Assessment _____ Group Assessment _____
Teacher Assessment _____ Other _____
Reader understands the person's influence and is convinced of its importance. _____
    or

Situation 29

Writer needs a more focused and detailed portrait of the person. _____

Writer must be clearer about the change. _____
Writer needs a better connection between the person and the change. _____

Writer needs more specific examples of behavior. _____
Other suggestions: _____

_____

30 · A Formative Situation

SITUATION 30

You and your friend continue examining the past. Now you are talking about situations: those interlocking sets of circumstances that we become part of, sometimes by choice, sometimes not. Your family is a situation that you are part of. A particular set of friends is a situation; so are a job, a class in school, a sports team. Think of a particular situation that has influenced your life, that has formed or changed you in some way. Write an account of that situation, describing its effect on your life.

GUIDELINES

1. Set up the situation. Give the background necessary to explain its place in your life.
2. Describe the situation in detail, expressing your basic feelings about it.
3. Identify the effect that the situation had on you.
4. Show the reader how the particular effect grew out of the particular situation.

ASSESSMENT

Writer _____
Self Assessment _____ Group Assessment _____
Teacher Assessment _____ Other _____
Reader understands the situation and its effect on you. _____
  or
Writer needs a clearer presentation of the situation. _____
Writer needs more details that express feeling. _____

Writer must identify the effect more clearly. _____
Writer needs to connect the effect to the situation more convincingly.
_____

Other suggestions: _____
_____

31 · Social Identity

SITUATION 31

You have just completed a job application that asked you to categorize yourself in various ways. You start to think: what groups do you belong to that help make you what you are? What group identifications really matter to you? Is it important that you are a student? Or a woman? Or that you grew up in a middle-class family? Or that you are an extrovert? Or a Republican? Choose one group you belong to that seems particularly important to your sense of identity. Write an account of what belonging to that group means to you.

GUIDELINES

1. Make clear your idea of the nature of the group. (For example, if you are writing about yourself as a member of the middle class, make clear what you mean by middle class.)
2. Show specific examples of how membership in that group affects your behavior. Choose examples that express the way you feel about belonging to that group.

ASSESSMENT

Writer _____
Self Assessment _____ Group Assessment _____
Teacher Assessment _____ Other _____
Reader understands why membership in the group is an important part of your identity. _____
    or
Writer needs a sharper definition of the group. _____

Situation 31

Writer needs more and better examples of the effect of the group. _____
Other suggestions: _____
_____

32 · A Wise Person

SITUATION 32

You and a friend are talking about people you admire, not so much for their specific accomplishments as for their wisdom, for what they seem to know about life and how to live it. Think of one such person—living or dead, a personal acquaintance or someone from public life. Write an account of your admiration for that person.

GUIDELINES

1. Focus upon and define the particular attitude that you admire in the person. What is it that makes the person wise?
2. Show the person in specific situations that demonstrate how he or she puts his or her wisdom into practice.
3. Explain why this person is particularly meaningful *to you*. How does his or her wisdom relate to your life and circumstances?

ASSESSMENT

Writer _____
Self Assessment _____ Group Assessment _____
Teacher Assessment _____ Other _____
Reader understands why you admire the person. _____
   or
Writer must define the person's attitude more clearly. _____
Writer must show the person in more specific situations. _____
Writer must connect the person's wisdom and the writer's life. _____

Other suggestions: _____

33 · Self-portrait

SITUATION 33

You are exchanging letters with a student in a foreign country. Your correspondent would like to know what you look like. Write a physical description of yourself for this person, who has never seen you.

GUIDELINES

1. Establish a general impression of your appearance. Try to give an overview, a sense of your appearance as a whole.
2. Fill in that general impression with specific details.
3. Order the details so that the reader can follow your description easily.

ASSESSMENT

Writer _____
Self Assessment _____ Group Assessment _____
Teacher Assessment _____ Other _____
Reader obtains a sharp visual image of you. _____
   or
Writer needs a clearer general impression. _____
Writer needs more specific details. _____
Writer needs a better order for the details. _____
Other suggestions: _____

34 · Your Home

SITUATION 34

The foreign student with whom you've been corresponding wants to know what your family's home looks like. Describe it.

GUIDELINES

1. Establish a general impression of your home. Give your reader an overview or general category into which he or she can fit your family's residence.
2. Fill in that general impression with specific details. If your home is a farmhouse, what distinguishes it from the typical farmhouse? Give the particulars that seem most essential to you.
3. Order your description by controlling point of view. In other words, don't randomly throw details at your reader. Give a systematic survey of the home; order the details so that a picture grows.

ASSESSMENT

Writer _____
Self Assessment _____ Group Assessment _____
Teacher Assessment _____ Other _____
Reader would obtain a sharp visual image of your home. _____
  or
Writer needs a clearer general impression. _____
Writer needs more specific details. _____
Writer needs a better order for the details. _____
Other suggestions: _____

35 · Explaining Your Politics

SITUATION 35

The foreign student with whom you've been corresponding is interested in your politics. Which major party do you belong to or generally favor? For what reasons? (If you don't align yourself with either party, explain why.)

GUIDELINES

1. Explain what philosophy you look for in a political party.
2. Show why the party of your choice most nearly meets your standards. Illustrate with reference to the party's stand on several specific political issues.

ASSESSMENT

Writer _____
Self Assessment __ _____ Group Assessment _____
Teacher Assessment _____ Other _____
Reader understands your political preference. _____
   or
Writer needs a clearer statement of standards and philosophy. _____

Writer needs more detailed, specific issues. _____
Writer needs a better connection between philosophy and specific issues. _____

Other suggestions: _____
_____

36 · A Family Portrait

SITUATION 36

Your sociology instructor has asked you for an anatomy of an American family, using your family. What are the most important characteristics of your family? What are the individual members like, and how do they relate to each other? What are the natural alliances in your family? How does your family make decisions? What values are expressed in the way your family lives? Write a portrait of your family and its way of dealing with life.

GUIDELINES

1. Draw brief portraits of the individuals in your family. What are their most important characteristics?
2. Show the interconnections between those individuals.
3. Generalize about what is most important to your family as a group. What values does it project?
4. Find concrete situations that illustrate the values you have identified.

ASSESSMENT

Writer _____
Self Assessment _____ Group Assessment _____
Teacher Assessment _____ Other _____
Reader has been given insight into your family and its workings. _____
  or
Writer needs more information about individual members. _____
Writer needs to show the interconnections better. _____

Situation 36

Writer needs a deeper analysis of values. _____
Writer needs more specific situations to illustrate values. _____
Other suggestions: _____
_____

37 · Thinking about the Family Portrait

SITUATION 37

You are thinking about the sociology paper in which you portrayed and analyzed your family. Assume that you will one day be raising a family of your own. To what extent do you want your future family to resemble the family you grew up in? In what ways would you like your future family to be the same? In what ways different?[5]

GUIDELINES

1. Again, identify what is most important about the way your family functions.
2. Evaluate that functioning. What is good about your family's operation? What is bad? What is both good and bad? What is the basis for your judgment?
3. Sketch how you would like your future family to operate. Compare and contrast the two operations.

ASSESSMENT

Writer _____
Self Assessment _____ Group Assessment _____
Teacher Assessment _____ Other _____
Reader understands your vision of ideal family life. _____
  or
Writer must better identify the important characteristics of his or her immediate family. _____

[5]The idea for this assignment is drawn from Mina Shaughnessy, *Errors and Expectations* (New York: Oxford University Press, 1977), p. 295.

Situation 37

Writer needs a clearer evaluation of the family's operation. _____
Writer needs a better statement of the reasons behind the judgment. _____
Writer needs a more detailed picture of the future family's operation. _____
Writer needs a sharper comparison and contrast. _____
Other suggestions: _____
_____

38 · A Travel Grant

SITUATION 38

You have won a travel grant enabling you to live abroad for a year, in the country of your choice. Your friends want to know where you are going and why. Write an explanation of your decision.

GUIDELINES

1. What makes the country of your choice unique? Explain its particular attractions (as opposed to the charms of living abroad in general).
2. Imagine in detail scenes and impressions of life in your chosen country, and give the reader its flavor.
3. Connect the country to your life and interests. What is it about you that makes this country the right place for you to live for a year?

ASSESSMENT

Writer _____
Self Assessment _____ Group Assessment _____
Teacher Assessment _____ Other _____
Reader understands your attraction to the country. _____
   or
Writer needs specific reasons (why this country is preferable to another).
_____
Writer needs more detailed scenes and images. _____
Writer needs a clearer connection to his or her life. _____
Other suggestions: _____

39 · A Textbook Critique

SITUATION 39

You are having problems using one of your textbooks; you feel that it is hindering rather than helping your learning. Write a letter of complaint to the publisher explaining your problem as clearly as possible. (Alternative: write a letter to a publisher praising a helpful text.)

GUIDELINES

1. Make clear the general problem or problems with the text. Characterize the kind of comprehension problem the text produces, and try to identify the source of the problem.
2. Cite specific sections or passages where the problem occurs. Bring up evidence to support your contentions about general problems.

ASSESSMENT

Writer _____
Self Assessment _____ Group Assessment _____
Teacher Assessment _____ Other _____
Publisher would understand your problem with the book. _____
  or
Writer needs a better statement of the general problem. _____
Writer needs more specific examples of trouble. _____
Writer needs better connection and coordination between general problems and specific examples. _____
Other suggestions: _____

40 · A Musical Debate

SITUATION 40

You are in the midst of a family argument about musical preference. Whatever music one person prefers, another says, "It all sounds the same." Write the strongest case you can for the kind of music you prefer (for example, country and western, new wave, nineteenth century opera); explain what appeals to you about that kind of music.

GUIDELINES

1. Define the kind of music you prefer. Find or set up a category that the reader understands.
2. Try to describe the particular qualities of that kind of music. What is it about that particular sound that attracts and pleases you?
3. Give examples of particular works and artists who fall inside your category and who particularly capture the qualities you like.

ASSESSMENT

Writer _____
Self Assessment _____ Group Assessment _____
Teacher Assessment _____ Other _____
Reader understands what kind of music you like and why. _____
   or
Writer needs to identify his or her category more clearly. _____
Writer needs a better analysis of the attractive qualities of the music. _____

Writer needs more and better specific examples. _____
Other suggestions: _____

41 · An Exercise in Charity

SITUATION 41

You have inherited a considerable sum of money and have set aside a large amount to contribute to a single charity or nonprofit institution. Explain what institution you would pick and why.

GUIDELINES

1. What makes a good charity? Explain what in your opinion makes a cause worthy.
2. Show why your choice meets your standards for a worthy cause.
3. Point out the particular qualities that make your choice more deserving than other, similar institutions.

ASSESSMENT

Writer _____
Self Assessment _____ Group Assessment _____
Teacher Assessment _____ Other _____
Reader understands the grounds for your decision. _____
   or
Writer needs to explain his or her standards more clearly. _____
Writer needs to show more convincingly why his or her choice meets the standards. _____
Writer needs particular reasons (unique qualities) that justify his or her particular choice. _____
Other suggestions: _____

42 · A Homecoming Speech

SITUATION 42

You have been asked to address the senior class at your high school. You are to give an account of the life of a college student. Write a draft of a speech for that occasion.

GUIDELINES

1. Think about your experience so far as a college student. What impressions stand out in your mind? Try to identify the problems, frustrations, changes, and successes that seem most important.
2. Of your experiences, which seem typical and common to many college students? Talk about these typical experiences in concrete, detailed terms.
3. Find a tone that is informative without being patronizing. Remember that you too were once a high school senior.

ASSESSMENT

Writer _____
Self Assessment _____ Group Assessment _____
Teacher Assessment _____ Other _____
Reader/listener would feel that you had provided useful insight into life at college. _____
   or
Writer needs more significant generalizations about college life. _____

Writer needs to describe experiences that are more typical. _____

Situation 42

Writer needs more examples and more detail. _____
Writer needs a humbler tone. _____
Other suggestions: _____
_____

43 · Specific Advice

SITUATION 43

You have made a speech to the senior class at your high school about the life of a student at college. In the questions that follow, someone asks, "If there is one skill or attitude that a new student should bring to college, what is it?" Write the answer you would give.

GUIDELINES

1. Identify and define a specific skill or attitude.
2. Offer a rationale for its importance. Why is the skill or attitude so important that you single it out above the others?
3. Cite from your experience specific situations in which the skill or attitude has been valuable.

ASSESSMENT

Writer _____
Self Assessment _____ Group Assessment _____
Teacher Assessment _____ Other _____
Reader/listener would be convinced that the skill or attitude is important. _____
   or
Writer needs clearer identification and definition of the skill or attitude. _____

Writer needs stronger arguments for its importance. _____
Writer needs more examples of specific situations. _____
Writer needs a better fit between arguments and situations. _____
Other suggestions: _____

44 · Commercial Consultant

SITUATION 44

Think about a current advertisement (from television, radio, or magazines) that has caught your attention, either because it amuses and delights you or because it annoys and irritates. Imagine that you have been randomly selected for a survey, and the advertising agency that made the ad is willing to pay you for your opinion. Write an assessment of the effectiveness of the ad.

GUIDELINES

1. Identify the ad in question.
2. Analyze the ad. How is it supposed to work? To what kind of people is it supposed to appeal? What is the appeal?
3. Describe your reactions to the ad. Does it work for you? How does it make you feel?
4. Discuss the reasons for your reactions. Why do you like or dislike the ad?

ASSESSMENT

Writer _____
Self Assessment _____ Group Assessment _____
Teacher Assessment _____ Other _____
The ad agency could make use of the response. _____
   or
Writer must identify the ad more clearly. _____
Writer needs a better analysis of the ad. _____
Writer needs a more detailed description of his or her reactions.

Writer needs a more thoughtful explanation of his or her reactions. _____
Other suggestions: _____

45 · A Resolution

SITUATION 45

Imagine that it's New Year's resolution time. What is one change you want to make in your life and habits? Phrase that idea into a resolution, and write an argument designed to persuade yourself to keep that resolution.

GUIDELINES

1. Identify a problem. What do you want to change?
2. Why is the problem urgent? Show its consequences in detail (for example, the hangovers brought on by a drinking problem), or cite specific instances of the problem (the party where you made a fool of yourself).
3. Is it possible to make a change? Present a convincing plan for carrying out a change.
4. What will be the results of the change? What benefits will you derive? What will be your reward for changing? Make the rewards as vivid as possible.

ASSESSMENT

Writer _____
Self Assessment _____ Group Assessment _____
Teacher Assessment _____ Other _____
Argument would be likely to move someone to action. _____
   or
Writer must identify the problem more clearly. _____
Writer needs specifics to make the problem urgent. _____

Writer needs a more practical and detailed plan. _____
Writer needs more vivid benefits. _____
Other suggestions: _____
_____

46 · Guest Critic

SITUATION 46

You have been asked to fill in for the television and movie critic on your school paper. Your assignment is to write a review of any current movie or TV show.

GUIDELINES

1. Establish the basic facts about the show under review. For a TV show give title, actors, network, time slot. For a movie give title, actors, director, theatre, length of engagement. Other facts may be important (for example, if a movie is in a foreign language with subtitles, say so).
2. Identify the *kind* of entertainment the show attempts to be. Situation comedy? Suspense thriller? Serious drama?
3. State your standards for judging the particular kind of entertainment. What do you like in a situation comedy? In a thriller? What makes a production of this kind good?
4. Cite evidence to show why this show meets or doesn't meet your standards.

ASSESSMENT

Writer _____
Self Assessment _____ Group Assessment _____
Teacher Assessment _____ Other _____
Reader understands why you are (or are not) recommending the show.
_____
   or
Writer must furnish more information. _____

Writer needs to establish the nature of the show. _____
Writer needs a clearer statement of standards. _____
Writer needs more discussion of the particular characteristics of the show. _____

Writer needs a more convincing application of standards. _____
Other suggestions: _____
_____

47 · A Letter to a Hero

SITUATION 47

Is there a figure in public life—perhaps an athlete, an entertainer, a politician, or an artist—whom you really admire? Write that person a letter expressing your admiration, and try to make it the kind of letter that will bring a reply.

GUIDELINES

1. Make the reasons for your admiration clear. What specific qualities or achievements do you admire?
2. Establish your knowledgeability. Show that you know about the person's life and work in detail.
3. Create a tone that expresses admiration without fawning. Sound sincere without overstating your feeling; there is a difference between tribute and flattery.
4. Show why the person's life matters to you. There must be something about you and your life that makes this person particularly important; what is it?

ASSESSMENT

Writer _____
Self Assessment _____ Group Assessment _____
Teacher Assessment _____ Other _____
Reader would be likely to respond to the letter. _____
  or
Writer needs to explain better his or her reasons for admiration.
_____
Writer must sound better informed about the person. _____

Writer needs to sound more genuine. _____
Writer overdoes the admiration. _____
Writer must bring out the person's connection to his or her life. _____

Other suggestions: _____
_____

48 · Looking Backward

SITUATION 48

Think back over the term. Are you the same person who started college? Or have you changed in some important ways over the term? Address the question seriously: if you think you are changed, explain in what ways; if you think you are essentially unchanged, explain what those essentials are that remain unchanged.

GUIDELINES

1. Identify some qualities or awarenesses that make you *you*.
2. Show how those qualities have or have not altered over recent months.
3. Cite specific situations in which the changes (or lack of change) demonstrate themselves.

ASSESSMENT

Writer _____
Self Assessment _____ Group Assessment _____
Teacher Assessment _____ Other _____
Reader is convinced of significant change (or significant continuity) in the writer. _____
  or
Writer must identify his or her important characteristics more convincingly. _____
Writer must show in what ways the characteristics have changed. _____

Writer needs more specific situations for illustration. _____
Other suggestions: _____

Appendix A · Five Studies in Revision

In the Introduction I said that rewriting is natural, continual, and necessary. From the moment you conceive an idea for a writing project until you submit the final manuscript, you are rewriting. As soon as you formulate ideas (in your head or on the page), you feel pressure to reformulate them, to reshape them, and your final product is almost always radically different from your initial conception. (That certainly is the case for me with this book.)

Let me make an arbitrary distinction between *rewriting* and *revision*: rewriting goes on throughout all writing; revision takes place when the writer finishes a draft of a project, stands back from that draft and considers it as if it were a final product, and then writes it over again.

Revision implies fresh start and fresh sight — returning to your project and literally *seeing it again*. Because this is often difficult, many students dislike revision, sometimes preferring to tackle a whole new task over revising a draft. They often confuse revision with copyreading for sentence-level problems and spelling and punctuation errors.

Situational Writing has not focussed on revision. This book moves writers through related situations with the hope that each situation helps prepare the writer for succeeding situations; the strategy is *incremental*. This is not to say that revision is not important, or that *Situational Writing* could not be used in a way that puts greater emphasis on revision.

To revise, you must be able to see how your draft falls short of your intention. *Situational Writing* should help you here, for a major aim of this book is to help you understand what didn't work when you have written unsuccessfully. Even after you identify major problems, however, you are still only part of the way home in revision. You need a new strategy for solving the problem, and you must be able to execute it. A number of things may happen when you revise: you may solve the perceived problem and dramatically improve your final product; you may solve some problems but create others while doing so; you may fail to correct the problem. Revisions are always risks—*necessary* risks when you want to bring a piece of writing to its full potential.

This appendix includes five revisions of original responses by the four student writers. Some are much more successful than others; in some cases, the writer needs to keep trying to achieve his or her purpose.

2 · A Time of Your Life

SITUATION 2

You are talking with a friend about a sport or activity you enjoy. Think back to a particular time or moment when you were totally involved in the activity, and try to write exactly what happened during that moment. Try not to talk about the "thrill of victory" or the *results* of the activity; focus on the *process*, on what actually happened while you were in action. Also, write about one specific time; don't write about what sometimes happens or what usually happens. Your description should establish why you enjoy the sport or activity.

TOM'S ORIGINAL RESPONSE

While at my first debate tournament I encountered a unique situation. As the first affirmative began his speech about the problem with the status quo, I suddenly realized I had no evidence on this subject.

After the first affirmative gives his speech about the problem in the status quo, I must refute his accusations with evidence. I had no evidence on this subject to refute his allegations, so I looked up at my partner and he just laughed at me. Quickly I found some evidence cards that vaguely fit the subject. After the debate the judge was wondering how I refuted this subject with such vague evidence for such a long time; I shook my head and said with a little luck and a lot of b.s.

Although it was a valiant effort, I did lose the debate. But, since the whole purpose of the thing was to have fun and learn something, I believe it was a good experience. I like debate because it poses a challenge that is exciting. I also believe it is a fun activity.

TOM'S REVISION

During my first participation in a debate tournament I was caught in a very unenviable situation. The team that was debating against us brought up a subject that we had no evidence to reply on.

The subject was emergency medical services. Knowing I had no evidence on this subject, I pulled out some general evidence cards and gave it a shot. During my speech I talked at length about a communist threat and how great America was, but nothing about emergency medical services.

Obviously we did lose that round, but I believe I had a lot of fun. The challenge of debate is like thinking on your feet or chewing gum and walking at the same time. This is why debate is such a good sport.

Tom and his group both saw a need for Tom to provide more specific details in his original response to show the reader what he likes about debate. Tom's revision moves in this direction: by filling in the situation, by telling the particular issue at stake and the content of his irrelevant rejoinder, Tom makes the situation more vivid and expresses his feeling for the activity. Tom should go even further: there is the potential for a fine comic scene if he details his feelings while speaking, the reactions of judges and opponents, the particular leaps of logic he found himself making, and so on. I was sorry that Tom omitted his partner's unsympathetic response to his predicament; Tom needs just such material.

SITUATION 2

LIZ'S ORIGINAL RESPONSE

Bicycling is a sport in which the mind can wander while the body remains firm but not tense. When I look back on my cycling life, I feel most excited when I recall the climb of a big hill. My body prepares itself by storing the needed energy. The heart begins to beat slower but with an invigorating force. A short glance tells me that I have an incline of about fifty feet. In my mind I calculate for a short time the difficulty of the challenge ahead of me. After all the calculations have been thought over and the bike is in the appropriate gear, it is time to free my mind of any thought. Music fills my ears and my legs respond to the never-ending beat. Although I never look up, my legs feel the rising roadway. I see in front of me only the cracks of the ever-swelling pavement. Sugary juices of energy pour through my veins to relieve the tormented tissues. But my mind continues to sing like a bird on a windowsill. Slowly the chains begin to quicken as the body bursts forth in a gallant finish. There is a oneness between my body and mind, one cleansing the other. With every breath the muscles revive themselves to go one step further. Then as the air grows lighter the legs grind much slower until finally an easy pace resumes. I lift my head to observe my new surroundings. Now I once again hear the sounds of the awakening life of nature. The heat from within is cooled by the beads of sweat. Now I am free of any physical or mental anguish. I am reborn.

LIZ'S REVISION

Bicycling is a sport in which the mind is freed of all tensions while the body grows firm and strong. When I look back on my cycling days the most fulfilling experience I see is that of the climb of a big hill.

My body prepares itself by storing the needed energy. In each breath my lungs grab for just a little more oxygen to strengthen every muscle. At the same time the heart begins to beat slower but with an invigorating force.

A short glance tells me I have an incline of about fifty feet. In my mind I calculate, for a short time, the difficulty of the challenge ahead of me and put the bike in the appropriate gear.

After the preparations for the bike and body have been made, it is time to free my mind of any thought. My ears become the receivers of KRNA, hearing only those songs to which my legs can follow the steady, forceful beat of the bass.

Although I never look up, my legs feel the rising roadway. I see in front of me only the cracks of the ever-swelling pavement. The sugary juices of energy begin to pour through my veins to relieve the tormented tissues. But my mind feels nothing as the radio plays on. Slowly the chains begin to quicken as the body bursts forth. With every gasping breath the muscles revive themselves to go one step further.

Finally the legs grind much slower as an easy pace resumes. It is time now to find my placement in the world. I glance forward to observe my new surroundings and once again rejoin my mind to my body. I feel the muscles relax as the heat from within is cooled by beads of sweat. The radio has left and reality has reappeared. In my short time away from the world I have broken away from all its tensions. Now I am back as a refreshed person.

Everyone was excited by Liz's original response because in it Liz was trying something hard—a description of her interior awareness, her state of consciousness during a crucial moment of a bike ride. Unfortunately, her response occasionally seemed confusing and contradictory. I felt particularly confused about the music and whether Liz's mind and body were opposed or united during the experience.

Liz's revision is a real improvement in terms of clarifying what is happening. The reader now understands how mind and body separate during the experience—the mind floating with the music, detached from everything, and the tormented, laboring body responding to the beat. Mind, body, and outer world all come back together when the hill is crested. Liz treats the experience with greater focus and clarity; in this version her paragraphing cues her understanding of the experience (paragraph four concentrates on mind; paragraph five on body; paragraph six on the reunion). Liz's writing is still held back from full effectiveness by occasional wordiness and awkward syntax (consider the two sentences in paragraph four, for example). I'm sorry that Liz changed her last sentence; I think "I am reborn" has more force.

SITUATION 2

RYOKO'S ORIGINAL RESPONSE

I have been missing going to the sea very much. I remember one day on which I went to the beach alone.

The waves were just rolling in as I arrived at the beach. I put down a lemon yellow blanket, set up a bright orange parasol to make a shadow, and threw my clothes and shoes on top of it.

The waves were calling me so strongly that I did not even sit down on the blanket. I grabbed my inner tube and ran toward the sea. The cold water covered me gently and the pebbles tickled my feet.

I swam far from the beach pulling the inner tube behind me. When I had gotten so far from the beach that I could not see the orange parasol, I mounted the inner tube and relaxed. In the cobalt-blue sky hanging over my head floated a few cumulus clouds that resembled marshmallows. The sharp, straight sunshine beat down on my body little by little as I lay with my eyes closed. The sea breeze whispered across the water, disturbing no one. The inner tube cradle let me indulge in daydreams. The seagulls floated through the sky, breaking the overwhelming silence of my peaceful world.

Although the sun was pleasant, it was too hot to tolerate. So I gradually let my body sink into the chilly water that surrounded my heated body very severely. I swam back toward the seaside. Before I reached the beach, I found a little pink seashell that made a wish come true.

When I walked on the sand, my chilled feet gradually turned to red. I ran to the blanket and fell on top of it. My eyes were so heavy that I could not keep them open. The lukewarm wind stroked my body and I dozed off.

RYOKO'S REVISION

In the light fog, the sun was slowly rising behind the mountains. I sneaked out of the youth hostel to go to the beach alone with my favorite novel in my hand. The road was wet from the early morning dew, and it was a little chilly on my bare feet. The wind kept bringing me the smell of the sea and the refreshing morning call of the seagulls.

I sat on a low concrete bank in front of the beach and watched the sea. The gulls were looking for their breakfast. As the fog lifted, the sea started changing color, brought to life by the sunrise. The wind from the sea blew upon me. I put my book on my lap and stared at the message from the sea, dark brown and dark purple; dark purple to navy blue.

The sun rose higher and higher; the wind grew warmer and warmer. The sky turned to violet-red from purple-gray. I stepped on the dry gray sand and walked to the waterside. The water was still chilly, but refreshing. The waves kept coming and leaving, touching my feet tenderly. I walked along the water's edge, step by step, and my footprints were half gone and half left on the dark brown sand.

I went to the beach cabin to get an inner tube. Children were arriving at the beach, laughing and shouting delightedly. The waves were calling so strongly in the bright sunshine that I put my book down on the beach and ran into the water.

The chilly water covered my feet and the pebbles tickled. I started swimming, pulling the inner tube behind me. Farther and farther I swam and the water got colder and colder. My hands pushed the water aside and the water pushed back at me. I flutter-kicked, attacking the water from both sides. I moved up and down against the rhythmical waves.

When I was very far from the beach, I lay on the inner tube and looked up at the sky. There were a few cumulus clouds that resembled marshmallows. The sharp, straight sunshine beat down on my body. I closed my eyes and listened closely. The sea breeze whispered across the water, disturbing no one. The inner tube cradle let me indulge in daydreams. I dangled my arms and legs in the water.

The waves gradually carried me away from the shore. My skin was getting brown as the sun got brighter and brighter. I slowly sank into the water, which shocked my burning skin. I swam back toward the shore. Before I reached the beach, I found a little pink seashell that people believe will make a wish come true.

In her revision Ryoko reworks, reshapes, and improves this already impressive narration/description. In the revision Ryoko sets up reader and atmosphere so that her experience in the inner tube cradle will have all the more impact. Her first paragraph introduces the main characters in the cast, the elements that she will be interacting with: sun, wind, sea. Paragraphs two and three show Ryoko's involvement with the elements as a developing process. In addition to her careful orchestration of the buildup, Ryoko also changes her ending. Though her first ending was good, I agree with her idea for moving the pink seashell into her final sentence; it is a perfect symbol for the whole experience.

5 · I Knew a Teacher

SITUATION 5

You are talking with a friend who wants to become a teacher. In the course of the conversation, you think of a teacher who made a strong impression on you, a teacher who was effective and inspiring or ineffective and perhaps even destructive. Write a portrait of this teacher, with the purpose of giving your friend a positive or a negative example.

RYOKO'S ORIGINAL RESPONSE

What? Are you going to be a history teacher? It reminds me of my teacher when I was a junior in high school. The teacher always embarrassed some particular students, including me, during his class, as if he were enjoying doing it.

The class president said to us, "Stand up" when the teacher came into our classroom. We made a bow to him and tried to sit down on the chairs. "Do it again," suddenly the teacher said. "Wait, wait. These guys. How many times have I told you to take off your caps in the classroom?" At that time, I had a hunch that the day was going to be bad for us. After some boys took off their caps, we made a bow to him again.

"Well, it was better than before. However, why can't you do it well the first time? You are not babies, so behave yourselves. Anyway. Last time we studied about the Middle Ages. And I gave you some work sheets, didn't I? Who forgot the homework?" He started checking our assignments, walking around the classroom, saying, "Come to the front if you cheated or forgot to do it."

It was a day right before the big carnival in school, so we were very busy getting ready for the carnival. However, he gave us four pages of work sheets. There were about eighteen students who forgot to do or did not complete the assignments, including me. "For Heaven's sake! How come there are so many lazy students in the class?" Complaining, he found me, standing in front of the blackboard. "I see. Ryoko. You are the class vice president, aren't you? Look at your classmates. They are imitating your bad example. Why didn't you finish your homework?" Even though I wanted to laugh at his nonsense words, I answered him seriously. "I was drawing pictures for tomorrow's carnival all day yesterday, so. . . ." "You should say that you are sorry. I don't want to listen to your explanation." It sounded so ridiculous to me that I grinned, looking at the floor, as if I were showing my apology.

"Everybody, turn your back and make a bow." Strange to say, he always had a very thick book. He began hitting our hips very hard with the book. When it was my turn to be hit, he said, "You are the worst in class. Do you think that I don't know that you are laughing?" Saying this, he hit me very hard three times He was enjoying it very much as if it were a kind of recreation.

Since I had not slept the night before, when he started the lecture, his low, monotonous voice sounded just like a monk reading a sutra. My eyes were getting so heavy that I could hardly keep them open. Suddenly something hit my head. It was a piece of chalk that the teacher threw at me. "Good morning," he said, grinning.

We students could hardly know what he was thinking or what he would do next. But, little by little, we figured out how to protect ourselves from his sudden emotional changes. But one thing we could do nothing about was that when he gave back our exams, he always read our scores loudly.

RYOKO'S REVISION

What! You've decided to be a teacher? Well, be careful. Teachers have such a strong influence on students, especially on junior high and high school students. I wish that all teachers were thoughtful, open-minded, accepting and understanding of youngsters' thoughts and feelings.

You know, I always tended to like or dislike a subject depending on the instructor. I had a very good math instructor and so I liked him very much. But I hated world history because of the teacher. Not only were his lectures boring, but he was also cruel. There's not much good I can say about him.

It was the day before the school carnival, a big annual event at school. Two days before, we had finished four days of midterm exams. Then we started getting ready for the carnival, making sets, practicing for plays and shows, and we were still attending classes regularly. Most teachers were considerate and didn't give us much homework, because they knew we were staying late at school, sometimes until nine or ten o'clock to set things up for the carnival. But Mr. T. gave us four work sheets right after the midterm exam.

As he came into class, we stood up and bowed. As we were sitting down, he shouted, "Do it again. . . . Wait, you guys, I mean you! How many times do I have to tell you to take off your caps in the classroom?" The boys took off their caps and we bowed again.

"Well, it wasn't too bad. Why can't you do it right the first time? You guys are not babies. Behave yourselves! Anyway. Yesterday I gave you some work sheets." He snickered. "Who forgot the homework?" He started walking around the room carefully checking our assignments, saying, "Go to the front."

There were about eighteen students who hadn't finished the homework. We walked to the front and stood in a line in front of the blackboard. "For Heaven's sake! How come there are so many lazy students in this class?" He looked at us and found me in the line. "Aha! I see. Ryoko. You are the class vice president, aren't you? Look at your classmates! Did they elect you to set an example like this? Aren't you proud of yourself? You all are too excited about the carnival. But don't act like four-year-old children. And don't follow Ryoko's example.

"Everybody, turn around, face the blackboard and make a bow." He began paddling us very hard with his thick book. When it was my turn, he said, "You are the best student in the class." Then he hit me very hard three times.

The way he treated us depended on his mood. And his reactions to our "misbehavior" were extremely cruel. He sometimes made up our faces with chalk dust from the eraser. Boys especially had a lot of trouble with him about their haircuts. Boys had to keep their hair to a certain length. Whenever Mr. T. found a boy with hair a little longer than the limit, he would clasp his hair with big wooden compasses and pull it.

I understand that he wanted to teach us good manners and make us noble-minded. However, he only insulted us and hurt our feelings. If his lectures had been extremely good, we could have respected him as a great teacher. However, he lectured like a monk reading a sutra, in a low, monotonous voice. He never gave us very important points but made very difficult quizzes and exams, and then would even read our test scores aloud.

Oh, it just makes me so mad every time I think about him. And he's the reason I don't know any world history. Of course, he meant well. But when you are trying to teach your students manners, and give them noble minds, and make them strong, remember, "You can catch more lightning bugs near sweet water than near bitter water." (The Americans say, "You can catch more flies with honey than with vinegar.")

Ryoko's original response was strong because it put the reader into the middle of Mr. T.'s classroom. Ryoko gave us immediacy, detail, reality. Both Ryoko and I were concerned with *interpretation:* it seemed that the situation was left too much to speak for itself; I wasn't sure exactly what Ryoko thought about the teacher, and I thought that the prospective teacher (the intended audience) might have a similar problem.

In her revision Ryoko is much more explicit about her attitude toward the teacher. She makes it clear that it is primarily the teacher's cruelty and enjoyment of the cruelty that she finds objectionable, and that his boring lectures and possible good intentions are subordinate matters. Ryoko structures the reader's reaction more clearly, which is appropriate because it is important that the reader understand the writer's judgment of the teacher.

6 · A Special Place

SITUATION 6

Sometimes place has a strong effect and influence on people. Describe a place that affects you strongly (a room, a building, an outdoor setting). Show the place so that the reader has its image in his or her mind's eye. The image should create a particular atmosphere and express a particular feeling.

KRIS'S ORIGINAL RESPONSE

My favorite place to go whenever something is bothering me is to my grandmother's house. It's an old farmhouse that sits along the back side of Lake McBride in Solon.

I don't think there's any place like it in the entire world. At least not a place that is as special to me as this one.

I enjoy walking down the hill behind the house to the edge of the water. It gives me a feeling of freedom and aloneness, yet I'm still aware of the life that surrounds me. It really is a breathtaking experience!

You walk down a hill covered with green grass and clover leaves, as if you were walking across the blanket of heaven. Never in my life have I seen a place that glows with such beauty and freshness. This glow of beauty and freshness is the same exact feeling I have after walking through the grass and clover leaves.

The atmosphere around you is so full of life, yet there is still a hushed relaxation, as if it were really two worlds in one. You can hear the rush of the water as it hits the banks of the land, yet you're not really aware of the life going on in the water. You can hear the birds sing, but they're more like a chime that lulls you into your own little world of peacefulness.

Above you there's a blue sky that's a cover from all harmfulness. There's a feeling of life unending, as if you can just go on forever. This feeling stems from the ability to see forever, as if the beautiful land doesn't end.

Walking back up the hill I carry a feeling of refreshment. It's as if you've been to the world beyond and now you're coming back as a new person. It's like no other feeling you've ever felt before. In fact, I'd say it's almost like a feeling of eternity.

KRIS'S REVISION

It's like a whole new world when you walk behind the farmhouse into the bright green meadow. The place I'm talking about is a place I go whenever something is bothering me. The place is my grandmother's farm at Lake McBride in Solon.

When emerging from behind the farmhouse and farm buildings, you are immediately greeted with a big green handshake, the handshake of a unique place where everything is free and alive.

When you walk into this green meadow and feel the soft, delicate grass, it's like walking across the blanket of heaven. The blades of grass press between your toes, leaving a feeling of freshness and coolness. The entire atmosphere is soft, delicate, and flowing. It's much like the picture people have designed to be heaven.

It's a place where you are alone, and free from all life's harms. You can go there to think and work out all the problems you are facing. It's like no other place I have ever been before.

The meadow turns into an unending body of water. You can hear the currents of the water hitting against the banks of the land, just knowing it's going to leave its etching of power in the side of the land. You can see the life in the water, but only in spurts—when a fish jumps, a bird dives, or a person goes in.

The area makes you feel that you're in a land of make-believe where no one can harm you or the beauty around you. This feeling stems from the ability to see forever, as if the beautiful land doesn't end.

Walking back up the hill and back into the real world, you have a feeling of refreshment. You can take a deep breath and feel as if your entire insides have been cleaned and are ready for whatever you have to face.

I find this place unique and exciting. It allows me to escape what is bothering me for a time. It's a place where I can get in touch with myself and prepare myself to face whatever comes my way.

Kris's original response was far too general; Kris needed many more specific details to help the reader experience her grandmother's farm as she experiences it. Kris is not successful in providing those specifics in her revision. Her first sentence locates the reader in a specific place, and she uses a striking new metaphor, "greeted with a big green handshake." But her details are not specific: "the soft, delicate grass," "a fish jumps, a bird dives, a person goes in." The scene is still nebulous. If Kris were interested in further improvement, I would suggest that she make a list of fifty memories and impressions from the lake, and not start a draft until she began to get specific detail.

Appendix B · Profiles of the Four Student Writers

Situation 24 asked you to review your writing and draw a portrait of yourself as a writer. There are four other writers that we know a good deal about because we have followed their work through twenty-four assignments and a revision or two. Let us see what conclusions we can draw about the prominent features of Liz, Ryoko, Kris, and Tom as writers.

LIZ

As a writer Liz is characterized by tenacity, force, and energy. Liz grasps the particular situation and then attacks the problem. Her natural sense of the purposive nature of writing grew during the course. Most of Liz's discussion of herself as a writer (Situation 24) circles around her new awareness of different types of writing. With her previous writing experience mainly in literary criticism, she says that she felt like a baby facing many of the situations—for example, spending four hours figuring out how to approach the first assignment. As writer, Liz is a determined problem solver.

Liz almost always produces full and specific development, unusual in freshman writers. Liz seemed to realize the importance of specific detail and specific examples from the beginning, and she regularly works at going beneath generalizations to *show* what she means. Good illustration and development involve some of the hardest work in writing; early on, Liz won the respect of the class (and me) for her obvious willingness to do this hard work.

Much of Liz's effectiveness comes from the speaker she consistently creates: she comes across as sincere, honest, and direct, and her writing has a dimension of authenticity and personal force. Consider her description of a crucial moment in bicycling (Situation 2), her portrait of her high school English teacher (Situation 5), her indictment of her high school (Situation 12), her letter to a friend with a drinking problem (Situation

13), her conciliatory appeal to the police officer (Situation 18), and her discussion of teaching excellence (Situation 23). Liz herself, projected through her language, becomes a major influence on the reader; the reader knows that Liz is trying to tell important truths to the best of her ability, and responds to that effort.

Given Liz's strong awareness of purpose, it seems somewhat surprising that she sometimes makes errors of judgment with respect to *audience*. In her original narration of the act of injustice (Situation 3), she leaves out essential information with the result that the reader has an inadequate context for the action. In her introduction to the jump shot (Situation 8), she writes at a level of complexity that would give a reader trouble, and the context of the instructions needs to be clearer. The same objections probably apply to Liz's job advice (Situation 9). In advocating group membership (Situation 15), Liz could better adapt her arguments to the particular friend she is addressing. In all these cases, Liz's characteristic concern with development needs to be tempered and guided by greater awareness of audience.

Closely related to audience awareness is Liz's problem with *readability*. This takes two forms: a need for clearer organization and a need for clearer and tighter sentences. Liz's organization problem is demonstrated in her penchant for long blocks of prose unbroken into paragraphs, as in her original description of her cycling experience (Situation 2), her description of the hotel room (Situation 6), and her job advice (Situation 9). The lack of paragraphing probably indicates that Liz has not planned her discourse in terms of sections; the result is that the reader does not receive enough guidance in terms of natural breaks in the discourse. (Liz does address the paragraphing problem in her revision.) In the theory situations where Liz deals with her job future (Situation 20) and the qualities that make a good teacher (Situation 23), there is an absence of plan or structure; these responses seem like random lists of ideas.

Liz has problems at the sentence level with wordiness, with awkward syntax, and with diction. Consider this short paragraph from Liz's revision of Situation 2.

After the preparations for the bike and body have been made, it is time to free my mind of any thought. My ears become the receivers of KRNA, hearing only those songs to which my legs can follow the steady, forceful beat of the bass.

Liz needs to cut words and restructure these sentences. A possible alternative:

Bike ready, body ready, I empty my mind. My ears are wired to KRNA, and my legs follow the steady beat of the bass.

Consider Liz's opening paragraph from this revision:

Bicycling is a sport in which the mind is freed of all tensions while the body grows firm and strong. When I look back on my cycling days the most fulfilling experience I see is that of the climb of a big hill.

This could become:

Bicycling frees the mind while firming the body. And there is one moment when the mind is freest and the body most challenged: the climb of a big hill.

But Liz might find better alternatives of her own.

Liz writes at length in Situation 24 of her problem with diction, of the frustration of not finding the right words to express her meaning. Consider the diction problem in this passage from an early version of her response:

I find it very difficult to express my feelings in speech and it is doubly difficult to find the words to write down. It takes a much deeper thought into my feelings than I would like to look at.

Liz has found that trying to put important truths into words is difficult and sometimes painful—not something that we exactly like, but something that we value.

RYOKO

In Situation 24 Ryoko does well at characterizing herself as a writer:

I like writing, especially when I describe my specific feelings, as if I were on the beach, or as if I were in the temples. I write many scenes passing through my head as if I were daydreaming.

I know that I like writing, but there are no readers in my writing; I am just writing for myself—entertainment.

Writing something in English takes a really long time and depends on my feelings. When I am fine, I can write better, but when I am not fine or am worrying about something, I cannot write anything good, making a lot of mistakes and misunderstandings.

As these remarks indicate, Ryoko likes to write expressive discourse — discourse centered in the self. The good expressive writer must like reaching inward to contact feelings. It is not surprising that Ryoko lives through scenes in her head, that her writing is very contingent on mood, and that she writes for herself — "no readers in my writing." Ryoko is *good* at expressive discourse — her descriptions of a beach experience (Situation 2) and a visit to a temple (Situation 6) are fine evocations of a particular state of mind. The pieces center beautifully around a mood, built up through skillful selection of specific detail. Ryoko has a strong aesthetic sense, a sense of what fits into each of these worlds. Ryoko revised her original responses to Situations 2 and 6, in each case heightening the mood and creating movement, building toward the climactic moment. Ryoko has an intuitive understanding of the essentials of expressive writing.

Another of Ryoko's gifts is her capacity for moral imagination. By this I mean the capacity to see the world as it looks to others, especially when that viewpoint is different from her own. In her re-creation of the act of injustice from the viewpoint of the opposition (Situation 7), Ryoko does a stunning retelling of a domestic clash from her mother's point of view. What stuns the reader is the thoroughness, consistency, and depth of her adaptation of the "other" viewpoint. She does something similar when writing about the situation of isolated students on a campus (Situation 19), and this same capacity for empathy (this time with her own students) gives an extra dimension to her job advice (Situation 9).

The converse of Ryoko's attraction to expressive writing and her ability to create worlds is her distaste for "reader" writing — and indeed, she has some problems with explanatory, persuasive, and theoretical discourse. One of Ryoko's main problems — one that bedevils many young writers of explanation and persuasion — is establishing context. Establishing the reader's initial understanding of the business at hand is a prime requirement of most explanatory and persuasive situations, and Ryoko does not do this early enough or clearly enough in her letter of recommendation (Situation 16), her complaint to a teacher (Situation 17), and her letter to the editor (Situation 19). In explanatory and persuasive situations, the writer must give the reader a sense of the larger picture before proceeding to details. In Ryoko's portrait of a bad teacher (Situation 5), her original version presented a vivid situation but an inadequate overview;

the meaning of the situation and Ryoko's attitude toward the teacher weren't clear enough. (Ryoko showed in her revision that she understood what was missing.)

Ryoko seems not to like, understand, or feel comfortable with theoretical writing. In her attempt to define excellence in an activity (Situation 21), Ryoko describes a ceremonial combat instead of making generalizations about the martial art. Similarly, in her response to Situation 23, Ryoko writes another teacher portrait instead of discussing excellence in teaching. (Though Ryoko says interesting things in her responses to Situations 22 and 24, these responses call for further development and connection.) Ryoko seems much more at home with specifics and moods than with abstract concepts.

Ryoko's difficulty with Situations 21 and 23 illustrates a further problem: her tendency to become confused about the rhetorical situation and the purpose of assignments. In her notes about herself and her future career (Situation 20), for example, Ryoko writes biographical background rather than exploring her thinking and intuitions about the future; she *presents* rather than *analyzes* herself. Understanding the involved act of injustice sequence (Situations 3, 7, 11, 18 or 18A, 22) also gave Ryoko trouble. This may be a problem with complex instructions in a second language, or it may be a problem in understanding complex rhetorical demands (or both). Disorientation about purpose seems to increase for Ryoko as the situations call for a higher level of generalization and abstraction.

In writing persuasion and theory, Ryoko seems to lose her sense of the need for supporting material, specifics, and evidence (so highly developed in her expressive writing). In her argument against a bad habit (Situation 13), her solicitation for a friend to join a group (Situation 15), her letter of recommendation (Situation 16), and her complaint to a teacher (Situation 17), Ryoko does not provide necessary specifics. This may be partly a consequence of the Japanese disinclination to advocate positions forcefully, which Ryoko writes about in Situation 24; in any case Ryoko should be able to make rapid improvement, for her work in expressive writing shows that she understands the principle of development in general. Ryoko makes a brilliant response to one persuasive situation. In her letter to the editor asking for attention for isolated students (Situation 19), Ryoko shows how skillfully she can put the reader into her writing. In that response she tactfully persuades the reader to act differently without making him or her guilty or defensive; she masterfully controls the rhetorical situation.

It is remarkable how well Ryoko does in English, and what she has the patience to do. Her gift for expression flourishes even in a language radically different from her first language. I wonder what her writing is like in Japanese?

KRIS

In Situation 24 Kris says that assignments that "use feelings and expressions seem to be easiest for me to write." On the other hand, the troublesome assignments are "ones that are supposed to contain a lot of detail." All her papers "start with an introduction, move to a body, and end with a conclusion." Kris is not easy to characterize as a writer, but these hints provide a start. What Kris says about her strong general sense of form (introduction, body, conclusion) is true. This may partially account for her ability to write good explanation, which puts a premium on clear organization and the immediate establishment of a clear context and an overview of the situation. When Kris writes job instructions (Situation 9), she successfully brings together overview, organization, and specifics. Similarly, in her instructions about hitting a softball (Situation 8), Kris establishes very clearly what she is going to do, and in her statement about the disorientation of the new freshman (Situation 12), she is clear in her general presentation of the problem. Establishing context is one of Kris's strengths; she understands the necessity of doing so in explanatory and persuasive situations.

Kris's sense of form occasionally leads to problems—for instance, a tendency to produce empty writing that is purely formal, a shell without content. This happens in her discussion of her job future (Situation 20). A sense of form as introduction, body, and conclusion can result in *formula* writing. Another result is occasional padding and wordiness—producing a beginning or an ending that doesn't say much, but is there because one "needs" an introduction and a conclusion. For example, the beginning of Kris's discussion of excellence in swimming (Situation 21) contains empty words and redundancy, largely because Kris wants a full paragraph introduction:

When you're looking for a champion in swimming, you are looking for a lot of things. The most important thing to look for, as you do in any sport, is a person who you can tell is really enjoying what he or she is doing. After you've found this, you start looking for the little things that might make that person the champion of the swimming pool.

The content of that paragraph might easily be reduced to a single sentence. Here is the conclusion to her speculations about excellence in teaching (Situation 23):

Many people may not have the same idea of a good teacher as I do, but then all people aren't exactly alike. We are all different, and all have different likes and dislikes. I guess that's what makes up people.

This paragraph adds nothing to Kris's paper; my guess is that she put it in for purely formal reasons.

Kris is correct when she says that she writes best when her feelings are engaged. For example, her plea for Roger to stop smoking (Situation 13) has great persuasive force, and her enthusiasm about cheerleading (Situation 15) is similarly effective. Kris is articulate when she explains her grievance about not being selected to the National Honor Society (Situation 3) and the teaching of Nancy M. (Situation 5). It seems paradoxical, then, that in situations that are primarily expressive (Situations 2, 4, and 6), Kris is unsuccessful. As she says, she has difficulty with specific details and also with figurative language (this is partly what makes Situation 2 seem flat). A lack of specifics also hinders her discussion of a student problem (Situation 12), and more specifics could increase the effectiveness of two good pieces of persuasive writing (Situations 13 and 15). "Use specific detail," the oldest writing advice in the book, is the advice Kris needs to heed, particularly in expressive situations.

Kris has trouble with tone when she assumes the role of adversary. With little inclination to try to see an issue from the other person's point of view, she tends to mount attacks rather than attempting to persuade. When asked to write the act of injustice from the opposite viewpoint (Situation 7), she writes around the assignment. Her letter to a teacher about a problem (Situation 17) is probably too hostile to produce the results she wants. Her original plea for redress (Situation 18) was more attack than plea, so she changed that response into a direct attack. Sometimes her hostile and aggressive stance is misdirected. Her letter to the editor (Situation 19) is rhetorically misguided because it becomes a personal attack and grievance inappropriate for her general audience. Even in writing to me about her writing (Situation 24), defensiveness and a sense that we are to some degree adversaries seem to limit what she can say. Kris needs to stretch to see other viewpoints and perspectives.

Finally, moving up the ladder of abstraction is a problem for Kris. In the situations that asked for theory (20–24), Kris has trouble generating interesting and useful generalizations.

TOM

Tom's writing profile has several prominent features, in terms of both what he does well and where he needs to improve. Tom's most obvious problem is development; most of his responses lack supporting material — specific details, examples, expansion and elaboration of generalizations. Tom apparently fails to understand that his reader usually needs more than a bare statement of a position. In a number of situations (2, 3, 4, 5, 6, 9, and 13), Tom's responses are painfully bare of detail. Other situations in the theory sequence (20, 21, 23, and 24) require more discussion. Tom generally needs to extend and illustrate his thinking when he writes.

Tom's strength is in strategy: Tom often finds a thoughtful approach for achieving his purpose in these situations. In his description of a moment in debate (Situation 2), he has selected an incident that emphasizes the one particular element of debate that he especially enjoys. In his instructions for a beginning debater (Situation 8), Tom provides a good analysis of the activity. First he effectively divides the activity into parts: he focusses the reader on the first negative speech. Then, in a further analysis, he states the three aspects of the affirmative's case that the speaker must cover. This clear setup is very helpful to the reader. Similarly, in his letter of job advice, Tom focusses the reader on conduct during a robbery; again, he divides and defines his subject in a way that facilitates reader understanding. While Tom often figures out an effective way to approach the writing situations, he is frequently unable to carry out and follow through his strategy because he doesn't develop with sufficient supporting detail. This happens in Situations 2, 8, and 9, where he fails to take advantage of his excellent setups.

Another major problem for Tom is tone, finding a stance that establishes the right distance between himself and his reader. The problem surfaces particularly in persuasive situations, where the writer's relationship to the audience is particular important. His "bad habit" letter (Situation 13) may be too bitter to win cooperation. His presentation of a problem to a teacher (Situation 17) is too stuffy and presumptuous to be effective. In his letter of recommendation (Situation 16) and his notes for an occupational interview (Situation 20), he might be taking a satirical stance, but the tone is too muddy for us to be sure. Tom likes working with an ironic stance, as he indicates in his identification of himself with Mark Twain and with the sly old country lawyer who pretends to be a simple soul (Situation 24). In this vein, he is proud (with some justification) of his "modest proposal" with regard to the physical education requirement (Situation 19). In general, however, Tom needs to work on tone.

Tom receives a mixed review on generating and handling generalizations. As his ability with strategy might indicate, Tom's work is often promising on the conceptual level. For example, he works with interesting ideas in his discussion of teaching excellence (Situation 23) and his self-portrait as a writer (Situation 24). But to compound his problem with developing ideas, he sometimes loses control over abstract language at the reader's expense. This happens in his explanation of the first negative speech (Situation 8), in the conclusion of his description of his room (Situation 6), in the inflated diction of his complaint to a teacher (Situation 17), and in his self-portrait as a writer (Situation 24).

As a writer, Tom seems to illustrate in a dramatic and exaggerated way a frustration all writers feel. We wish that the words on the page could come closer to doing justice to the conceptions in our heads. Tom must work harder to realize his ideas in language.

Appendix C · Classifying the Situations

I. PURPOSE

Situational Writing draws on James Kinneavy's *Theory of Discourse*[6] to classify discourse into *expression, explanation,* and *persuasion.* (I do not use Kinneavy's fourth category, literary or poetic discourse.) Remember that all writing is to some degree expressive, explanatory, *and* persuasive, so that this classification really lists the *predominant* purpose. Situation 1 is listed in all three categories, because all three purposes are strongly operative there.

    A. Expression
       1. As I Begin the Writing Course
       2. A Time of Your Life
       3. A Victim of Injustice
       4. Job Talk
       5. I Knew a Teacher
       6. A Special Place
       7. On the Other Hand . . .
     18A. A Tongue-lashing
     19A. Madman or Fool
     25. Meeting an Old Friend
     26. A Way You Were
     27. A Major Change
     28. At a Crossroads
     29. A Formative Influence
     30. A Formative Situation
     31. Social Identity
     32. A Wise Person

[6]James Kinneavy, *Theory of Discourse* (Englewood Cliffs, N.J.: Prentice-Hall, Inc., 1971).

37. Thinking about the Family Portrait
48. Looking Backward

B. Explanation
1. As I Begin the Writing Course
8. The Expert Instructs the Beginner
9. Job Advice
10. Teacher Portrait
11. A News Story
12. A Student Problem
20. Peering into the Future
21. A Particular Kind of Excellence
22. A Definition of Justice
23. The Good Teacher (Or, The Good Student)
24. Self-portrait of a Writer
33. Self-portrait
34. Your Home
35. Explaining Your Politics
36. A Family Portrait
38. A Travel Grant
39. A Textbook Critique
40. A Musical Debate
41. An Exercise in Charity
42. A Homecoming Speech

C. Persuasion
1. As I Begin the Writing Course
13. I Hate to Bring This Up, But . . .
14. The Better Way
15. To Join or Not to Join
16. Letter of Recommendation
17. A Student Complaint
18. Righting a Wrong
19. Concerned Citizen
43. Specific Advice
44. Commercial Consultant
45. A Resolution
46. Guest Critic
47. A Letter to a Hero

II. THEMATIC SEQUENCES

In *Situational Writing*, students regularly return to certain subjects, writing about them from a number of perspectives and for a number of purposes. Some of the situations can thus be divided into groups connected by subject or theme.

A. Writing
   1. As I Begin the Writing Course
   24. Self-portrait of a Writer

B. A Sport or Activity
   2. A Time of Your Life
   8. The Expert Instructs the Beginner
   14. The Better Way
   21. A Particular Kind of Excellence

C. An Act of Injustice
   3. A Victim of Injustice
   7. On the Other Hand . . .
   11. A News Story
   18. Righting a Wrong
   18A. A Tongue-lashing
   22. A Definition of Justice

D. Work; Job
   4. Job Talk
   9. Job Advice
   16. Letter of Recommendation
   20. Peering into the Future

E. School and Education
   5. I Knew a Teacher
   10. Teacher Portrait
   12. A Student Problem
   17. A Student Complaint
   19. Concerned Citizen
   19A. Madman or Fool
   23. The Good Teacher (Or, The Good Student)

F. An Overview of Your Life
   25. Meeting an Old Friend
   26. A Way You Were
   27. A Major Change
   28. At a Crossroads
   29. A Formative Influence
   30. A Formative Situation
   31. Social Identity
   32. A Wise Person
   48. Looking Backward

G. Correspondence with a Foreign Student
   33. Self-portrait
   34. Your Home
   35. Explaining Your Politics

Classifying the Situations   255

    H. Advice to High School Students
        42. A Homecoming Speech
        43. Specific Advice

III. TRADITIONAL MODES

(Some situations may be listed under two categories.)

    A. Description
        1. As I Begin the Writing Course
        4. Job Talk
        5. I Knew a Teacher
        6. A Special Place
        10. Teacher Portrait
        12. A Student Problem
        18A. A Tongue-lashing
        24. Self-portrait of a Writer
        25. Meeting an Old Friend
        26. A Way You Were
        28. At a Crossroads
        29. A Formative Influence
        30. A Formative Situation
        33. Self-portrait
        34. Your Home
        36. A Family Portrait
        42. A Homecoming Speech
        47. A Letter to a Hero

    B. Narration
        2. A Time of Your Life
        3. A Victim of Injustice
        7. On the Other Hand . . .
        8. The Expert Instructs the Beginner
        11. A News Story
        27. A Major Change
        28. At a Crossroads

    C. Exposition
        9. Job Advice
        20. Peering into the Future
        21. A Particular Kind of Excellence
        22. A Definition of Justice
        23. The Good Teacher (Or, The Good Student)
        27. A Major Change
        29. A Formative Influence
        30. A Formative Situation

31. Social Identity
32. A Wise Person
37. Thinking about the Family Portrait
48. Looking Backward

D. Argument
13. I Hate to Bring This Up, But . . .
14. The Better Way
15. To Join or Not to Join
16. Letter of Recommendation
17. A Student Complaint
18. Righting a Wrong
19. Concerned Citizen
19A. Madman or Fool
35. Explaining Your Politics
38. A Travel Grant
39. A Textbook Critique
40. A Musical Debate
41. An Exercise in Charity
43. Specific Advice
44. Commercial Consultant
45. A Resolution
46. Guest Critic

IV. LEVEL OF ABSTRACTION

The assignments in *Situational Writing* generally progress from concrete to abstract. Let me apply three categories from James Moffett's *Teaching the Universe of Discourse*[7] to classify this movement. (I am not using Moffett's category of recording.)

A. Reporting (what happened)
2. A Time of Your Life
3. A Victim of Injustice
4. Job Talk
5. I Knew a Teacher
6. A Special Place
7. On the Other Hand . . .
10. Teacher Portrait
11. A News Story
18. Righting a Wrong
18A. A Tongue-lashing
33. Self-portrait
34. Your Home

[7] James Moffett, *Teaching the Universe of Discourse* (Boston: Houghton Mifflin, 1968).

B. Generalizing (what happens)
    1. As I Begin the Writing Course
    8. The Expert Instructs the Beginner
    9. Job Advice
    12. A Student Problem
    13. I Hate to Bring This Up, But . . .
    15. To Join or Not to Join
    16. Letter of Recommendation
    17. A Student Complaint
    19. Concerned Citizen
    19A. Madman or Fool
    24. Self-portrait of a Writer
    25. Meeting an Old Friend
    26. A Way You Were
    27. A Major Change
    29. A Formative Influence
    30. A Formative Situation
    31. Social Identity
    32. A Wise Person
    35. Explaining Your Politics
    36. A Family Portrait
    38. A Travel Grant
    39. A Textbook Critique
    40. A Musical Debate
    41. An Exercise in Charity
    42. A Homecoming Speech
    44. Commercial Consultant
    45. A Resolution
    46. Guest Critic
    47. A Letter to a Hero
    48. Looking Backward

C. Theorizing (what may happen)
    14. The Better Way
    20. Peering into the Future
    21. A Particular Kind of Excellence
    22. A Definition of Justice
    23. The Good Teacher (Or, The Good Student)
    28. At a Crossroads
    37. Thinking about the Family Portrait
    43. Specific Advice

V. AUDIENCE

The assignments in *Situational Writing* also move from addressing an intimate and friendly audience to a more remote, impersonal, and general audience—from private to public discourse.

A. To a sympathetic and receptive friend
   2. A Time of Your Life
   3. A Victim of Injustice
   4. Job Talk
   5. I Knew a Teacher
   7. On the Other Hand . . .
   8. The Expert Instructs the Beginner
   9. Job Advice
   10. Teacher Portrait
   23. The Good Teacher (Or, The Good Student)
   25. Meeting an Old Friend
   26. A Way You Were
   27. A Major Change
   28. At A Crossroads
   29. A Formative Influence
   30. A Formative Situation
   32. A Wise Person

B. To the writing teacher
   1. As I Begin the Writing Course
   24. Self-portrait of a Writer
   48. Looking Backward

C. To the class
   6. A Special Place
   31. Social Identity
   37. Thinking about the Family Portrait
   41. An Exercise in Charity

D. To a friend who is neutral or in disagreement
   13. I Hate to Bring This Up, But . . .
   14. The Better Way
   15. To Join or Not to Join
   21. A Particular Kind of Excellence
   38. A Travel Grant
   40. A Musical Debate

E. To an adversary
   18. Righting a Wrong
   18A. A Tongue-lashing

F. To an authority or institutional representative
   12. A Student Problem
   16. Letter of Recommendation
   17. A Student Complaint
   20. Peering into the Future
   39. A Textbook Critique
   44. Commercial Consultant

Classifying the Situations

G. To the community or its representatives
   11. A News Story
   19. Concerned Citizen
   19A. Madman or Fool
   22. A Definition of Justice
   46. Guest Critic

H. To a foreign student
   33. Self-portrait
   34. Your Home
   35. Explaining Your Politics

I. To a sociology teacher
   36. A Family Portrait

J. To an assembly of high school students
   42. A Homecoming Speech
   43. Specific Advice

K. To yourself
   24. Self-portrait of a Writer
   45. A Resolution
   48. Looking Backward

L. To a hero
   47. A Letter to a Hero

Bibliography

Britton, James, and associates. *The Development of Writing Abilities (11–18).* London: Macmillan Education, 1975.

Gibson, Walker. *Persona.* New York: Random House, 1969.

Kinneavy, James L. *A Theory of Discourse.* Englewood Cliffs, N.J.: Prentice-Hall, 1971.

Lloyd-Jones, Richard. "Primary Trait Scoring." In Charles R. Cooper and Lee Odell, eds., *Evaluating Writing: Describing, Measuring, Judging.* Urbana, Ill.: National Council of Teachers of English, 1977.

Moffett, James. *Teaching the Universe of Discourse.* Boston: Houghton Mifflin, 1968.

NCTE Commission on Composition. "Teaching Composition: A Position Statement." *College English,* 36 (Oct. 1974), 219–20.

Progoff, Ira. *At a Journal Workshop.* New York: Dialogue House, 1975.

Shaughnessy, Mina P. *Errors and Expectations.* New York: Oxford University Press, 1977.